John Patrick's CRAPS

"So You Wanna Be a Gambler"

By JOHN PATRICK

A Lyle Stuart Book
Published by Carol Publishing Group

To my Mother and my Father.
To my daughters Lori and Colleen.
How I love these four people!

Carol Publishing Group Edition, 1997

A Lyle Stuart Book
Published by Carol Publishing Group
Lyle Stuart is a registered trademark of Carol Communications, Inc.

Editorial, sales and distribution, rights and permissions inquiries should be addressed to Carol Publishing Group, 120 Enterprise Avenue, Secaucus, N.J. 07094

In Canada: Canadian Manda Group, One Atlantic Avenue, Suite 105, Toronto, Ontario M6K 3E7

Carol Publishing Group books may be purchased in bulk at special discounts for sales promotions, fund-raising, or educational purposes. Special editions can be created to specifications. For details, contact Special Sales Department, Carol Publishing Group, 120 Enterprise Avenue, Secaucus, N.J. 07094

Manufactured in the United States of America
ISBN 0-8184-0554-6

15 14 13 12 11 10 9 8 7

PREFACE

This book covers Bank Craps. Its purpose is not only to teach you how to play, but How to Win. In case you're one of the eighty-two billion people who think gambling is an exercise in fun and excitement, this book may be a revelation to you.

I'll teach you everything you need to know about the table, the lay-out and the odds. But mainly I'll teach you Money Management and Discipline. It will lead to winning.

If you're not interested in winning, all of my suggestions will be a useless monotone of wasted words, and won't reach you.

But if winning is your game, the systems and methods in this Craps book will give you a new insight into gambling, and a strong push on the road to victory.

Read these chapters with an open mind. The Discipline methods are very strict, but very successful. They offer a new approach to playing the game of Craps.

So You Wanna Be a Gambler??? Well, be a good one and a successful one. I think you'll like the approach. It works.

CONTENTS

INTRODUCTION TO CRAPS

1. So You Wanna Be a Gambler! 1
2. The Big 4 3
3. Little 3 5
4. Need 7
5. Vigorish 10
6. Craps Terms 14
7. Summary on Introduction 17

BANKROLL

1. Bankroll, What Is It? 19
2. Bankroll — How Important Is It? 21
3. Loss Limits 24
4. Win Goals 27
5. Wrapping Up Bankroll 30

KNOWLEDGE OF THE GAME

1. What Is Knowledge? 31
2. Bank Craps 33
3. The Lay-Out 35
4. Dealers and Pit Bosses 38
5. The Buy-In 43
6. The Game 45
7. Pass Line 51
8. Free Odds 53
9. Double Odds 57
10. Three-Unit Bet 59
11. Come Bets 60

12. Place Bets 65
13. Place Bets vs. Come Bets 71
14. Don't Pass 74
15. Odds on the Don't 77
16. Theory on Laying Odds 81
17. Double Odds on the Don't 83
18. Don't Come 85
19. Buying the Number 90
20. Laying Against the Number 93
21. Field Bets 95
22. Big 6 and Big 8 97
23. Proposition Bets 100
24. Any Seven 102
25. Any Craps 103
26. Three-Way Craps 106
27. Yo 109
28. Horn Bet 112
29. Hopping 114
30. Hard Way Bets 116
31. Wrapping Up Proposition Bets 121
32. Summary on Knowledge 123

MONEY MANAGEMENT

1. Money Management—What Is It? 125
2. Sessions 127
3. The Series 131
4. Systems in Craps 133
5. Basic Right Betting 136
6. Betting Progression for Place Numbers 139
7. Aggressive Place Betting 145
8. Superaggressive 149
9. Comment on Right Betting Method 155
10. Come System 157
11. Single Bet 160
12. Pass Line Control 162
13. 1,2,3,4 System 166
14. Follow the Trend 168
15. Variations for the Trend 171

16. Forcing the Bet 174
17. Reading the People 176
18. Field Place System 178
19. Six and Eight System 182
20. Regression System 186
21. Up and Pull 190
22. Martingale System 193
23. Summarizing the Right Side 195
24. Simple Don't Pass 196
25. Three Number Don't 199
26. Aggressive Don't Betting 203
27. Advanced Two-Unit Don't 206
28. Choosing a Method 208
29. Removing Your Bet 210
30. Off-Setting the Don't Six and Eight 212
31. Accepting the Small Return 216
32. The Don't Bettor 218
33. The Hedge Bettor 220
34. $41 No Ten 224
35. The Simple Hedge 227
36. The Double Hedge 231
37. Extended Hedges 236
38. The Patrick System 238
39. The Patrick System—Step Two 241
40. Theory of the Patrick System 243
41. Two and Three Unit Bets (Patrick System) 246
42. Using the 7 Both Ways 248
43. Trends and the Patrick System 250
44. Hedging the Trend (Patrick System) 254
45. Synopsis of the Patrick System 256
46. You and Money Management 259
47. Wrapping Up Money Management 263

DISCIPLINE

1. Discipline—What Is It? 265
2. Discipline and the Dentist 268
3. How Do You Walk? 270
4. The Casinos and Discipline 272

5. The Set Amount 276
6. The Professional Gambler 278
7. The Big Shot 282
8. Charting a Table 285
9. Learning How to Win 287
10. The Author and Discipline 290
11. Discipline: The Name of the Game 292
12. Wrapping Up Discipline 295

ODDS AND ENDS

1. Tipping 297
2. Comps 303
3. Etiquette 309
4. Crooked Dice 312
5. Luck in a Casino 315
6. Streaks 317
7. Intimidation 319
8. The Ultimate Goal 323

ACKNOWLEDGMENTS

I'd like to take a minute to thank some people who have assisted me in the completion of this book. I don't wanna sound like the guy who wins an Oscar and ends up thanking everybody from his nursery school nurse, to the guy who delivers his weekly pizza. But there are a few people I'd like to mention. Ted Butner, my partner, and one of the best craps players in the country. My associate Lynn Niglio, who must do all the dirty work of running around, setting up lectures, meetings, and countless sessions of research. She is priceless. To Jeff Mitchell, for keeping a close eye on this project.

Thanks to Diane and John Guibas. Also to Frankie Keilly, a beautiful girl who has done much to coordinate the various theories that have to do with this intricate game. Her contributions were invaluable.

Finally, my deep thanks go to the finest group of instructors you could find. I have been associated with these professionals for several years, and am indebted to them for their help and knowledge, but mostly in their ability to teach these games. These men have no equals, and I truly respect them: Mark Zimmer, Les Scally, Ron Ludden, Charlie Zimmerman, Carl Bajor, Jeff Dalia, Irv Hyatt, Greg Lantz, Austin Kosik, Jim Gilrain, Jack Klarman, Bob Nash, Leon Ackerman, John Sullivan, Barry Urban, and Howie Goldstein. It is my privilege to know and work with these people.

1 INTRODUCTION TO CRAPS

So You Wanna Be a Gambler?

This book covers Bank Craps. The kind that is played in casinos all over the world. You think you know how to play craps? Great! I'm proud of you. But what this book does, is teach you how to win. That's the difference. Most people play to play. I want you to play to win.

I'll explain the entire table, the odds, the vigorish and all the pertinent information needed for you to intelligently attack this game. But most of all I'll show you how to win. If you follow the methods, you'll reduce your losses, and when you get ahead, you'll know when to walk.

It's called learning how to win. Try it—I think you'll like it.

Craps is a fascinating game. It's a fast game, where a multitude of bets can be made after every throw of the dice, regardless of whether you are a right or wrong bettor.

Walk into a casino sometime, and listen to where all the noise is coming from. Right over at the craps tables. The winners are whooping and yelling up a storm. Every throw of the dice causes these players to let off steam, to evoke emotion.

The losers are cursing and moaning, screaming for the shooter to throw the dice. People are able to yell their heads off at the craps table. Not so at Blackjack or Roulette, or Baccarat. At those tables, it's considered bad taste to show any emotion, let alone speak of how rotten your streak is going.

Notice how in Blackjack you make hand signals to let the dealer know if you want a card or not? You could play Blackjack for three straight days, and not utter a word. In Craps, they let it all hang out. People talk to the dice as if they are human, pleading, screaming, begging, chastising—anything to get their number to show.

It appears that things are moving so fast that it is a complicated exercise in mathematical calculus. It's not. As you proceed through these chapters, you'll see how basically simple the whole game is. The main point is this: I'll show you how to play—and I'll show you how to win.

Ah!!! Now I've got your attention. That little word: WIN!!!

2 INTRODUCTION TO CRAPS

The Big 4

Before I go one step further, let's get right to the basic needs you must have—to gamble successfully. I call them the Big 4. It doesn't matter if you play Craps, Blackjack, Baccarat, Poker, Bingo, Sports Betting, or toss pennies in the gutter. If it's a form of gambling, you must have the Big 4.

After these chapter's on introduction to Craps, you'll see the book broken into four sections, with each section covering one of these items. All facets of the Big 4 are dependent on the other three ingredients, and if you are lacking even one part, you might as well wrap up your gambling career right now. It's good as over.

Well, what is this magical formula? Very simple:

1. Bankroll
2. Knowledge of the Game
3. Money Management
4. Discipline

That's it! That's your whole key to winning at gambling. If you have all four, you will reduce the house's edge to the barest minimum, and be in a position to pick up some consistent wins.

BANKROLL: This is the amount of money you bring to battle. It is your own business what that bankroll may be. Five thousand is a bankroll, so is one thousand. So is seven hundred. So is two hundred. If you take $200 to the game of your choice, that is your bankroll. Every monetary decision you make that day is based on $200. The amount you will set to win, and the limit you set on your losses is based on that $200. Not on your own silly inflated dreams.

KNOWLEDGE OF THE GAME: Knowledge is golden. Knowledge is wealth. Knowledge is everything. Well, I wouldn't go that far. But, you get the point. You need knowledge in most everything you do. And especially in gambling. If you don't know everything there is to know about the game you are competing at, then you shouldn't play. And I don't mean you should have just an idea of the game—I mean you should be perfect. And why not?

MONEY MANAGEMENT: This is the ability to manage that bankroll that you started with. You could have a six figure bankroll, but if you don't have a masterful Money Management system of betting it, your lack of direction and control will eventually wear you down. Every single bet you make, following either a win or a loss, should be predetermined. My method of Money Management will minimize your losses, and enable you to take full advantage of winning streaks.

DISCIPLINE: Last, and most of all, this is the bottom line of gambling. This is the ability to walk when you are losing, and walk when you are winning. It separates the good players from the boobs. If you think you'll never get it, quit gambling right now. You're a born loser.

There you have the Big 4. Having just two or three of them will eventually crush you. Having all four gives you a decent chance.

I believe that utilizing the Big 4 will make you a perfect player. Let's face it, you have to get tired of losing. Well, give these systems a good shot. I think you'll be surprised at the results.

The Big 4 is effective. It works. I'll refer to it throughout this entire book, and maybe you'll start to see the importance of each of these steps, as you climb the four pronged ladder to success.

INTRODUCTION TO CRAPS

3

Little 3

I've explained the Big 4, and without it, you haven't got a prayer of winning consistently in gambling. But right in back of the Big 4 is another set of items that you should be aware of. It's called the Little 3:

1. Theory
2. Logic
3. Trends

THEORY: Theory is an opinion that you might have on a subject. But, naturally, if you do not know everything about a certain subject, who gives a rat's tail what your opinion is. So, it behooves you to conquer item number two of the Big 4, Knowledge of the Game. When you are perfect at the game you choose to bet on, then the manner in which you approach it—is your theory. And theory, when you have complete knowledge, is never wrong.

LOGIC: In gambling, everything has a logical explanation. For instance, for the non card counter in Blackjack, a proper move would be to take a hit when you have a sixteen against a dealer's Ace, because if you stand, the dealer has the opportunity of turning over eight cards, (6, 7, 8, 9, 10, Jack, Queen or King), and beating you. So, the logical move would be to take a hit. During the course of this book you will see logical approaches to all situations. Whenever you gamble, look for the logical solution, or explanation, to stand out. It'll end up being the best move.

TRENDS: In gambling, trends dominate. Streaks occur more than you might think. An illogical approach to gambling is bettors thinking something should happen because the opposite has occurred on the previous decision, or decisions. For instance, in Roulette, the color black comes up four times in a row. The novice rushes up to bet on red, because he thinks red is due. Garbage. That kind of thinking gives you no logical reason as to why you should risk good money on a silly theory like that. That's a crazy assumption, that something is due to occur, for no other reason than it is "due." That law does not work on any set number of rolls, or hands of cards, or throws of the dice. The professional gambler is more likely to bet on the color black coming up again. There's no way of explaining why streaks happen, but they do. Get in the habit of looking to take advantage of streaks. Take a baseball team. Watch how many times it will get into a streak of consecutive wins or losses. And this dominance of streaks, or trends, is prevalent in all forms of gambling. Look for these trends to happen, and then climb aboard. You'll get a lot of smooth rides.

There you have the Little 3. Don't discount them. All of these things add up to the arsenal of ammunition you need to compete at gambling.

INTRODUCTION TO CRAPS

4

Need

Why do people gamble? Why do you gamble? There's got to be a reason, because so many people do. Successful people, born losers, rich people, poor people, young and old, men and women. Most everyone gambles.

My opinion is that people gamble out of need. Not greed, but need. They need the money, or they need the excitement, or they need the outlet from their everyday lives. But need is the underlying factor behind the reasons that drive people to bet. But the need so overshadows logic, that the bettor loses all touch with reality.

Willie Gettsomdoe just has to get money together to meet his $450 mortgage payment. He has a hundred dollar bankroll, and heads for the casinos. He sure as heck won't accept doubling his money, or even tripling it. Nothing short of $450 will please this boob. His need is $450, and nothing less than that will do. Willie Gettsomdoe better get some brains.

Phil Miday is bored most of the time. His excitement comes from playing Craps, and betting gives him his thrills. He has a good job, a pretty penny stashed away, but craves the excitement of gambling. He is more interested in playing—than winning. Actually, he doesn't know how to win. He just wants his thrills from the action of the game. He invariably gets whacked, and his day is another loss.

Bordwith Selff is a typical visitor to the casinos. He works hard five days a week, from eight to five. His wife doesn't communicate with him, the kids are in college. He doesn't bowl, ski, play golf or have any interest in sports. In short, he is bored with himself. He is looking for something to do, and a weekend trip to the casinos is his outlet. He brings down money in excess of what he can afford to gamble with, and plays Blackjack, a game he knows very little about. He continuously gets taken for his wad, but also continues to come back the next week. His explanation is that it is his only vice. Of all the crap.

Are you among any of these examples? If you are, then step back and take stock of your gambling habits. The need for money, or excitement, or outlet, should not be an excuse to gamble. Especially if you are not perfect at the game you attack.

I, personally, disagree with the hordes of people who gamble, simply for the previously stated reasons. I think it is an expensive way of satisfying your so-called needs.

Naturally, I'm not trying to discourage you from gambling, but only trying to make you aware of what you're up against. This so-called need of yours can be tempered, by mastering the Big 4, and turning gambling into an entertaining and profitable experience, rather than the satisfying of a lofty, illogical craving.

You probably thought that people gambled because of greed. No, greed only takes place after you get ahead. The anticipation of making a bet excites people, and they are hoping to win a small amount at a given game. But, once they get ahead, they think they're geniuses, and have the gorgeous lady luck sitting on their shoulder. That's when greed takes over and pushes them to try and win astronomical amounts of money. Vigorish, stupidity, and dumb bets, replace the hot streak, and the greed erodes the small profits that were accumulated, and leads to disaster. Has it happened to you? You bet your sweet tooth it has.

How many times have you been ahead in a casino, and instead of quitting a winner, you poured your profits back to the house, and also your original starting bankroll?

It's been estimated that 70% of the people who gamble, are ahead at one point in their play, yet 90% of that number pour it all back—looking for bigger profits, more excitement and the continued thrill of being able to compete.

If you number yourself in this group, you're on a one way trip to consistent losses. Temper your need, and acquire control. Your betting forays will take a complete 180 degree turn.

INTRODUCTION TO CRAPS

5

Vigorish

If you've been around gambling for any length of time, you've surely heard the word vigorish, or vig. It's the edge, baby, the hammer the house has over you. It's the amount of money we pay for the right to make a wager.

The casinos, or race tracks, or your local bookie, all must have this vig working for them, otherwise, they'd be in a position of gambling, and that's something the house does not like to do. For that reason, you, the bettor, are subjected to a charge, or vig, for the right to make a bet.

For example, let's use the roulette table. There are thirty-six numbers shown on the lay-out, plus 0 and 00. Suppose you place a chip on the number 8. If 8 shows, the house pays you thirty-five chips for every one you wagered. Since you had only one chance of winning, (#8), and thirty-seven other numbers that could beat you, the true payoff should be 37-1. The difference between what they pay you (35-1), and what they should pay you (37-1), is called vigorish. Those extra two numbers, that the house holds back on, results in a vigorish of 5.26%, in their favor.

The house sets vigs on any game they allow you to bet on. It is your responsibility to play only those games where the vig is not prohibitive. Let's take one more look at how vigorish works for the house.

Suppose you wanted to call your local bookie to place a small bet on a football game, and your next door neighbor was dialing the same number, to place his wager. As it turns out, you were both interested in a game that was on TV that day, the Giants playing the Jets. The man on the phone announced that the line was: Jets, favored by three points.

You figured the Jets would win by at least three points, so you tell him: "Give me the Jets minus 3, five times." A "time" stands for a $5 bet, so when you say five times, you are looking to win $25. But to make that wager, you must not only lay the three points, you must risk $6 for every $5 you wish to win. In this case, you are putting up $30 to win $25. That extra $5 is called vigorish.

Your neighbor thinks the Giants will beat the Jets, so he tells the same bookie that he wants a five timer on the Giants. He gets three points, but must also lay $30 to win $25.

The bookies sheet for these two transactions will look as follows:

(Caller A)	Jets minus 3	30-25
(Caller B)	Giants plus 3	30-25

Let's assume the Jets win 28 to 20. You collect $25 and your neighbor loses $30. The bookie made $5 on that particular bet. Actually, he was in a no lose position. Whichever team won, he would pay $25 out, and collect $30. That $5 is his vigorish.

In this instance, let's say you and your neighbor were the only two people to bet on that game—(an unlikely happening, I assure you), but you get the point. That $5 charge that is tagged on, is the bookies edge. It is the hammer over every bettors head.

Naturally, the bookie hopes that he gets about $5,000 wagered on both sides, and just sits back and waits to collect his "juice." Sometimes he gets equal action on both sides, and sometimes he doesn't. But one thing is certain, he gets his vig on every bet.

Vigorish is a big part of gambling, and the less you have to lay out, the longer your bankroll will remain intact. Go back to the bets you made on football. Suppose, over a period of time, you made twenty bets. Ten times you won, for a profit of $250 and ten times you lost, for a deficit of $300. In other words, you won just as many times as you lost, but the vigorish got into you for $50. That's because you were laying $30 to win $25—a 20% bite. That's a healthy whack in the gut.

During the course of this book, I'll be trying to get you to make wagers, only where the vig is not a percentage of the national debt.

Look at the chart on the next page. The third column shows the vig you are fighting for each different bet. It's not necessary to try and comprehend the whole list right now, as we'll be referring back to it in future chapters. But at least get an idea of the edge the house has in it's favor on these different bets.

CASINO'S ADVANTAGE ON CRAPS BETS

BET	CASINO PAYS	CASINO ADVANTAGE %
PASS LINE	EVEN MONEY	1.41
PASS LINE & SINGLE ODDS	EVEN MONEY & ODDS	0.84
PASS LINE & DOUBLE ODDS	EVEN MONEY & ODDS	0.60
DON'T PASS (BAR 12)	EVEN MONEY	1.40
DON'T PASS & SINGLE ODDS	EVEN MONEY & ODDS	0.83
DON'T PASS & DOUBLE ODDS	EVEN MONEY & ODDS	0.59
COME	EVEN MONEY	1.41
DON'T COME (BAR 12)	EVEN MONEY	1.40
PLACE BET ON 4 or 10	9-5	6.67
PLACE BET ON 5 or 9	7-5	4.00
PLACE BET ON 6 or 8	7-6	1.52
BUY THE 4 or 10	2-1 (5% commission)	4.76
LAY BET vs. 4 or 10	1-2	3.03
LAY BET vs. 5 or 9	2-3	2.50
LAY BET vs. 6 or 8	5-6	1.818
FIELD* (2-1 on 2 and 12)	EVEN MONEY	5.56
FIELD* (3-1 on 12), (2-1 on 2)	EVEN MONEY	2.70
ANY SEVEN	4-1	16.67
ANY CRAPS	7-1	11.10
ELEVEN	15-1	11.10
HARD WAY 4 or 10	7-1	11.10
HARD WAY 6 or 8	9-1	9.09

INTRODUCTION TO CRAPS 6

Craps Terms

You ever hear the word "Jargon"? It's a fancy six letter word that stands for jive talk. Since jive talk is not accepted in a Craps game, it is better that you use the craps terms that go with this fast game.

The dealers in the casino like you to use the terms that allow the game to move right along, so I'll touch on all the parts of the table, including the terms that apply to the various bets that can be made.

1. Lay-out	The cloth containing all of the various bets.
2. Craps	When the total of the two dice is either 2, 3, or 12.
3. Pass Line	Place on the lay-out, where bettor puts his chip, to indicate he is betting that the shooter makes his point. (Made before game begins.)
4. Don't Pass	Place on the lay-out where bettor puts his chip to indicate he is betting that shooter will not make his point. (Made before game begins.)
5. Right Bettor	Pass Line or Do bettor. He is playing that shooter keeps making his point.
6. Wrong bettor	Bets on Don't Pass, against the shooter.
7. Buy In	When you come up to a table, and place your money down, and wish to buy chips.
8. Come-out roll	To begin a new game, the first roll of the shooter is called his come-out roll.

	He keeps throwing a come-out until he establishes a point number of either 4, 5, 6, 8, 9, or 10.
9. Stickman	One of three dealers who work the table. Dealer with the stick calls the game for the time he is in that position, usually twenty minutes. He is called the stickman.
10. Natural	7 or 11 on the come-out roll.
11. Hard Way	Two like numbers appear on the dice: 5-5, or 4-4, or 3-3, or 2-2. The total of the two like numbers is called "hard."
12. Easy six	5-1, or 1-5, or 2-4, or 4-2 is an easy six. (same holds true for easy eights, fours or tens)
13. Yo	Slang word to indicate 11.
14. Place bets	Player has opportunity to make bets on the 4, 5, 6, 8, 9, and 10, any time he wants.
15. Come bets	Same type bet as Pass Line, except that it affects the rolls of the dice after the point is established.
16. Press	When you place a number, and it hits, and you do not wish to take the profit, merely tell the dealer to "press" your existing bet, and he will increase it by the amount of money called for on that wager.
17. Odds	Once a point is established, you have opportunity of taking the true, or free odds on that number. If the number is made before a 7, you are paid off on the correct odds.
18. Proposition Bets	One roll action bets and hard way bets that you may make at any time. They are located on the lay-out, right in front of the stickman.

19. Box man	Seated at the table, opposite the stickman. Checks all buy-ins, and acts as referee of the game, in event there is a dispute. Makes sure pay-offs are correct.

This list is not in any order, as I want you to take the time to study each different explanation. It is also not the complete list, but the ones that are sure to get you started at this game. The other parts of the table will be explained in due course.

INTRODUCTION TO CRAPS 7

Summary on Introduction

All right, I've touched on a couple of points that will be covered in detail in later chapters, but at least you'll have an idea of some of the things I'll be expounding on.

Of all of the chapters in the book, there is none more important than the one on understanding the Big 4. If you haven't memorized the Big 4, and the individual meanings, head back to Chapter 2 right now. You can scoff at my attempts to over dramatize the need for control, but if you are interested in winning, then you'd better program yourself to accept the restrictions that are needed.

Also, if you're not going to follow the discipline regulations, you're wasting your time reading this book, or any book on Craps. I'll show you how to play, but that in itself is not enough. Get into your head that gambling is a tough business, and that winning small amounts consistently, is better than going for the big kill. You'll have your big days, but the main thing in gambling is minimizing the losses. If you minimize your losses, by the money management and discipline techniques I advise, you will see how much longer your bankroll will stay active. And as long as you have the bread to compete, you're a threat to the casinos.

Watch how the different facets of the Big 4 intertwine with each other. The sections in this book are broken down into four separate categories, each one containing chapters on that particular part of the Big 4.

Remember one thing about gambling in general, and craps in this particular case. Even if you're perfect in your Knowledge of the Game you're betting on, your chance of winning is still never better than 50-50. Do you realize that?????

Then how the devil can you play a game, that at best gives you a 50-50 chance of winning, and try to double and triple your starting bankroll? It's an illogical assumption that you should try to double your bankroll, just because you're a great player. Yet that is the goal that many people set for themselves.

Well, enough on introduction, let's get to the meat of playing Craps.

BANKROLL 1

Bankroll, What Is It?

Don't think that a bankroll means a gigantic wad of money. It doesn't. A bankroll is the amount of money that each individual brings to the casino. It can be $5,000, or $1,000, or $500 or $100. Whatever you, yourself, have in your kick, it's a bankroll.

And with that bankroll comes all of the monetary decisions you will make that day. The bankroll tells you how much you should use as your win goal, which value table to play at, and how much your initial series of bets should be. It also is the guide that determines the limit of your losses that day.

Suppose Berta Bigbucks brings $2,000 to the casino and plunks down $25 as her initial bet. Standing next to her at the table is Sidney Smallcents. He brought $150 as his bankroll. Do you think he has the right to bet the same amount? Of course not. He must play within the confines of his smaller wad. But usually, the Sidney Smallcents of the world use little sense, bet with their wild dreams, and start laying out big amounts.

A few disastrous streaks against them, and lack of sense and cents, will destroy them. Sure, they'll cry all the way home about how rotten their luck was, but it's the old story of not having enough bread to stay in the game.

Bankroll decides your play. In the chapters on Money Management, I'll go over the betting series, but right now, get it into your head that you don't have to push a wheelbarrow of money up to the tables to compete. If your bankroll comes in the form of a fistful of $20 bills, so be it. Naturally, there are minimums that you should have, and you'll get those figures later, but an intelligent look at your past flimsy approach to casino games is the object of discussion right now. Whatever your starting bankroll, you must play within that structure.

Let me tell you what destroys a lot of bettors. It's the minimum bet. Do you know what that is? It means the house sets a minimum amount that you must put in play on every hand, or roll of the dice. In Atlantic City, most minimums are $5. That's steep for most of the patrons. That means they must bet at least $5 on a hand of Blackjack, which will take fifteen seconds to play.

Some of these people drive fourteen miles to save a thirty-five cent pay-out on the Parkway, and now they're asked to plunk down $5 for the right to play a hand of Blackjack. You don't think it's a sweaty palm that places that chip on the lay-out? Think again! Watch some of the dealers wipe their hand from time to time. It's to dry off their paws, from handling a couple of chips, from a player who is down to his last few dollars.

Some people lose three straight bets and almost melt off the chair—they're so burned up. That's because they're playing with short bankrolls. And they're not alone. Many people are in this same position, and it's caused by these high minimums.

In Las Vegas, there are $3 dollar, $2, and even $1 minimum tables. I've played at ten cent roulette games, and twenty-five cent craps games. That gives players a chance to compete. But the higher minimums knock your socks off. With a $100 bankroll, you can intelligently compete at a $2 table. But as soon as the minimums call for $5 bets, the people with short bankrolls are in trouble.

I will address my theory to cover the $5 table, so as to cover a multitude of casinos, and if you're fortunate to find a lower minimum table, just adjust the percentages. You wanna play at a higher table, just make the adjustments the other way.

BANKROLL 2

Bankroll—How Important Is It?

How important is bankroll? It's the beginning, baby, and without it, you can't compete. It's the first step of the Big 4. Money is what you need to compete, and naturally everyone does not have thousands of dollars to take to the casinos.

So, most people take whatever they can lay their hands on, and think that luck, and law of averages and other illogical theories will eventually allow them to win. It just ain't so. It just ain't possible.

A small bankroll causes people to play scared—to make moves that coincide with their lack of money. A small bankroll affects a player so much, that he makes moves that allow him to just "stay in the game," instead of taking advantage of the house when he has them in trouble with a hot streak.

How many times, playing Blackjack, have you had a $10 bet on the table and get dealt an ace and a 4, versus the dealers up card of 5? You check your stack of chips and find three lousy red ones sitting there. If you lose, then you're finished for the day. So, instead of doubling down, and investing another ten dollars, which you should do when that dealer is in trouble, you merely take a hit, because you're scared to invest those extra two chips. See what your lack of bankroll has done to you? Affected your play, and made you adjust your Knowledge part of the Big 4 because you didn't have the Bankroll part.

Right now, think of how many times you allowed scared money to affect your play. I don't care what game it was: Craps, Blackjack, Roulette, Poker, Horse-Racing, Sports,

Bingo, you name it. If you played scared, chances are you had a short bankroll.

Rule number one for the first part of the Big 4. If you don't have the right amount of money, you've got to have the guts to avoid playing. Oh, it'll hurt, cause you want to play so bad. But if you play short you will play bad.

Coming up, I'll be giving you loss limits and win goals, but right now let's go over the proper amount you should have in your bankroll.

The figures will raise a rash on your tender spots, but remember, they are merely the amounts you will "bring" to the table. They are not the amounts that you will risk for that particular session. (Following is minimum at most Atlantic City Casinos.)

BLACKJACK: When you sit at a table, you should have forty times the amount of the minimum bet at that game. But, because of the higher set of minimum bets at many casinos, I have adjusted those figures to thirty times. That means at a $5 table, you must have at least $150.

BACCARAT: Since the vigorish against you in Baccarat is only 1.17% on bank, and 1.38% on player, and since there are no decisions to be made as to whether you you want to hit or stand, it is impossible for you to make a mistake, because the rules are predetermined. In fact, you don't need any knowledge to play the game. A lot of you ought to be right at home. But this chance to play a game that is almost 50-50, without having to make decisions, allows some leniency in your starting bankroll. In Baccarat, you can take twenty times the amount of the minimum to battle, although, if possible, begin with thirty times. That means a $5 table can be attacked with a nice easy $100 session stake. A $10 minimum table needs only $200, and so on.

ROULETTE: For the inside numbers, where the minimum bet may be $3, use fifty-cent chips, with a starting session amount of $50 as your absolute smallest starting figure. The outside bets usually call for $5 minimums, and you should have thirty times that minimum, or $150. Remember, the proper amount is always supposed to be forty times the minimum, but my reducing that figure is simply to conform to the times that some people can just not raise that much money. That may sound silly to you big shots, but this lack of betting bankrolls is a tremendous percentage of the cause of people getting wiped out.

CRAPS: At a $5 table, you should have ten times the amount of what you bet on the first shooter. Suppose you're a right bettor, and your wagers on the first shooter throwing the dice call for a $5 pass line bet, with odds, and a $6 bet on both the 6 and the 8. You have $22 at risk on that shooter, which means you need $220 for that table. This will be expounded upon later on. But the theory is, that it takes one shooter in ten, to have a hot roll, and you need enough of a bankroll to bet the same way for the next ten shooters, as you did for the first one. Otherwise, you will become an erratic bettor, adjusting your bets to coincide with the money you have to play with. If you think the proper amount of money to bet on that first shooter was $22, then the same amount should be the proper figure for the remaining shooters at that session.

Don't minimize the importance of the bankroll. It is the starting point for any gambling endeavor. The proper bankroll allows you to play intelligently and confidently.

In Las Vegas, you have the chance to play at tables where the minimums are sometimes $2 and $1. There you have the chance to stay in the game, until a trend or hot streak comes your way. With the systems I will give you, and the Money Management methods, playing in Vegas with the low minimums, will give you a tremendous chance to pick up some consistent wins.

BANKROLL 3

Loss Limits

Don't skip over this, or the next chapter. They're hands down, the two most important chapters in the entire book. It is the lack of a Loss Limit and a Win Goal that destroys most gamblers.

A Loss Limit is exactly that! You set a limit on what your losses will be for a certain day, or game, or table. It is the limit you will lose. Never, ever, never bet down to your last chip.

That session should last until either your win goal is accomplished, or your loss limit is reached. When you lose that predetermined amount, your play at that table is over. Period! Not one single dollar more should be invested.

Ever watch the patterns of people in a casino? Many of them have the same illogical approach to gambling as the next boob. They are captivated by the desire to play, rather than to win.

Some famous quotes:

"I only come down once a month, so I want my money's worth of playing time."

(They would rather play than win!)

"I've got $200 of the casino's money. I'm ahead, so I don't have to worry about losing."

(Doesn't this jerk realize that when he wins, it is not the casino's money anymore, but his own? No one is just looking for an excuse to keeping playing.)

"I'm ahead $300, and I'd like to quit right now, but the bus doesn't leave for another four hours, so I may as well keep playing."

(Sound typical? Of course it does: This person has no

control—no Discipline—and no idea of what gambling is all about.)

"I'll just bring an amount of money to the casino that I can afford to lose."

(This is the coup de grace in stupidity. Show me a person who can afford to lose money, and I'll show you a full-grown nut. Yet, you hear this statement over and over. Beats me why people actually believe they have to lose.)

You've heard these words before. I just hope you don't use any of them.

Finally, one more example of an undisciplined player. Freddy Fumble Fingers has been at the craps table for two hours. He has already lost the $250 he brought, the $500 credit marker he drew, and another $100 he borrowed from his buddy. So what's he doing now? Fumbling through his pockets to try and find another $10 or $15 to continue playing. He feels if he can just get a few more dollars to stay in the game, he'll get hot and recover all of his losses.

The trend (Little 3) on this day was against him, but he is still trying to stay in action. If he had set a Loss Limit, he'd have money to play with the next day. But he's too stupid to realize that, until he's on the way home, and reality finally hits him. He got completely wiped out that day—and he is sick.

Loss Limits at every single game of gambling will completely eliminate any possibility of your ever going broke. Depending on the game you play, your loss limits will be set.

Following is the Loss Limits for any casino table that you attack:

Blackjack	40%
Craps	50%
Baccarat	50%
Roulette	50%
Slots	60% per machine, or up to 30% of your total bankroll.

This means you can lose anywhere up to that figure, but never to exceed it. For instance, in Craps, you can lose 50% of the total you take to the casino, but never in excess of that 50% amount.

The reason you take more with you than you will put at risk, is to eliminate playing with scared money. If the temptation to play with this extra money is too great—then you have no discipline whatsoever.

You don't have to play until you lose exactly 50% in craps. You may set your own Loss Limit, depending on how comfortable you feel with the percentage you set.

You could make it 40%, or 30%, or even 25%. But you absolutely must set a limit. And where is this figure set? Outside the casino, before you even enter the battlefield, and get swayed by the aura of the moment.

Again, if you set 40% of your bankroll as your Loss Limit on a particular day, and things are not going too well, you don't have to sweat out those last few whacks. If you've lost 30%, and that table is really going against you, get the heck out of there. You don't have to wait for your exact percentage to be reached. When I start losing at a certain table, and can't get going, I don't need a hammer to hit me on the head to realize I'm in the wrong spot. I'm ready to run at the first hint of doom.

By following my theory (Little 3), it is absolutely impossible to ever go broke in gambling. Suppose you start with $1,000 as your bankroll, and 30% is your loss limit. If you lose 30% or $300, that day is over, and your next trip has a $700 bankroll with another 30% of that figure as the Loss Limit. If you lose 30% of $700, or $210, that day is over, and $490 will be your starting cache on the next trip. If you adhere to this strict rule, you'll always have a backroll in reserve, however small it may be. That's because your loss can never exceed 30% of what you started with.

BANKROLL 4

Win Goals

Just as important as the Loss Limit, in your disciplined approach to gambling, is the Win Goal. This is the amount of money that you set as the goal you wish to reach.

Now, the win goal should not be set after you get ahead, but must be decided upon before you make your first bet. Before you enter the casino, this Win Goal figure must be uppermost in your mind. Naturally, it must be based on your starting bankroll. A player with a $200 bankroll cannot set the same goal as the patron with a $2,000 bankroll. Here is where percentages come in.

When giving lectures on the subject of gambling, one of the questions I ask the audience is how much they would like to win, with a $500 starting bankroll.

The answers range from $300, to double your money, to $3,000. Some merely say: "as much as I can." Some say they play until it's time to leave. Most have no idea at all as to a certain amount.

The Win Goal, in my opinion, should be easily attainable, not a high amount, that is very difficult to reach. My reasoning is 10%, with 30% as the absolute highest goal you should set.

Remember, you are playing games that, at best, only offer you about a 49-51% chance of winning. Then how can you intelligently hope to consistently win large amounts at gambling, when the chances are never in your favor?

Look at this logical example. Have you ever taken $100 to the casino, and gotten ahead $10? Of course you have. Many times. OK, if it's so easy to win $10 with $100, then it should be just as easy to win $100 with $1,000, or $1,000 with

$10,000. It's the exact same percentage. But no, you don't want to risk $10,000, and yet logically, there is no mathematical deviation. The problem is you don't want to accept just a $10 profit, because that's beneath you. You want the big bucks, but aren't willing to put up the kind of money it takes to satisfy those desires.

Go a step further. If it's so easy to win $10 with $100, then it ought to be a snap to win $5 with that same $100. That's a 5% return. Using that same percentage table, a minuscule 5% return, which is very easy to reach, increase your bankroll to $5,000. Play until you get that 5% goal. That is $250 profit per day. Suppose you went to the casino two hundred times a year. That's a $50,000 profit, taking just 5% returns.

I'm not telling you to do this. I'm telling you to approach these games logically. These comparable examples offer you the exact percentage returns, but your lofty desires are tempered by your meager amounts of working capital.

Another point about the Win Goal. It is not a Win limit, merely a *goal.* Notice how the previous chapter talked about a Loss *limit.* That's a stopping point. You never want to put a stopping point on your winning. Don't limit your wins, but merely set your goal, in order to make sure you show a profit, most of the time.

The Win Goal is merely a point you wish to reach, and then guarantee your profit for that day. In the chapters on money management and discipline, you will see a deeper look into the method of handling your money. Right now, zero in on the intelligent handling of your bankroll.

The Win Goal applies to every game in the casino, and every gambling endeavor you undertake. Get into the habit of setting these goals. They are more important than you might think.

I know it is hard to quit when you are losing, and still have money in your pocket. But that is following your Loss Limit. I also realize it is hard to quit when your goal for the day has been reached, and the total cache does not come up to your prior lofty victory desires.

But, I never said winning was easy. It isn't, but it sure as heck beats losing.

Win Goals. You must have them. They must be made small, so you can attain them easily, and then go for the bigger returns, but only after you make sure that each day puts a few sheckels in your pocket.

BANKROLL 5

Wrapping Up Bankroll

I think by now you realize that the bankroll does not have to be big, but it should also be the whole determining factor for your play on a given day.

I don't expect everyone to agree with my theory, which, admittedly, is a conservative approach. It would be easy to tell you to look for double and triple your starting bankroll, but I know how hard that is to accomplish.

You will have good days with my system, but my primary concern is minimizing your losses. The longer you are able to stay alive in a game, with a good bankroll, and complete knowledge, and a strong Money Management system, the better your chances of being a winner will be.

To summarize the handling of your bankroll at Craps:

1. Put together a bankroll. I would prefer it to be $600, to play at a $5 table. (The Loss Limit will protect you from a wipeout)
2. Set your Win Goal—preferably 20%
3. Set your Loss Limit—no more than 50% (anything up to that is fine)
4. Look for the lowest possible minimum table
5. Concentrate on playing to win—look forward to leaving the table with more money than you started with
6. Don't play with a short bankroll
7. Don't play with a scared bankroll
8. Learn How to Win

Bankroll, it's the first thing you need to compete. Make sure you have a decent one. It's step one.

KNOWLEDGE OF THE GAME

1

What Is Knowledge?

We move into the second part of the Big 4, Knowledge of the Game. It doesn't matter what game you like to play, but it is imperative that you are perfect at it.

I, personally, am the best player in the casino. Hands down, the best player. I know how to play every game. I know the basic strategy of Blackjack, and am also a card counter. Every single part of the Roulette wheel is memorized, and I know the payoffs and vigorish of both the Baccarat and Roulette games, including all of the rules. In Craps, I understand the payoffs and odds, and have mastered over twenty different systems for play at that table. There is nothing I need to know about any of these games.

So what!!!!! Big deal!!!! I only know what I'm supposed to know, what every single person who risks a dollar in the casino ought to know. It's the Knowledge of the Game they're playing.

OK, what does this knowledge do for me? What does it get me—being aware of all of these things? Not too much. By having all of this knowledge, my chances of winning are still only 50-50 . . . at best. That's all . . . 50-50. And that's being perfect. The house still holds the hammer with the vigorish. But at least I won't make any percentage mistakes at the games I undertake.

Well, if I'm perfect, and I don't win all the time, how about the poor player who is not perfect? What's his chance of winning?? You tell me. If the perfect player, the professional gambler has only a 50-50 chance, then the novice must be operating at quite a disadvantage. How true.

Knowledge is only 25% of the Big 4, and yet you need it—badly. Being good is not good enough. Being very good is OK, but it's still not enough. Be perfect in the Knowledge of the Game you play. Why not?

I've actually heard people come up to a craps table and ask the other players: "What game is this?" or "Where should I put my money?" This same dope wouldn't give a quarter to a starving man, but will plunk $5 down on a table, at a game he doesn't even understand.

You wanna gamble? Learn how to play. How can you have the audacity to bet hard earned money on anything at which you have only a sprinkling of knowledge?

I know people love to bet on the Sunday football games. The big day arrives and our hero grabs the paper to do his handicapping. First of all, he checks the TV section to see which games are on the tube. All the other contests are disregarded. Even if there are several games that stand out as good wagering possibilities, they are discounted because our hero wants to see the game he bets on.

It turns out to be New England at Kansas City. This dope can't name three people on both squads combined, but he still has to bet that game. He can't decide. So he leafs through the sports page to find out what the local writer has predicted. So far, for this season, the writer has a won-loss record of 22-47 in making selections. But, what the heck, his analysis of the game sounds good, and maybe he's due to pick one right.

So, the weekend watcher bets $100 on the opinion of the writer—just so he can have the "fun" of watching the game on TV. He's been doing this for eleven years. So far he's lost over 80% of his bets, and he still hasn't taken the time to study the teams that he might have to get on.

Are you one of these guys? Tch! Tch! Tch!

I refuse to bet one lousy dime on any gambling enterprise, unless I make my own judgment, based on my own information and knowledge. You need Knowledge of the Game. Maybe it is only 25% of the Big 4. But it's still a big important 25%.

KNOWLEDGE OF THE GAME

2

Bank Craps

Remember when you played craps in the back room of a store, or on a stretched-out bed cover? That was called street craps. The shooter would establish a point, and everyone stood around until he made his point, or sevened out.

In the casinos, the game is called Bank Craps. That is because, while the basic idea is the same, the opportunity to make numerous other bets is allowed.

The game is covered, or "banked" by the house, or casino. There are a multitude of bets that can be made, which differ from the ordinary game of street craps. You can bet the Pass or the Don't Pass Line, the Come or Don't Come Line, make place bets, or bet the hard ways, the field, or any one of several proposition bets. You can increase, or reduce, or take your bets off any time you like. You have a complete handful of variations that you can apply to every wager. (Pass Line and Come bets cannot be removed.)

In other words, there are a great many variations of bets that can be made during the course of one game. And herein lies the trap.

Bank Craps offer so many opportunities to make three, four, five different bets on one throw of the dice, that the lack of bankroll, lack of Money Management, or lack of Discipline will get to the player, and wipe him out. And we're not even covering his probable lack of knowledge of the game. The opportunity to make various bets, at the same time, is very tempting, and eventually the undisciplined player falls prey.

Each of the succeeding chapters will take a different part of the table, explain how it can be played, and what it's disadvantages are. This section on Knowledge will explain the game itself. The chapters on Money Management will show you how to attack those sections of the game.

You pick the systems that best suit your style of play, but only after you understand the entire table.

KNOWLEDGE OF THE GAME

3

The Lay-Out

The game of Craps moves so fast that the novice has a hard time keeping up with the flow of action. Even the lay-out looks complicated. But, in reality, it is a very simple game.

Both sides of the table are identical. In this way, more people are able to play at the same time. In this chapter, there's a typical lay-out. Check the description below with the corresponding letter:

a. Pass Line	Bet is made before dice come out.
b. Come	Bets are made after the original point is established, and allows you to have additional bets working.
c. Don't Pass	Bet is made before point is established. Opposite of pass.
d. Don't Come	Bet made after point is established. Looking for additional numbers to have working for you.
c. Place Bets	Numbers 4, 5, 6, 8, 9, 10. May be placed, or taken down any time you wish.
f. Big 6 and Big 8	Available in Las Vegas Casinos. Not on Atlantic City layouts. Even money payout for 6 and 8.
g. Field	One roll bet on listed numbers that can be made any time.
h. Hard Way Bet	Proposition bet that number will appear "hard," before a 7 or an "easy" combination of same number. Covers 4, 6, 8, or 10.

i. Any Seven	Bet that a combination of 7 will show on next roll. Worst bet on the table, in fact, worst bet in the casino, tied with the Big Wheel, and the blackjack player that doesn't have complete knowledge of Basic Strategy.
j. C or E	One roll bet on either designation. (C) stands for craps, (E) stands for 11.
k. Any Craps	Could be 2, 3, or 12. It is a one roll bet, paying 7-1.
l. Horn	Combination of the three craps bets, and also the 11.
m. Dealer	His position at the table.
n. Stickman	His position at the table.
o. Boxman	His position at the table.

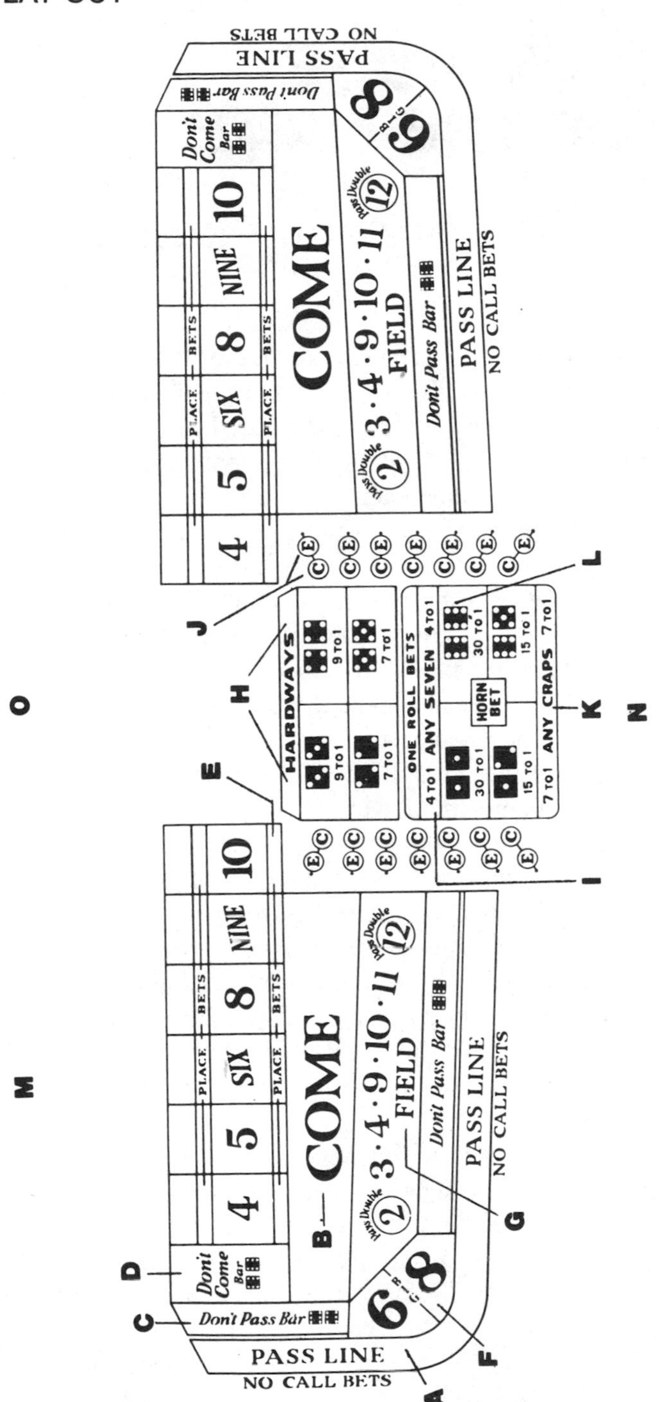
PASS LINE
NO CALL BETS
Don't Pass Bar
Don't Come Bar
PLACE BETS
4
5
SIX
8
NINE
10
COME
Pass Double 2
3 · 4 · 9 · 10 · 11
Pass Double 12
FIELD
BIG 6 8
HARDWAYS
9 TO 1
7 TO 1
ONE ROLL BETS
ANY SEVEN
4 TO 1
30 TO 1
15 TO 1
HORN BET
ANY CRAPS
7 TO 1
C E
A
B
C
D
E
F
G
H
I
J
K
L
M
N
O

KNOWLEDGE OF THE GAME

4

Dealers and Pit Bosses

Let's touch on the management side of the table, by explaining about the personnel who run the game. In a casino, there are sometimes four, six or eight tables in one section. Walking behind these tables, checking the customers, the dealers, and the flow of each game, are the pit bosses. These are usually ex-dealers, who have been around for some time, and they are sharp.

In the event of a dispute that cannot be handled by the boxman, the pit boss will step in and make the final decision. These pit bosses have a tremendous grasp of the game, are secure in their jobs, and have the best interests of the house in their hands. They realize that it is important to keep the customers happy, and that sometimes a dealer can make a mistake, which goes against the player.

For that reason, you will find that the decision of the pit bosses, many times, will be in favor of the player. It is a good public relations move, and makes that casino look good. I've seen many, many times when a dispute arose between a dealer and a player, and the pit boss was called in. Invariably, the decision would go to the player. If you have a problem, where you are positive you are correct, don't hesitate to ask for the final decision of these pit bosses. You will get a good shake, most of the time.

A final word on these pit bosses. I said they were sharp, and some of them can scan a table of fifteen players, and in a matter of five or six rolls of the dice, size up every player. They can tell the strong player, the novice, the ones with scared money, the big shot, the junket player, the pro, all in the space of a few minutes. You ever have a problem at the craps table, ask for a decision by these people. They've already studied your play, and the outcome will not be prejudiced. Hey, don't get the idea that I am a shill for the casino. Hardly. They are the enemy, and you better look at them as such. But every enemy has vulnerable spots, and strong points. I am simply trying to alert you to all of the things you will encounter in your trips.

Next we have the boxman. It might be a man or woman, and there may be one or two of them handling a table, depending on the amount of action at a particular time. He or she is seated opposite the stickman, in a position to observe the whole table. He is a sort of referee for that game, making sure the players' bets, and the dealers' payoffs, are correct. The boxman counts all money coming into the game, and places the cash into a drop box, which is situated right in front of him. It's sort of a boring job, but the step before becoming a pit boss. The boxman does not share in the tips for the dealers, but he is shortly removed from being a dealer himself, and allows a certain amount of levity in seeing things that may go in favor of the player. This is explained more in the chapter on tipping.

And then there are the dealers, who usually work in groups of four, with three of them handling a table, and one on a break. After twenty minutes, the oncoming dealer will replace the stickman, who then moves to one of the dealers' spots. That dealer then takes his twenty-minute break, and the process is repeated for that entire shift. A dealer usually works forty minutes on, and twenty minutes off. The pay, at this writing, in Atlantic City, is minimum wage, and all the dealers on a shift share in whatever tips are accumulated during that time. It's an exciting job in the beginning, and then, like any other job becomes just that. Technically, you become a sort of robot, dealing out cards in Blackjack, spinning the ball in Roulette, making payoffs in Craps.

The dealers with outgoing personalities can turn their day into either a drab experience, or a fun time, depending upon their rapport with the different players who come to their table.

So many people blame the dealer for the flow of the cards, that they show their ignorance of gambling, by assuming that a dealer can effect what cards come out of a shoe, or show on a set of dice.

A good dealer will assist you at the table, usually reminding you of the correct amount of money to be wagered on the odds, or, after noting your style of play, bring up the fact that you may have forgotten to place a certain number. Then again, a slow dealer can antagonize the players by slow and sloppy payoffs.

When there is a lot of action at a table, and some patrons are making exceptionally high wagers, in off amounts, the pit boss may replace a slow dealer with a sharp veteran from another table, to handle the play from that side of the table. That's to keep the flow of the game sailing along. A strong craps player, who knows exactly what he's doing, will become very aggravated if he is saddled with a slow dealer, who has trouble making split second payoffs on a series of high, multiple valued bets. The pit boss will immediately bring in a fast dealer to keep the action going. This type move shows that player that the casino values his play, and wants to keep him comfortable.

It's no trouble spotting the good dealers. They are fast, accurate, courteous. They would rather see you win than lose. In that way, they may be in line for a toke. If you are the type of person who automatically hates the dealer, because you think he represents the house, take another stock of your opinion. They are human beings who have no inner desire to wipe you out. Get them on your side. They can help you more than hurt you.

The stickman runs the game. He calls out the point, checks the other dealers, in the event they may miss a bet, and controls the proposition bets in the center of the table. He will not return the dice to the shooter until his two dealers have finished handling all of the bets for their respective players.

Due to the superstition bug that grips many players, you will notice that the stickman will not present the dice to a shooter with the total of seven showing. A lot of players consider that bad luck, and so in order not to irritate anyone, the stickman will make sure that any number but 7 is showing when you receive the dice back.

It might be nice to mention one other person who could be considered part of the casino personnel. That would be the shill. This person is retained by the casinos, when business is slow, to play at a table in an attempt to draw customers. A lot of people won't venture up to an empty table, but don't ask me why.

To offset this empty feeling, a shill will be sent to the table, and immediately given a stack of chips from that table, and begin to play. He'll stay at that table until enough customers are involved in the game. Then he'll merely return the chips to the dealer, leave that table and wait for a new assignment. Shills are used mostly in Las Vegas, because there are so many casinos and so many tables. Right now, Atlantic City does not have to resort to shills, due to the tremendous crowds that are usually there.

I used to work as a shill, to get enough money to build up another bankroll. Don't get me wrong, the pay is lousy, but the work isn't too strenuous. Remember, you're not risking any of your own money. Of course you don't get to keep your winnings, but it's not so tough on the nerves.

I worked as a shill, many years ago, when I was running bad. Looking back now, it seems that I put in a lot of shill time. I could be playing craps for three or four days, and get whacked. So I'd grab a job with a casino, to work as a shill, and would you believe all of a sudden, I'd turn into the hottest shooter in the desert, and naturally no way to benefit from it. When I set aside a few dollars to get back into action, my shilling would end—at least until my winnings diminished, and it was time to eat again. Those were the days when I never knew there was such a thing as Discipline. I never knew when to quit. I could never win enough, never. Eventually I'd lose it back, and then begin the process over again.

There was never a time when I risked money that I borrowed, to gamble. I just love the action, the thrill of the chase, the walking on the edge. When I was broke, which was often, I worked as a dealer, or a shill, accumulated some capital, and started out again. Finally, I learned about Discipline and Money Management, and a new door opened. It will with you too.

I remember one time in particular, after an unusual run of bad dice over a few weeks' span, I decided to swallow my pride and get a job as a shill. The pay was $10 a day. At the time, I figured swallowing some food would be a lot more beneficial to my health.

While working the tables as a shill, the dice came to me. All we were supposed to do was put a chip on the Pass Line, and not get fancy. I placed my chip on the Pass Line and started my roll. One hour and fifty minutes I held the dice. I threw points, numbers, hard ways, 7's and 11's on the come-out, everything. You name it, it showed on the dice.

Remember now, none of this money was mine, but the rest of the table was whooping up some storm. The table was packed. Everyone was winning, and winning big. Finally, the roll ended and I got a rousing ovation. I do recall one thing though. A couple of the high rollers at the table knew I was a shill, and not benefiting from the roll. They threw me a couple of chips during the play, and again at the end. When I left the table after that roll, I had over $150 in tips, and the next day was back in action on my own.

But never before, and not since that day, have I had such a hot roll. Maybe there's a message in that. Perhaps I was born to be a shill.

KNOWLEDGE OF THE GAME

5

The Buy-In

When you go up to a craps table, you are able to enter the game as soon as you want. If a point has not been established, you will see the black side of the puck, which marks the pass line number, sitting in the "off" position, on the side of the lay-out, in the section marked: "Don't Come." That means that a number has not as yet been established. The game has not begun.

You could make your bet on either the Pass or Don't Pass Line, and get into the initial flow of the upcoming game. But, even if the white side of the puck indicates a point number has been established, because it is on one of the place numbers, and the side of the puck that says "on" is showing, you are still able to immediately get involved.

Let's say you walk up to a table and want to wait to begin betting, only from the come-out roll. Great, merely wait until a decision has been reached on the game in progress, and then start your series of bets. As long as that puck stays in the "on" position, on top of one of the place numbers, that game is live. When the shooter either makes that number, or 7's out, the puck is returned to the Don't Come box, and you can now start your betting sequences, because a new game will now be starting.

The first thing you do is drop your "buy-in" cash in front of you. Don't try to hand the money to the dealer. He cannot take it from your hand. You must place it on the layout. He knows what it's for. When the dealer has a player try to hand him the cash, he knows right away the person is a novice.

The dealer will take your buy-in money, and place it in front of the boxman. Let's say it is $200. The boxman will count it out on the table, and inform the dealer how much in chips he is to give you. In this case it was $200. The dealer will count out $150 in red, $5 chips, and two green $25 chips.

Notice that the house will keep trying to increase the valued chips they want in front of you. If you've got some green chips in your stack, you may feel too intimidated to ask the dealer to break them down to $5 chips, and start betting the higher amounts. We'll cover intimidation later. With a $200 session amount, you are a $5 bettor.

As soon as the dealer places your $200 in chips in front of you, grab them, count them, and place them in the rack in front of you. If there is a mistake, immediately call it to the dealer's attention.

Since you will be using $1 chips (usually white), in your play, drop a couple of $5 chips on the lay-out, and ask the dealer for: "Change please," or "Check change, please," or "Break it down, please," or "Some whites, please." He will count out ten white $1 chips, and place them in front of you.

You have completed your "buy-in," and are ready to swing into action.

KNOWLEDGE OF THE GAME

6

The Game

I know that the speed of Bank Craps, and the constant betting of the patrons, confuses many people. They're intimidated by all the action, and instead of zeroing in on the game itself, they find themselves trying to comprehend the various moves of the dealers.

Let's break down the entire exercise of Craps—to the object of the game:

A shooter picks up the dice, tosses them to the other side of the table and tries to establish a point number, either 4, 5, 6, 8, 9, or 10. He must throw that number again, before a 7.

That's it!!!!! That's the entire object of Craps. There are a multitude of side bets that can be made, but it all reverts back to the basic idea of making your number, before a 7 shows.

Examine a set of dice. There are six numbers on each die, and when that set of dice are thrown across the table, there are thirty-six possible combinations that can be made.

NUMBER THAT SHOWS	COMBINATIONS	WAYS TO ROLL IT
2	1-1	1
3	1-2, 2-1	2
4	1-3, 3-1, 2-2	3
5	1-4, 4-1, 2-3, 3-2	4
6	1-5, 5-1, 2-3, 3-2, 3-3	5
7	1-6, 6-1, 2-5, 5-2, 3-4, 4-3	6
8	2-6, 6-2, 3-5, 5-3, 4-4	5
9	3-6, 6-3, 4-5, 5-4	4
10	4-6, 6-4, 5-5	3
11	5-6, 6-5	2
12	6-6	

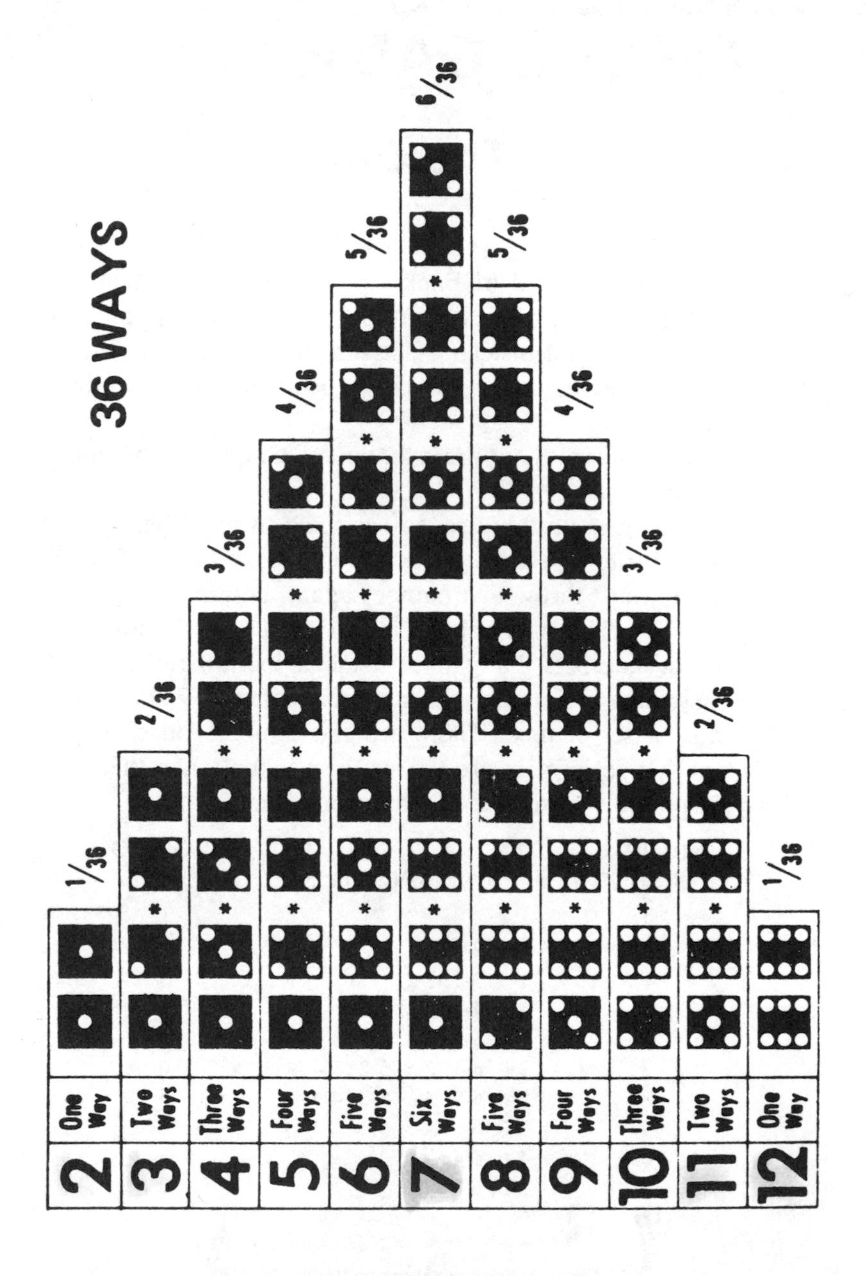
36 WAYS
2 One Way 1/36
3 Two Ways 2/36
4 Three Ways 3/36
5 Four Ways 4/36
6 Five Ways 5/36
7 Six Ways 6/36
8 Five Ways 5/36
9 Four Ways 4/36
10 Three Ways 3/36
11 Two Ways 2/36
12 One Way 1/36

For example, on the 11, there are two ways for that total to show. Six on one die, 5 on the other. Then reverse it, because the first die could turn up 5 and not 6. Then, the second die could be 6, and not 5. I've seen guys actually get into fist fights, arguing over this explanation. And yet the answer is so logical, and so simple to understand.

Check back to how many ways that 7 can be made (6). It is the power number in dice. If the dice were to come out, one at a time, no matter what that first number was, it is half way to a 7. This does not hold true for any other number. Suppose the first die showed a 2. There is nothing on the second die to allow a 9 or a 10 to appear, but the 5 will cause 7 to be the total of the two numbers. As you get deeper into this game, remember that little fact. The right bettor is always fighting that powerful 7, after his point is established.

Each shooter takes his or her turn throwing the dice, or he or she can pass up the chance to throw the dice, by merely waving the dice to the next shooter. But, most people love to throw those dominoes. It's so funny. A guy could be playing Pass Line at a table, and betting $5 on every shooter. Finally the dice are passed to him. He immediately drops $15 on the line. He feels that he is gonna get hot, and wants to pour it in. Typical illogical thinking.

The game begins when the black and white marker, or puck, is in the off position. The stickman will push five dice in front of thc next shooter. He chooses two of them. The stickman returns the other three dice to the bowl in front of him and says, "We're coming out." That means the game is beginning. The first roll of the dice, by this new shooter, is called the "come-out roll." He is "coming out" with the dice, trying to establish a point, or throw a 7 or 11 on that first roll.

Let's assume everyone is betting on the pass line. They don't have to bet, except for the shooter, but in this case, everyone at the table is betting that this shooter will have a hot roll. They each place a $5 bet on the pass line. They are right bettors.

The shooter could throw any one of the previously mentioned thirty-six combinations. If he throws:

1. 7 Pass Line bettors win even money
2. 11 Pass Line bettors win even money
3. 2 Pass Line bettors lose
4. 3 Pass Line bettors lose
5. 12 Pass Line bettors lose

Notice the Pass Line bettors will win even money on their bets eight times (7 and 11), and lose four times (2-3-12), on the come-out roll. That's big 8-4 edge they have going for them.

6. 4, 5, 6, 8, 9, 10 That is their point, and must be made again, before the 7.

The shooter will hold the dice, until he is unable to make his point, by sevening out. Don't call it crap outs. When he establishes a number, let's say 6, he could throw for three days, just as long as a 6 or 7 doesn't show. If the 6 comes, he has made his point, and a new game begins by repeating the above procedure. If the 7 comes before the 6, the game is over, the dice pass to the next player, and he in turn will begin the next game.

Incidentally, when throwing dice, use a little class. Throwing those little monsters doesn't take much intelligence or strength, yet over a hundred times a day, someone will throw one of the dice off the table. Both dice must hit the opposite side of the table, and just a little flick of the wrist will give you a nice soft throw. It is very easy to keep the dice on the table, and keep the game moving right along.

Also, try not to hit the stacks of chips in front of the far dealer. Some players intentionally aim for them, for no other reason than to satisfy their own curious humor.

Another crazy habit is trying to set the dice a certain way, before throwing them. When they hit the other side of the table, all the fixing in the world won't help you, as the dice will just bounce around in an uncontrolled pattern. I've seen people drop the dice in front of them, 4, 5, 6, 7 times, trying to "get rid of the 7's," before throwing them. This really antagonizes both the dealers and the other players.

Make your bets as soon as you can, and get your hands back off the playing area. Don't leave your arms hanging over the sides. Invariably, the shooter will hit your hand, and if the number that comes out is unfavorable for the majority of that table, you'll hear about it. Make your bets immediately after the previous roll and step back.

Each part of the table will be covered separately in upcoming chapters, but after you know the object of the game, all these other pieces will fall in line.

In summary: the game begins when the shooter, on the come-out roll, throws either a 4, 5, 6, 8, 9, or 10. He continues throwing the dice until his point, or a 7 appears. Naturally, after every throw of the dice, the house allows time for all players to make additional bets, as they see fit. On the come-out roll, 7 or 11 is an automatic win, and pays even money. Two, 3, or 12 is called Craps, and if it shows on the come out roll, results in an immediate loss to the right bettors. In the case of Craps, the shooter still retains the dice.

When the shooter is "coming out" with his first throw, the puck is in the "off" position in the Don't Come box, with the black side up. As soon as the dice present a point, the stickman announces the result. His dialogue could be as follows:

1. If 7 or 11 shows: . . . "Winner, winner on the front line. Pay the do's and take the don'ts." (That means the right, or do bettors are automatic winners. He is telling the dealers to take the bets from those who bet on the Don't Pass, since they lose, if the natural appears on the come-out roll.)
2. If 2, 3, or 12 shows: . . . "Two (3 or 12), Craps, line away. Take the do's and pay the don'ts. Twelve is barred." (The right, or do bettors lose, if Craps shows on the come-out roll. In the case of the 2 or 3, the don't or wrong bettors automatically win even money. If the 12 shows, the do bettors lose, the don't bettors get a push, or tie. They don't win or lose.)
3. If 4, 5, 6, 8, 9, or 10 shows: . . . Stickman will announce that particular number, such as: "Five, five, mark the five. We're out on five." (It's self-explanatory. He is

telling both dealers, and the whole bevy of players, that the 5 "came" on the come-out roll, and the pass line bettors need a 5 to "show," before the 7. The don't bettors want the 7 before the 5. The two dealers immediately take the puck, turn the white, or "on" position face up, and place it on the number that showed, in this case the 5. The game has begun.)

Keep looking for the logical explanation to everything that comes up at that table. After awhile, you'll see how simple this game really is.

KNOWLEDGE OF THE GAME

Pass Line

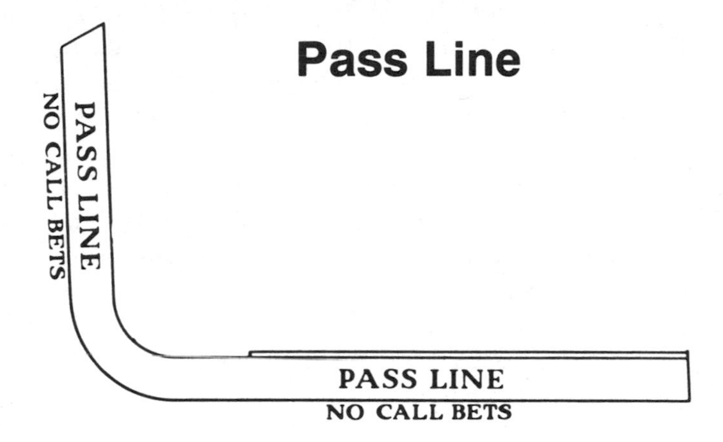

One of the most popular plays on any craps table is the Pass Line. The vigorish against you is only 1.41% and after the point number is established, you can take free odds, which reduce the vig against you to .8%.

Your bet on the Pass Line indicated you are going with the shooter—playing that numbers keep coming out, and hoping that the shooter gets a red hot roll, and holds the dice for a good long time.

Most players bet the Pass Line. They are called do bettors, or right bettors, or Pass Line bettors. It is not for me to say which is the smartest player, the right bettor, who continuously looks for the hot roll, or the wrong bettor, who is playing for that 7 to keep appearing after the shooter establishes his point. It will always come down to how you manage your money, regardless of which side you prefer.

After a player drops his bet on the Pass Line, and the shooter establishes his point, either 4, 5, 6, 8, 9, or 10, that bet is locked. He cannot remove it from the table, until a decision is reached. Either that number is made, or the 7 beats him.

Pass Line bets are paid off at even money. Suppose you come up to a table, after the point has been set. For example, 10 was the point. You can place a $5 chip on the Pass Line, and another $5 free odds bet behind the line, even though the game began before you arrived. If the 10 shows, you receive $5 for your pass line bet, and $10 for your 2-1 odds bet. That's a total of $15. However, you could have "placed" the whole $10 on the number 10, and if it hit, get a payoff of 9-5, for a total win of $18. That extra $3 is the reason why it is better to place your bet on the number, instead of the Pass Line, but only in the event you wish to cover the point, and arrive too late to take advantage of the come-out roll, where the 7 and 11 give you an 8-4 edge on Craps showing.

If you don't understand the previous paragraph, go back and read it again, until it sinks in. I want you to take this game in degrees. It is not hard to play, but the multiple variations of bets make it important that you know what your options are.

A final word on the Pass Line. Like I said, most players bet the Pass Line, and many of them do it simply because that's what the majority is doing. The vigorish against you is only .8% when you take free odds, so it is an excellent bet. But, you do not have to bet the Pass Line. You can bypass the come-out roll, and then place the numbers you desire. Of course, you lose the 8-4 edge that the 7 and 11 has over the 2, 3, and 12 on the come out, but you also eliminate the possibility of getting stuck with the 4 and 10, the two numbers that are difficult to make.

You then have the opportunity of placing the 6 and/or 8, which, logically, has a better chance of showing, than the 4 or 10.

But don't make your decisions yet. Just keep an open mind until you reach the money management section.

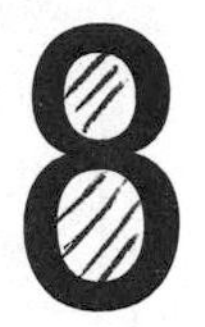

KNOWLEDGE OF THE GAME

Free Odds

Before you start this chapter, clear your brain, take a strong shot of ice water, and move all other thoughts out of your head. This is, by far, the most complicated part of the game, and yet the explanation is so logical, it's hard to believe that so many people have trouble grasping it.

It is called free odds, or true odds, and I shall explain it, as to how it applies to the right bettor.

The table is not marked, where this bet is allowed, and that is because it is the only bet in the casino, where the house does not have a vigorish working for them. Usually, the lay-out will read something like, "No Call Bets," where the free odds are to be placed.

Incidentally, "No Call Bets" means exactly what it states. You cannot go up to a table and call out a bet. Your money must be on the table, and the dealer, or boxman, must acknowledge your bet. Suppose you did not have any chips, and the dice were coming out. You drop a $100 bill on the table and tell the dealer, "Ten dollars on the Pass Line." If he acknowledges this with, "You've got a bet," or "Ten they do," or "You've got action," or simply "Bet," you've got yourself a bet. If neither the dealer or boxman acknowledges your request, you do not have anything going.

This is to stop people from yelling out a bet, and if the roll does not show a favorable edge to the caller, he could disappear into the crowd. I've seen guys in Vegas call out a bet on the come-out roll like this: "Two hundred on the Pass Line!" hoping that a 7 or 11 shows. A three craps comes up, and all Pass Line bettors lose. The guy with the mouth turns and runs.

(It's a contest as to whether he or the difference gets to the parking lot first.) If he suddenly develops a broken kneecap, you have to assume he lost the race. Atlantic City takes all the fun away from guys trying that play, by barring the "call bet."

Back to the free or true odds bet. You put a $5 chip on the Pass Line and a 10 shows. That is your point. You want a 10 to appear before the 7. Let's see what your chances of winning are.

Checking the chart in Chapter 6, you find that a 10 can be made only three ways, while there are six ways for the 7 to show. You are only paid even money for the Pass Line bet and yet the odds against the 10 coming are 6-3, or 2-1. You're not in such great shape. But, the house allows you to take what is called free or true odds, by placing a chip behind your Pass Line bet, for an amount equal to what your Pass Line bet is. This is called single odds. In this case, you put a $5 chip behind the first $5 chip that you have on the Pass Line.

If the 10 shows, you are paid even money ($5) for your Pass Line bet, and true odds for your free odds bet. Since the true odds are 2-1, and you took $5 odds, the payoff is $10. That $10 that you received for your odds bet, make for a total payout of $15. What the free odds have done are increase the value of your Pass Line bet. By not taking free odds, you receive only $5 for your $5 bet, and yet the chances of a $10 showing are 6-3 against you. But, by taking the free odds, you are now paid $15, for the $10 you risked, or $7.50 for each $5 wagered. It is always a good idea to take the free odds in order that your Pass Line wager is increased in value.

Since the 4 and 10 can both be made three ways (6-4, 4-6, 5-5, for the 10, and 1-3, 3-1, 2-2, for the 4), they are called sister numbers, and the odds on one, are exactly the same as on the other.

Suppose the 6 was the point. Let's work out the formula for figuring what odds you can take. Since the 6 and 8 can both be made five ways, the explanation on one will suffice for the other.

OK, you've bet $5 on the Pass Line, and the 6 showed. There are five ways to make the 6 (1-5, 5-1, 2-4, 4-2, 3-3), and six ways for the 7 to appear (1-6, 6-1, 2-5, 5-2, 3-4, 4-3). That means your chances of winning are 6-5 against you. So, by placing a $5 chip behind your pass line bet, after the 6 showed as the point, you have single odds working. If the 6 comes before the 7, you'll be paid even money for the Pass Line bet, and true odds, $6 to $5, for the free odds, making a total payoff of $11, for the $10 at risk. Notice how you increased the value of your even money Pass Line payoff from $5 to $5.50, merely by taking the free odds.

Finally, we come to the 5 and 9, and a little extra thinking is needed here. You drop a $5 chip on the pass line, and the 5 shows. There are four ways to make the 5 (1-4, 4-1, 2-3, 3-2), as opposed to six ways of making a 7. That makes the odds, against you making your point of 5, 6-4, or 3-2, or 9-6, or 7½-5. All of these percentages are exactly the same, and I show them here, to alert you to what the correct payoff should be. The example of this payoff is based on the 5 as the point, but it also applies to the 9. Since the 9 can be made four ways (3-6, 6-3, 4-5, 5-4), the odds are also against you, and the payoffs will be the same as on the 5.

Since you bet $5 on the line, in a craps game that allows single odds, you are able to take free odds for the amount of your pass line wager. With a $5 chip on the pass line, and a $5 chip behind the line, as odds, the house would be obligated to pay you true odds on that second bet, calling for a payout of $7.50, because that would be the true payoff. That means they would have to deal in half-dollar chips, and they are not interested in that maneuver. So, in the case of a $5 Pass Line bet, where the point is 5 or 9, there is a slight adjustment in the odds you may take. The house allows you to place an extra $1 chip on your $5 odds bet, making a total of $6 odds. Then, if the 5 (or 9, if that is the point), is made, they can pay you the correct odds of $9, for the $6 you risked. Breaking the payoff down, it comes to $3 for every $2 you bet. If you were to break the $6 odds bet into three separate piles of $2 each, the odds of 3 to 2 could easily be applied. You would risk three piles of $2 each, and be paid three piles of $3 each. This comes to $9 for the $6 you laid out. Simple, eh?

See how logical every one of these moves are? Just another part of the Little 3. If you sometimes forget to take your extra dollar odds, on the 5 or 9, the sharp dealers will remind you so as to make sure you receive full value for your bet.

However, if the dealer reminds you to increase your odds bet from $5 to $6, and you refuse, because you don't understand, or are not interested, then you're on your own. If the 5 (or 9, if that is the point), is made, you will receive $5 for your Pass Line bet, and only $7 for your odds, not $7.50. That's why it is better to put out that extra dollar, for it amounts to a 2-1 payoff for that extra buck. You will be paid $9 to $6, instead of $7 to $5.

Odds bets are the best move in a casino, because you are receiving the true payoff, in relation to your chances of winning or losing. The house has no vigorish attached to this bet. Take your free odds.

Following is the amount of odds you are allowed to take on the 5 and 9, when you bet an uneven amount:

PASS LINE WAGER	MONEY ODDS TAKEN	ODDS PAY-OFF
$ 5	$ 6	$ 9
$15	$20	$30
$25	$30	$45
$35	$40	$60

This allows the dealers to quickly pay off the true odds wagers, and actually allows the players to pick up a couple of extra dollars in free odds. Later on, I will go over the three-unit bet, which allows you to consistently pick up the free odds edge.

Also, in a later chapter, you will see an option you have in the case of the taking or not taking of free odds, in the case of the 4 and 10. For now, concentrate on the fact that you should always take free odds, and then the options off of these moves will be entirely up to you, but only after you understand the theory of the bet.

KNOWLEDGE OF THE GAME 9

Double Odds

There are some casinos, but not all, that allow double odds (or more) to be taken. Since the house does not gain any vig on the odds bets, you might ask why they would permit the player to take these extra shots at the casino's money. The reasons could be:

1. To draw the craps player to that particular casino
2. To realize that players lack of Money Management and Discipline will eventually break him

I'll give you my comments on this, later in the chapter. For now, let's go over the plus factors for double odds. It merely means that you are allowed to bet twice as much on the free odds, as you have wagered on the pass line. If you have the proper bankroll, this is an excellent edge for the player. It reduces the vigorish against you from .8% to .6%, the best move you can expect at the casinos, with the exception of the card counter in Blackjack.

Suppose you bet $5 on the Pass Line. No matter what number showed as the point, you are allowed to take $10 free odds behind the line. This gives you an increased value for the Pass Line wager, which will only be paid off at even money.

Another edge for the player comes from a $10 bet on the Pass Line, and the point is 6 or 8. The house allows you to take $25 free odds behind the line. This opportunity to take double odds, definitely helps the craps player—but only if he can afford it. If your bankroll does not measure up to my method of play—forget double odds.

I've listed two reasons why the house gives you this bonus,

and the first reason is self explanatory. That particular casino is looking to lure all of the high spending, big rollers to their games.

The second reason is a spin-off of the first. Most people who gamble—do not have strong Money Management and Discipline techniques. The casinos realize this, and base their hopes on this lack of control breaking the player, before he reaches a hot roll. Since Bankroll is the first step in the Big 4, the lack of it, regardless of the double odds, will prohibit you from taking advantage of this edge, as you will see in the Money Management sections. If you lack the proper Bankroll, double odds are a no-no.

KNOWLEDGE OF THE GAME

Three-Unit Bet

A little known fact, even by astute craps players, is the benefit a player gets from betting three units at a time on the Pass Line. That's because with a three-unit bet, in a single odds game, the house allows you to take higher free odds.

Remember, in a single odds game, you are allowed to take free odds for an amount equal to your Pass Line wager. Of course, in the case of the 5 or 9, you may add $1 to your odds bet.

To be able to bet heavier odds, the house allows you to get more money in action, if you bet in these aforementioned three-unit bets. For example, if you bet $15 on the Pass Line (three units), and the point is 6 or 8, the house allows you to take five units in free odds ($25). This way they can pay you 6 to 5, or $30 for the $25 wagered. Following are some examples:

PASS LINE WAGER	POINT	AMOUNT OF ODDS (SINGLE ODDS)
$15	6 or 8	$25
$15	5 or 9	$20
$ 6	6 or 8	$10
$ 6	5 or 9	$10

It behooves you to take advantage of these little edges. Naturally, you cannot do it if you lack the proper bankroll, but then again, you shouldn't be in the casino in the first place, unless you are properly prepared.

KNOWLEDGE OF THE GAME

11

Come Bets

COME

Notice on the lay-out, the space on both sides of the table, that is labeled COME. This bet is exactly the same as the Pass Line, and is used by the right bettor. You cannot bet the come box until a point number is established.

On the first roll of a game, the come-out roll affects the bet you have on the Pass Line. The same is true for the Come bet. After a point number is established, you may place a bet in the Come box. Just as on your pass line wager, the next roll of the dice will affect that chip.

Suppose you placed a chip on the Pass Line and the 4 showed. That is your point. You took $5 free odds behind the line. Since Bank Craps offers you the opportunity of making multiple bets, you want additional numbers going for you. Drop a $5 chip in the Come box. The next roll is a 7. You lose your Pass Line bet and odds, because the 7 showed before the 4, but since that roll affected your Come bet (which is exactly the same as the Pass Line), you would win $5 for the $5 you had in the Come box.

Following is actually a repeat of what could happen to that particular bet (4 is the point):

1. If 7 showed, you lose your Pass Line and odds bet, but win even money on the Come wager
2. If 11 showed, you win $5 even money for the Come

bet—the Pass Line bets remain

3. If 2, 3, or 12 showed, you lose $5 Come bet—Pass Line bets stay
4. If 4 showed, you win your Pass Line and odds bet. The 4 "came," and that Come bet chip is then moved to a spot in the place number box 4, and becomes a separate wager on its own, to be affected by only the 4 or the 7
5. If 5, 6, 8, 9, or 10 shows, it becomes a bet, separate from the Pass Line bet, which in this case was 4. This Come bet will be affected only by that number appearing again, or the 7, which means you get paid if it repeats, and lose if the 7 shows first.

Take it step by step. You don't have to be a genius to understand what happens to your Come bet if 2, 3, 11, or 12 shows. The 7 is equally logical. You automatically win the Come bet, but since the 7 showed before the 4, which was the point, your Pass Line bet is lost, the puck returns to the OFF position, you pick up your Come bet and winnings and start over with a bet on the Pass Line.

If the 4 showed, while you had that Come chip in action, it means the point, or Pass Line bet was made. The dealer would complete that transaction, by taking all bets that were on the Don't Pass, and then paying all of the Pass Line wagers, because the 4 was made.

However, your $5 chip is still in the Come box, and that is now a new bet. Even though the puck is moved to the "OFF" position, to signal the end of that game, the bet that came through the Come, now becomes a new, separate wager.

A word here regarding where the dealer will place that chip. Since there could be three or four different players having money in the Come box, the dealer distinguishes whose bet it is by lining the chips up—in the place box, after a number shows, to coincide with where you are standing at the table. For instance, if you are standing right next to the stickman, your Come bet chip is placed in the 4 box, right next to the dividing line of the 4 and the 5. If that dealer leaves the table, the new dealer knows exactly which Come bet belongs to each player, by merely lining them up with where you are standing around the table.

Just as in the case of the Pass Line wager, the first thing you do, when a point is established on the come-out roll, is take your free odds. The same should be done here. However, you cannot touch the bets in the place box, or Come box section of the table. So, you merely drop your chip in the Come box, and tell the dealer: "Odds, please!" You are telling him you wish to take odds on your Come bet. Due to the sparse room in that box, they do not put the odds bet behind the Come bet. Instead, the odds bet is placed on top of the Come bet, although edged over the side, to show how it is separate from the base Come bet. In this particular instance, since the 4 that showed on the Come was the same as the point bet, you do not have to immediately take odds, because the prior game ended when the 4 was made. On the next roll, which will be a come-out roll for the next game, your Come bet will "work," but odds are off on the come-out roll. Wait until a new number is established as the point, and then you can take odds of that Come bet.

If the 5, 6, 8, 9, or 10 showed on that second roll (example 5), that would be a new number working for the players, who put a chip in the Come box. The dealer will take that chip (let's say it was an 8), and put it in the number 8 box, at a place in that section, that coincides with your position at the table. Now you have two numbers working for you, the point number 4, and the Come number 8. Suppose you want another Come bet working for you. Drop a chip into the Come box. The same procedure is repeated. Then the following could occur:

1. If the 4 shows, point is made, and Come bet moves to the 4
2. If the 7 shows, you lose pass line bet on 4 with odds, and previous Come bet and odds on the 8. But you win $5 for the present come wager
3. If 11 shows, you win present Come bet
4. If 2, 3, or 12 shows, you lose present Come bet
5. If 5, 6, 9, or 10 shows, dealer moves your Come chip to that number (let's say it was a 5). You immediately drop $6 on the lay-out, and tell him: "Odds on my five,

please." He lays the $6 on top of the Come bet—off to the side. You now have Come bets of 5 and 8, along with the pass line bet on the 4.

6. If 8 shows, the dealer pays you $5 for your previous $5 Come bet on the 8, plus $6 for the odds you took on the 8. (That bet immediately comes down.) He then puts the present Come bet into the 8 box, and you drop a $5 chip to cover odds on that 8. You once again have a Pass Line bet with odds, and one Come bet, with odds.

I'll go over the theory behind Come betting in the Money Management section, so right now the main thing is to know all the ins and outs of this part of the game.

A brief review of the main points:

1. Come bets can only be made after Pass Line point number is established.
2. Come Line rules exactly the same as Pass Line.
3. Come bets are positioned in place number box, in such a way that they coincide with where bettor is standing at the table.
4. Odds on Come bets are placed on top of original bet, overlapping to the side, to indicate odds are separate from basic bet.
5. Come bets, like the Pass Line bet, cannot be taken down until a decision is reached, although odds can be removed any time.
6. Come bets work on the come-out roll, but the odds are OFF.
7. Payoffs are even money on basic bet, and true payoff on odds bet.
8. Come bets can be made, even though you have no bet on the Pass Line.
9. Come Bets can fluctuate in value, as long as they are within minimum guide lines of that particular table.
10. Just as in the case of Pass Line bets, you do not have to take full odds. For instance, if you bet $10 on Pass Line, or Come Line, and the 10 shows, you could opt to take just $5 (half odds), or none.

That's about it for the Come Line. It is not complicated, and the rules are exactly the same as apply to the Pass Line. Should you play the Come??? I, personally, do not advise it, but again, digest the method, and we'll get into opinions later on. I just think there is a better way to play Craps.

KNOWLEDGE OF THE GAME 12

Place Bets

This is a big part of Craps, and is becoming more popular with players, due to the fact that place bets can be put up, and taken down, at any time during the course of the game, allowing the player a tremendous amount of flexibility.

You have to look hard to find the place bet sections, as it is written in black, surrounding the place box numbers.

		PLACE	BETS		
4	5	SIX	8	NINE	10
		PLACE	BETS		

When you "place" a bet, it is put by the dealer in the spaces so marked, in deference to the Come bets, which are positioned right in the numbered box. In effect, the place bets are a gamc within themselves, since they do not work on the come-out roll. They can be taken down, or placed, at any time the player wishes, have their own set of payoffs, and can even be "called off" for a roll of the dice, at any time. Also, unlike the Come bet, which, after it is hit, is given back to the player, along with the profit, the place bet can stay up, or taken down, or increased. Again, this is all at the discretion of each individual player.

Obviously, you get the idea that this is an important part of Craps, and may end up being the sections you will concentrate on completely.

We'll start with the payoffs, which are not the same as true odds. That's because the house must apply a certain amount of vigorish, to each bet, to insure its profit. Refer back to the odds chart, to see the difference in the percentages. Following is a breakdown for comparison purposes:

PLACE BET	TRUE ODDS	PLACE PAYOFF	HOUSE VIG
4	2-1	9-5	6.67%
5	3-2 (7½-5)	7-5	4.00%
6	6-5	7-6	1.52%
8	6-5	7-6	1.52%
9	3-2 (7½-5)	7-5	4.00%
10	2-1	9-5	6.67%

Suppose you wish to place a $5 bet on the 4. Merely drop the chip on the lay-out and tell the dealer, "Place the 4, please." The dealer will place the chip in the Place box section, again to coincide with where your position at the table is. The place bet sections are on both sides of the number, to allow enough room to cover every players space, on either side of the table.

When placing a bet on one of the six numbers, you can bet all of them at once, or singularly, as you desire. Naturally, a 7 wipes you out.

There's a big reason why a lot of craps player prefer the place bets over the Come bets. Assume two players were at the same table, and each had a different theory as to how to bet. The Come player puts his chip in the Come box, and the place bettor merely puts $22 on the table and announces, "Inside bets, please." The dealer places $5 on the 5 and 9, and $6 on the 6 and 8.

The 6 shows, and the place bettor is immediately paid his $7 profit. The Come bettor, even though he had the possibility of winning his come bet, if the 7 showed, now merely has his bet moved to the 6. He must have that 6 hit again, to receive a profit. There are different theories on this comparison, and my views are expressed in the next chapter.

The vigorish is heavy on the placing of the 4 and 10, since you are paid $9 instead of $10, for a $5 wager. That's a 6.67% whack, and a dollar *profit* for the house on every bet. Think about that!!!!! The casino retains a 50-cent profit on the 9 and 5, by paying you $7 on a $5 bet, instead of $7.50.

The least amount of vig is on the placing of the 6 and 8. You are paid $7 for every $6 wagered, instead of $6 for every $5. With this place bet, you are paid $6 for your initial $5 bet, and $1 for the extra $1 you must lay down to place the 6 or 8. They should be paying you $1.20 for that extra dollar, and the twenty cents is their vig, or edge, making the percentage only 1.52% against you. That is not too shabby a bet. That is why sharp craps players, who are "right" bettors, always keep that 6 and 8 working for them. You should too, if you're a "do" bettor.

The 4 and 10 are considered outside numbers, while the 6 and 8 are called inside numbers. The 5 and 9 bounce back and forth. It is important that you use the jargon of the table when making your bets. The dealers like the fact that you request your bets in the manner that allows a fast handling of your wager. Suppose you wanted to make a couple of place bets. This is how you would make those requests. Drop your chips on the table and say:

AMOUNT YOU ARE BETTING	NUMBERS YOU WANT	JARGON
$12	6-8	Inside, please
$22	5-6-8-9	Inside, please
$10	4-10	Outside, please
$20	4-5-9-10	Outside, please
$32	4-5-6-8-9-10	$32 across please

Suppose you bet the Pass Line, and wish to make additional place bets:

POINT NUMBERS	AMOUNT YOU ARE BETTING	NUMBERS YOU WANT	JARGON
4	$15	5-9-10	Outside, please
4	$22	5-6-8-9	Inside, please
5	$15	4-9-10	Outside, please
6	$16	5-8-9	Inside, please
9	$12	6-8	Inside, please
10	$27	4-5-6-8-9	$27 across please

You get the idea. The dealers like to handle the bets of players, who pop their requests right out. It keeps the game moving. Know ahead of time what your play will be, and the proper way to ask for those bets. You'll see the respect the dealers will show you.

When you place a number, and that number shows, you should know how much you're supposed to receive. The dealer knows, and as he goes around the table making the appropriate payoffs, he would like each recipient to indicate what should be done with the profit. It would be well to use the following terms:

1. **"Same Bet". . .** .Take your profit and leave same bet on that number.
2. **"Take me down"**. . . . Take your profit, and also take your bet down.
3. **"Press it"**. . . . Use the profit to increase your bet on that number. Example: You have $6 on the eight and it shows. By saying "press it," the dealer increases the bet, on the 8, from $6 to $12, and gives you the extra dollar.
4. **"Press it all the way up"**. . . . You have a $12 place bet on the 6 and it shows. You have $14 coming. The dealer will increase the place bet by $12, making the total now $24 on the 6. He then gives you the extra $2 from the $14 win.
5. **"Press it up one unit"**. . . . You have a $10 place bet on the 9, and it shows. You have $14 coming. The dealer will go up one unit, making your place bet $15, and give you the extra $9 from the win.
6. **"Make it look like six"**. . . . You have an $18 place bet on the 8 and it shows. You have $21 coming. The dealer will give you the $21 win, and break your place bet down to $6, by returning you $12 from your place bet on the 8.
7. **"Off on this roll"**. . . . Suppose you had place bets on the 5, 6, 8, and 9, and a point of 10 working. Naturally, you cannot call off your pass line bet, but the dealer will place an "OFF" button on top of one of your place bets,

to indicate they are not working on the next roll. After each roll you should indicate whether you are still "OFF." When you decide to have them in action again, merely tell the dealer: "working again," or "back on." When you let him know the place bets are back in action, he'll remove the "OFF" button.

NOTE: Superstitious players usually call their place bets off when the shooter throws one of the dice off the table . . . a silly excuse for this move. Their theory is that when that happens, the 7 will show next. I refuse to argue with a person's theory, but I haven't met a set of dice that can tell the difference between the floor and a table. My own personal response to this move . . . Garbage!!!!!

8. **"Go up one unit on my eight"**. . . . In this case, you have $12 placed on the 6, and $6 on the 8. The 6 shows, making for a win amount of $14. The dealer will increase your placed 8 to $12, and give you $8 from your win.
9. **"Press up my inside numbers"**. . . . You have $10 placed on the 4, 5, 9, and 10, and $12 placed on both the 6 and 8. The 10 shows, and you have $18 coming. You drop $4 on the lay-out, to add to the $18 win amount, and the dealer increases your place bets on the 5 and 9 to $15 each. He increases your 6 and 8 from $12 to $18 each, using up the $22.
10. **"Break all my bets down to one unit"**. . . . In this case, you have $15 on the 4, 5, 9, 10, and $18 on both the 6 and 8. The 9 shows, for a $21 win. The dealer passes you the $21, plus breaks all of your bets down to where you now have $5 on the 4, 5, 9, 10, and $6 on the 6 and 8. This additional $64 is passed over to you.
11. **"Move me to the five"**. . . . You have the 6 and 8 placed, for $6 each, and the shooter has just made his point of 4. The puck is placed in the OFF position, as the shooter comes out with a new roll, and naturally the place bets are off. On the come-out roll, for the next game, the shooter throws a 6. You have a $10 bet on the

Pass Line, so it is not necessary to place the 6 also, as you can take $10 odds behind the point. The dealer will take your $6 place bet from the 6 box, move $5 of it to the 5, and return $1 to you.

12. **"Go up on my eight"**. . . . Same situation. You have $6 on both the 6 and 8, and the point of 9 is made. On the ensuing come-out, where the place bets are off, lets say the 6 becomes the point. The dealer will move your $6 place bet from the 6 to the 8, thereby increasing that wager to $12.
13. **"Down on my five**. . . . You have all of the numbers placed when the shooter makes his point. On the new come-out roll, the 5 is the new point, but you have a bet on the Pass Line, and do not wish to increase any of your other place bets. The dealer will return your $5 from the placed 5.

Get in the habit of handling yourself with the highest amount of class in a casino. Knowing what you want to do, and properly informing the dealer, is a big, big plus. For now, don't worry about the winning part of Craps. We'll get to that later. Concentrate on understanding the game. These examples that I've just given to you, are based on situations that will arise throughout a normal game. You must have it already decided upon, ahead of time, exactly what move you will make, based on the Money Management plan that you will be armed with.

Every single winning or losing roll in Craps, calls for a certain move, and if you know what your next bet will be, the simple terminology explained here will help you. It's called Knowledge of the Game. It's important, and a big 25 percent of the Big 4.

KNOWLEDGE OF THE GAME 13

Place Bets vs. Come Bets

This section is devoted to Knowledge of the Game, but before we get to the systems of winning, I might as well give my theory as to which is the better bet: the come bet, or the place bet. I'll list the pluses and minuses, and you can make your own evaluations.

Come Bets (Pluses)

1. Vigorish is only 1.41% without taking odds
2. Vigorish is only .8%, with single odds.
3. Vigorish is only .6% with double odds
4. You win when you have bet the Come, and 7 or 11 shows.

Come Bets (Minuses)

1. You have no control over what number you get on the Come roll
2. On a red hot roll by the shooter, as soon as your Come number hits, you are paid off, and if you did not have another chip in the Come, you must reestablish your bets, by coming through the Come, again
3. The number has to appear twice, before you start getting paid. It has to show once to be established, and again to effect a payoff
4 Even though edge is 8-4 in favor of 7's and 11's, when Craps appears on the dice, while you are betting in the Come, your bet goes down.

Come bets work on the come-out roll. Suppose a shooter holds the dice for a long period of time, making his point, plus the box numbers. Somewhere along the line, he may throw one, two, or even five 7's on his come-out roll, which is great for your Pass Line bet, but wipes out all your Come bets. (Odds on your Come bets do not work on the come-out roll, so they do not go down.) It is just too hard to build up a heavy bet on the Come, without exposing your bets to the 7 on a come-out roll.

Place Bets (Pluses)

1. You have opportunity to pick numbers you wish to place (come bettor must take the number that "comes")
2. You may take your Place bet down at any time
3. You may increase your Place bets whenever you choose
4. Place bets are off on the come-out roll, giving you opportunity to stay with a hot roll, and manage your money any way you like. The come bet has to immediately come down, after it hits.

Place Bets (Minuses)

1. Vigorish on placing 4 or 10 is 6.67%
2. Vigorish on placing 5 or 9 is 4%

OK, you can see that each has some good points, and some bad ones, so it is up to the individual player to decide which way he would like to bet. There is absolutely no question in my mind that the place bet is a better move than the come, but this is strictly opinion, or theory.

Many crapshooters will disagree with this theory, but in the past few years, some die-hard crapshooters are swinging over to this place betting method. I am fully aware that the Come bet is the same as the Pass Line bet, so why not follow the teachings that have been handed down for years, of having a Pass Line bet, and two Come bets. The answer is in the fact that those Come bets work on the come-out roll, and every hot roll will usually have a few 7's show up on a come-out. Bang!!! Down go the Come bets.

I give seminars on casino games. Not one single Come bet system is taught. Yet, I teach a multitude of systems covering the Place numbers. Since I strongly adhere to a conservative way of betting, the variations of moves on the Place bets allow me to lay out powerful winning formulas due to the opportunity of being able to pull bets down, whenever I want.

Master both modes of play, and then come up with your own theory. I will stress the Place betting systems in the Money Management sections, and you will see the flexibility that you have in making Place bets. With all due acknowledgment to the Pass Line, I firmly believe that Place betting is the true barometer of winning or losing at Craps. It all has to do with Money Management, Discipline, and Learning How to Win.

KNOWLEDGE OF THE GAME

14

Don't Pass

Don't Pass Bar ⚅⚅

The Don't bettor!!!!! You've heard about him. For some reason, he is the hated man in the casino. Since 90% of all crapshooters are right bettors, it is only natural that the Don't bettor is in the minority.

At a craps table, you'll hear the screaming and yelling, the constant venting of emotions by the right bettors, who become louder and louder as the red-hot Pass Line bettors give vocal support to the player throwing the dice.

The quiet guy, standing off in the corner, never utters a sound, even when the table is ice cold. He wouldn't dare—since he's probably the only Don't bettor at that table. In fact, the poor guy hardly even looks up, even when he's winning.

What the Don't bettor does is go against the flow of the dice. He is betting that the shooter does not make his point. He is the complete opposite of the right or Do bettor.

First off, get that silly notion out of your head that the Don't bettor is betting with the house. I hear that comment over and over. Suppose there were ten players at the table, and every one was betting wrong, even the shooter. Whenever anyone got the chance to roll, they bet against the dice, even if they were the shooter. Tell me, who is the house then? In this particular case, the house, or casino, would be bucking the wrong bettors, and in effect would be betting right. The casino merely books all bets, no matter if it's right or wrong. This cockeyed thinking, that the wrong bettor is "betting with the house," is pure nonsense.

It just happens that most crapshooters are Pass Line bettors, and that's where that silly idea started. But you can believe one thing about don't betting. It is a grind. A slow, tedious, monotonous grind, and you won't win all the time. The wrong bettors rarely win gigantic sums of money. That's because of the constant swing of hot and cold streaks, with those six-sided monsters.

After you master the systems on both the right and wrong theories of playing Craps, the side you choose is up to you. And neither side belongs to the house. They are merely opposite to whatever bets a player makes. Let's get back to basics.

Right next to the Pass Line is a thin space, spanning both sides of the table, with black letters stating: "Don't Pass Bar 12." This is where the Don't bettor places his bet, when the dice are coming out. It is exactly opposite to the Pass Line. Simply reverse all of the rules for Pass Line play, and you have the Don't Pass object of the game.

The Don't bettor:

1. Loses, if 7 or 11 shows on the come-out roll.
2. Wins, if 2 or 3 shows on the come-out roll.
3. If 12 shows on the come-out roll, the wrong bettor does not win or lose. The 12 is "barred." There is no decision either way for the Don't bettor. This is the edge that the house has going for it. They win from the right bettors, and push with the wrong bettors.
4. If 4, 5, 6, 8, 9, or 10 shows, on the come-out roll, that is the point, and the Don't bettor will win—if a 7 shows, before that number repeats. At this point, the odds favor the wrong player.
5. Wrong bettor is bucking vig of 1.41% to the house, the same as the right bettor. The kicker is in that 7 or 11 showing on the come-out roll. That is some whack to the Don't boys.

Actually, there's no real edge for either the right or wrong bettor, as both fight a vig of 1.41% to the house. The bottom line, in any, and all forms of gambling, are Money Management and Discipline. The object of gambling is winning. What method you use, or what game you play, is immaterial.

Usually, the wrong bettor passes the dice, and bets only against the other players at the table. By placing a bet on the Don't Pass section, before the come-out roll, you are fighting that dreaded 7 or 11.

But once a number is established, the edge swings over to the wrong bettor. If you can get past that come-out roll, where the 7 or 11 will beat you, the edge definitely swings over to the wrong bettor.

Suppose the point is 4. There are only three ways that you can lose: 1-3, 3-1, and 2-2, against six ways of making the 7. You collect even money, yet in the case of the 4 or 10, the odds are 2-1 that the 7 will appear before the 4. With the 5 and 9, the odds are 6-4 in your favor, and the 6 and 8 offer a 6-5 edge to the Don't bettor—always based on whether he can beat that 7, or 11, on the come-out. If he does—then he's in the driver's seat.

A point to remember, when you are betting wrong. Unlike the Pass Line, and Come bets, you are able to remove your Don't bets, at any time. In fact, if you wanted to take your Don't bets down, the house will bend over backwards to help you.

Naturally, there's a logical explanation for this. Once the Don't number is established, you always have more ways of winning—than losing. That's why the house loves to have you take your Don't bet down. They don't like being on the short end of the stick. Even in the case of the 6 or 8, numbers that come up quite often (five ways), the 7 is still stronger. It can be made six ways. Yet, I see stupid Don't bettors take down their 6's and 8's because they're scared. Fact is, they're too dumb to realize that they have an edge on the house at that time. Even the Don't 6's and 8's offer you a 17% (6-5) edge. Don't give it up.

Should you ever take down a Don't bet? Never, never, never, never, ever, ever, never, never. . . .

KNOWLEDGE OF THE GAME 15

Odds on the Don't

This chapter will be easy to understand, since it is exactly opposite to *taking* odds on the Pass Line. This is *laying* odds on the Don't Pass Line. When you bet the Pass Line, you "take" odds on the number. The house will pay you an amount of money, based on the true percentage chances of your making that number, before the 7 appears.

When you bet the Don't Pass, you have the opportunity to "lay" odds on that number. You must put up an amount of chips, based on the chances of the 7 beating that number. As a Don't bettor, you have the 7 working for you, and after a point is established, your chances of winning are greater, since the probability of a 7 showing is always greater than any other number.

Take the case of the 4. The right bettor takes odds of 2-1, since he has six ways of losing against three ways of winning. The Don't bettor lays odds of 2-1, since he has six ways of winning, and only three ways to lose.

Here is the list of odds against the various bets, assuming you have bet $5. It also shows how you place your chips on the basic bet, to indicate that it is an odds bet. (You are allowed to lay your own bets on the Don't Pass Line.)

POINT NUMBER	AMOUNT BET	TRUE ODDS	YOU LAY	TO WIN
4, 10	$ 5	2-1	$10	$ 5
5,9	$ 5	3-2, 6-4 7½-5, 9-6	$ 9	$ 6
6, 8	$ 5	6-5	$ 6	$ 5

POINT NUMBER	AMOUNT BET	TRUE ODDS	YOU LAY	TO WIN
4, 10	$10	2-1	$20	$10
5, 9	$10	3-2	$15	$10
6, 8	$10	6-5	$12	$10

Notice with the 5 and 9 you lay $9 to $6, which is a ratio of 3-2. It is the opposite of what you "take" on these numbers, when you bet "right."

When you bet the Don't Pass, and a number is established, you lay your own odds. It doesn't matter how much your Don't Pass wager is, you'll always lay the odds, in increments, based on the true odds of either 2-1, 3-2, or 6-5 for the respective numbers.

You can take off, or place your odds, at any time. When you bet right, you may also put on, and take off your odds, any time you please. The reason the casinos allow this is that they have absolutely no edge in their favor on the odds bet. That is because odds payoffs are based on true percentages, and the payoffs reflect the true amount of money, as respects the true chances of that particular number appearing.

Naturally, you cannot bet the Don't Pass Line after a number or point is established. The casinos would be nuts to allow you to wait until a number is established as a point, for example the 9, and then allowing the Don't bettors to place their chip on the Don't Pass Line. This way, you would have a good chance of winning, with the odds 3-2, or 6-4, in your favor. That method would allow the player to offset the possibility of losing their Don't Pass bet, if the 7 or 11 showed on the come-out.

Do you have to lay the odds? No, it is up to you whether you prefer to lay odds, or just stick with your Don't bet. I teach both methods, but leave it up to the individual as to what he or she wishes to do. Strong theories prevail for both sides of that argument.

I, personally, lay the odds, only when protecting my bet on the Don't Come—a move that will be discussed later. The only other time I lay odds is described in the chapters on the Patrick System, a very advanced method, which is also covered in detail in upcoming chapters. But, when betting a simple Don't Pass method, I never lay the odds. Let's look at a few of my theories.

Suppose two people were playing "wrong," and each had a $5 wager on the Don't Pass. The 10 became the point. Player A laid $10 odds against the 10, while player B did not lay the odds.

If the 10 shows, player A loses $15, and must win three units to come even. Player B loses $5 and must win only one unit to come even. Go back to establishing the number, in this case the 10, as the point. Both players have the house against the wall. They have six chances of winning, with the 7, and only three chances of losing if the 10 shows. And they will be paid even money for their wagers, even though the odds, or chances of their winning, are decidedly in their favor. An excellent situation to be in—even if you do end up losing—which does happen.

Player A, by laying the odds, will win an extra $5 if 7 shows, but now he is laying $15 to win $10. He has reduced that heavy edge he had against the house, by laying that extra $10. His payoff is higher, but why risk $15 to win $10, when you already will be paid $5 to the $5 you had at risk? That's a 100% return, with 2-1 odds in your favor. Many, many, many times I have discussed this theory with lifetime craps players, and the majority have recognized this move as being in the best interests of the Don't bettor—as to NOT laying the odds. There are probably many strong craps players reading this page right now who will disagree with me. That's OK, I'm not telling you that your way is wrong—only that this way has been very successful for me over the years, and naturally I am partial to it.

My humble opinion would be to not lay the odds. When I have the house in trouble, I want them to literally squirm. If I'm playing Don't, I want that strong edge working with me, all the time.

Neither player is wrong in the method of play. However, my theory is NOT how much you win, but how you minimize your losses. I believe the losing player is so affected by the losing, that he panics, and makes stupid, illogical moves. Stop going for that big kill all the time, with your silly approach of super aggressive play, with a microscopic bankroll. The next time you approach a craps table, with your session money of $200, take a gander at the money the casino has ready to combat your best shot. They operate with a cache of over $7,000, ready to do battle against your arsenal. And if you do put a dent in their bankroll, they merely bring fresh money into play. They put up thousands—to fight your hundreds. Yet, you bet hundreds, trying for the thousands. Somebody is wrong, the house, or the player. And I have never heard of any casino applying for federal aid to recoup losses. Maybe, just maybe, their idea of grinding out small wins from the customers is the smarter move.

In any event, I try to hold my losses down, and accept smaller, conservative wins. It's called a grind, Learning How to Win. It's an art, my friend, and one you should master. The amounts are not important—only the plus results.

Will you listen to me? Nah!!!!! Not all of you. You want the left wing of the casino every time you play. You play to play, not play to win. There is a difference.

But, I'll get you someday. I'll reach you with my theory, and get you to win a few times, and the habit will become contagious. Will you enjoy it??? You bet your bag of bad breaks you will.

One final point on laying odds. You do not have to lay full odds, if you don't want to. Suppose you bet $10 on the Don't Pass (or Don't Come) and the 4 becomes the point. Instead of laying the full $20 of odds, to win $10, you could opt to lay just half. In other words, you could lay just $10 odds, to win an additional $5. The dealer will announce this move, by stating to the boxman: "Laying ten to five," or "Laying half odds!"

Remember this option, as there are systems that will call for this maneuver.

OK, that's the story on odds. It's very logical and easy to comprehend. It is also an optional move. Before making your decision, weigh both sides.

16 KNOWLEDGE OF THE GAME

Theory on Laying Odds

In the previous chapter, I gave you an example of the benefits of laying or not laying the odds, when the point was either 4 or 10. Naturally, the same logic would apply to any of the other numbers.

I just feel, that since I went to such pains to explain to you about theory, and logic, as a part of the Little 3, being such a big influence on gambling, it is wrong if I do not give my opinion on laying against the numbers.

As I said, my opinion will smack right at the feelings of many experts, who believe that laying odds against the point, or Don't Come wagers, reduces the house vig from 1.41 to .8%, and that laying double odds reduces it to .6%. I can see this on the right side method of playing, but on betting against the dice, I just don't buy it.

I am not a mathematical wizard, or even a mathematical half brain. I am simply trying to look at a dollar and cents return, on a bet where I have the house in trouble, and where I am told to loosen the grip on his throat so as to be able to kick him harder. It doesn't wash. I don't believe the laying of odds causes a bigger punch in the gut to the house. The possible damage to the player is actually greater than the possible additional loss by the house.

As I explained in the example shown in chapter 15, if I have a $5 bet on the Don't Pass, and the 10 shows, I'm in great shape. I have six ways to win and three ways to lose. Agreed, betting an additional $10 odds against that 10 gives the house no vig, as this is true odds, but I weaken my original position.

Most people lose in gambling because they have a small

bankroll, no knowledge of the game, no Money Management at all, and not even a thought of Discipline. I feel that holding losses down, keeps players in the game longer. In this case, why should I, the Don't player, risk another $10 to win $5, since the odds are 2-1 anyway, so I am really gaining nothing by the additional bet, yet still have to lay out ten extra dollars.

Additionally, while the odds stay the same, 2-1 in my favor, one thing does go against me. The $5 I bet on the Don't Pass Line will return a $5 profit if I win. That's dollar for dollar value, with the percentage of 2-1 in my favor. But, by laying that extra $10, puts me in a position of getting $10 profit, for a $15 risk. My percentage is still 2-1 in my favor, but now I am risking $15 to win $10. I've lost a little off that initial lock I had on the house's throat.

Contrary to bucking the long established opinion of many experts, that say you should always lay the odds, I am taking the other side of the road. Except in the few instances where I lay the odds to make the 7 work for me, which you'll see in the Money Management section of the Don't Pass methods, this is my advice: don't lay the odds on your basic Don't Pass and Don't Come bets.

You can make your own decision, but don't make it based on the silly explanation that you want to win as much as you can, as soon as you can. Laying, or not laying odds, is a tricky mishmash of theories. And until someone can prove to me that lessening my initial edge against the house, by laying odds, is beneficial to me, then I'll stand by my opinion. As I've said, you check out all the facets, come up with your own solid theory—and follow it.

17 KNOWLEDGE OF THE GAME

Double Odds on the Don't

Just as in the case of the Pass Line, you may double your odds, if you like, and if it is so allowed by the casino where you are playing. But remember, you do not lay twice what you bet, but twice what the pay-off for that bet would be.

Suppose you bet $5 on the Don't Pass Line, and four became the point. You may lay $20 to win $10. If double odds are allowed, you may lay $40 to win $20.

Following is a breakdown of possible double odds bets:

POINT NUMBER	DON'T PASS BET	IF LAY DOUBLE ODDS
4, 10	$ 5	$20 to win $10
5, 9	$ 5	$15 to win $10
6, 8	$ 5	$12 to win $10
4, 10	$10	$40 to win $20
5, 9	$10	$30 to win $20
6,8	$10	$24 to win $20

When you lay odds, just like the right bettor who takes them, there is no vigorish against you. However, you are effectively reducing the statistical edge you have over the house on your original Don't bet. You've already beaten the 7 and 11 on the come-out roll, which is the house edge on a Don't bet.

I've already voiced my opinion of laying odds, fully aware of this theoretical reduction in the vig. It all comes back to the Big 4, and the Little 3.

1. Do you have the bankroll to do it—and the stomach? Remember, that's quite a lot of money to wager for only a percentage return.

2. What is your logical theory as to how you manage your bankroll?

Remember, the bottom line of winning at gambling, is based on the fact that all factors of the Big 4 and Little 3, rely on each other to produce successful sessions. Putting up great deals of money, and then suffering a loss, cuts into your available capital, and may affect the way you will then play. Think about it!!!!!

We'll do a quick example of laying double odds, and let you see what you're up against. You drop $5 on the Don't Pass, and 9 becomes the point. You lay $15 odds, and drop a $5 chip in the Don't Come. Four shows, and now you lay $20 odds against the 4. You decide to go for one more Don't number, and drop another $5 chip in the Don't Come. Six appears, and you lay $12 odds against that number

You take stock of your situation. The three Don't bets, with odds, called for you to lay out $62 so far, and that took only three rolls of the dice. If you entered that session with a $200 buy-in, you've already got one third of it at risk, and you haven't sipped your first drink yet. Suppose two of those numbers go down, and you must replace them with two more Don'ts, with double odds?

You think you're gonna stand there with that silly grin on your face, acting like you got the world by the tail? It's more likely you'll be reaching for your Rosary beads, looking for a little Divine assistance.

A guy who lays out $62 on that first shooter, should have $620 per session to play like that. And if you have a mind to play three sessions, that comes to a bit over $1,800 as your needed bankroll.

You got that much with you. Big Shot??? If not, then drop down to the level of play that your bankroll will allow.

Double odds on the Don't are not for everyone. I'm not even sure they're for anyone.

KNOWLEDGE OF THE GAME

18

Don't Come

We arrive at the last phase of Don't betting, a part of the game that many craps players don't comprehend, and yet a very flexible part of the game for the wrong bettor. It is called Don't Come betting.

Just like the Come bets for the right bettor, the Don't Come bets cannot be made until after the point is established. It has the exact same rules as the Don't Pass, except that it affects the bet *after* the Don't Pass point has been set.

You bet $5 on the Don't Pass, and the point became 8. You wish to have additional numbers working for you, and to get them (just as in the case of the Come bet for the right bettor), you must establish that number to get it in action. When that 8 became the point, you then placed another $5 chip in the Don't Come box, which is situated right next to the Place Number 4.

1. If the 7 or 11 shows, you lose
2. If the 2 or 3 shows, you win
3. If the 12 shows, it is a stand off
4. If 4, 5, 6, 8, 9, or 10 shows, that becomes it's own separate bet, and is affected only by the number reappearing, wherein you will lose, or the 7 showing, wherein you will win even money.

Just as in the case of the Come bet, if one of the place numbers (4, 5, 6, 8, 9 or 10) shows, the dealer will take your chip and put it behind (above) the number that appeared. It is a rectangular type box, small in size, and the bet is placed in the box in such a position as to coincide with where you are standing at the table.

If you desire to lay odds on that bet, just drop your chips onto the lay-out and tell the dealer, "Odds, please." Suppose the Don't Come number was the 5. Drop him $9, and he will position that $9 over your bet to signify that it is odds. You may remove the odds, and then replace them, whenever and as often as you like. Odds "work" on the come-out roll, unless you tell the dealer, "Odds are off on the come-out."

At this point, I would like to get in a little dig at the players who prefer to lay the odds at all times, claiming that it is in the player's best interests.

I've just informed you that the house allows the odds against the Don't Come wagers to "work" on the come-out roll. That means that if a 7 is thrown on the come-out roll, and a player has a Don't Come bet, with odds, still in play from the previous game, the bet and the odds would both be "working." This differs from the right bettor, who has a Come bet still sitting there, after the shooter has made his point. The upcoming come-out roll will affect only the basic Come bet, and not the odds that he has taken.

If, in fact the house has no edge, one way or the other, why do they bar the right bettor from collecting a payoff on his odds bet, yet allow the odds for the wrong bettor to "work" on the Don't Come bets. Maybe, just maybe, the house does not consider the laying of odds to be that detrimental to it, and allows the wrong bettor the opportunity of laying out more money than he can collect, even though the bet for the odds is paid off at the true chances of making a particular number. It's food for thought, O ye of aggressive play. There's got to be a message there somewhere.

There is no restriction as to how much, or how often, you place your bet in the Don't Come box, after the original point has been established. Naturally, you can't exceed the table limit, but you can bet in higher or lower amounts than your original Don't Pass bet, depending on your own preference.

Here are the two questions you've been dying to ask:

1. If you disagree so much with the Come bet that prohibits your picking the number you wish to have going for you, why not just place the Don't Come bet, and take the no 4, or no 10 all the time?
2. Instead of fighting the 7 and 11 on the Don't Come, why not just bet your $5 against the rough numbers of 4, 5, 9, 10, and just relax with those great odds working in your favor?

Great questions, but the house is not stupid, for it'd be destroyed in a matter of months. For that reason, it put in a rule that will answer both of these questions.

Answer to No. 1—You can place the Don't bet behind the line, anytime you like, but not for $5, or $10, or even $20. In order to bet against the number of your choice, for example the 10, you must bet enough to win four $5 units, or $20. And, you must lay the correct odds on that number, not just even money. In this case, to win $20 on the No Ten, you must lay $40 to win $20, plus you must pay the house a 5% vigorish, for the right to make that bet. Five percent of the $20 you would win is $1. So, if you want to bet No Ten, you must lay $41, to win $20 (minus that $1, which is a 5% vigorish which you pay, win or lose). A lot of $5 bettors do not have the bankroll to sustain several losses. So, they shy away from laying out that much money.

Answer to No. 2—See above answer.

So you see, there are certain barriers put up to discourage the logical move by the $5 bettors. This particular rule strikes right at the heart of most players. The house is telling you that you must bet a certain minimum amount, in order to take advantage of that 7. Actually, the odds are still the same, but most players, and I say that again for emphasis—most players do not have the bankroll to put this much money on a single move. Actually, most players do not have the proper bankroll to even compete, but I'll elaborate on that in different chapters.

The bottom line is that this rule puts a different light on this don't come betting section. But don't be discouraged, there are ways of offsetting all of the obstacles that the house sets up. Just be patient, and you'll start to see the different methods.

Do not discount the house's knowledge too. It sets the rules that attack the weaknesses of the individual player. It's aware that some people would turn blue if they lost three $41 bets in a row. And don't think that 10 doesn't show, two, three, four and even five times in a row. I've seen it, and I've suffered through it. Does it hurt? Oh, my, does it ever!!! You figure after two straight 10's it can't happen again, and then after three, it's nearly impossible for it to show for a fourth time, and bango—up pops the 10, soft. Whack!!! You feel it right in the pit of your gut. And when it happens, you die a little. You show me a guy that says it wouldn't bother him, and I'll show you a first-class jerk.

Let's get back to the Don't Come. In Bank Craps, as I explained, you have a tremendous amount of options, and this phase of the game allows you the chance of getting several numbers working for you, although a good hot shooter will destroy a Don't Come bettor, unless that particular person realizes the shooter is hot, and stops bucking him.

In summary, let's go over the basic play:

1. Don't Come bet is made, after the Don't Pass number is established,
2. Put your bet in the Don't Come box,
3. Next roll of the dice affects that wager,
4. If 4, 5, 6, 8, 9, or 10 shows, the dealer will move the chip, behind that number, to a place on the lay-out that coincides with where you're standing,
5. Laying odds is optional, and if they're desired, drop chips on lay-out and instruct the dealer: "Odds, please."
6. The Don't Come bets lose, as each individual number is thrown. But, suppose through a series of Don't Come wagers, you end up with No Six, No Eight, and No Ten. If a 7 shows, you win all of these bets, even if that 7 shows on a subsequent come-out roll.

That's it. Now how you manipulate your bets will determine your conservative or aggressive style.

19 KNOWLEDGE OF THE GAME

Buying the Number

You've heard the term: buying the number. This is to help reduce the vig against the player, especially the ones betting higher amounts. You're already aware of the vig against you when you place the numbers, as a right bettor:

6 or 8	1.52%
5 or 9	4%
4 or 10	6.67%

Now, just roll that 6.67% bite, around in your mind a little. Take a dollar bill, drop it on the floor, and pick up ninety-three cents, then drop ninety-three cents on the floor and pick up eight-six cents, then drop eighty-six cents on the floor and pick up seventy-nine cents. It's not too long before that 6.67% vigorish eats away that dollar.

The same is true with any heavy bet. Based on gambling being a 51-49 proposition at best, in favor of the casino, you've got to stay away from the higher vig games, as much as you can.

Along that line, the casino allows you the option of buying a number, instead of just placing it. However, you must pay a 5% charge, or vig, for the right to buy a number. Since you can place the 6 or 8 for $6, and only fight a vig of 1.52%, it would be crazy to pay a higher percentage of 5% to buy those numbers. So, you would never buy the 6 or 8, merely place them.

The same is true for the 5 and 9. On these two numbers, the house vig is 4%, and even a mathematical dope like me can see that it's better to place those numbers for 4%, than buy them for 5%.

Finally, we slide to the 4 and 10. Since placing these numbers gives the house a 6.67% bite, you could save yourself a healthy 1.67%, by buying the 4 or 10, if you want to play those two numbers.

Before you start making out your shopping list, get to understand the drawback of buying the 4 or 10. Not everyone can do it. You must bet at least five units, or $25, to be allowed to take advantage of this savings. Notice how many of the come-on bets are predicated on the player having to lay out higher amounts. A lack of a bankroll (Big 4) would stand in the way of the majority of players.

This is a way that the house tempts you, to get the player to deviate from money management and discipline. A guy placing $15 on the 4 or 10 figures, "what the heck," for another lousy $10, I can buy the number instead of placing it. So he throws out the extra $10, increasing his bet to the point where he saves the 1.67%, but then puts a strain on his already tight bankroll. Since Bankroll and Money Management go hand in hand, you have no right to damage one for the other.

Your bankroll tells you if you can buy the 4 or 10. Not your own illogical, misconceived, assumption, that knowing the difference between buy and place, gives you the right to weaken the session money that you are working with.

Incidentally, when you buy a 4 or 10, the dealer will so indicate the bet, by placing a "buy" button on the top of your chips. Naturally, just like any place bet, you may remove your buy bet anytime you like. Just say, "Down on my buy, please."

For a quick comparison of the break the casino gives you, by allowing a buy on the 4 and 10, examine the following possibilities, based on a $50 bet.

	BET	PAYOFF
Place the 4 or 10	$50	$ 90 for $50
Buy the 4 or 10	$50 plus 5%	$100 for $50

By risking the 5% charge, instead of the 6.67% vig for placing the numbers, you can see what a difference there is in the payoff. It is definitely to your advantage to buy those numbers, when your wager is at least $25.

Finally, my opinion. As I do throughout all of my books, I repeat statements, not to fill space, but to make a point. I intentionally repeat certain items that I believe should be absorbed by the reader.

I am a conservative bettor, and stress the fact that gambling should be an endeavor of winning, not just playing. The term winning does not necessarily mean a Hope Diamond price tag every session. My idea of winning is leaving that game with more than I started with—based on my starting bankroll, and my percentage Win Goal.

To win consistently, you must have a good chance of winning every bet you make. My idea of making a four or ten, opposed to a 7, breaks down to three chances of winning and six chances of losing.

That ain't good odds, just like it ain't good English. Forget the payoff being in relation to the possibility of winning, the odds are against that number showing.

I, personally, do not approve of the normal buying of the 4 or 10. Why should you? The 5, 6, 8, and 9 can be made more ways, and the house vigorish is not as steep.

When you get to the point where your bankroll allows substantial bets across the board, and I mean during the run of a particularly hot roll, then I will agree with buying those numbers. Until then, let's work up to those instances in a moderate, controlled sensible fashion.

You don't have to fully agree with my theories, but until they are proven to be disastrous, at least keep them under consideration.

KNOWLEDGE OF THE GAME 20

Laying Against the Number

Just as the "right" or "do" player is called a front line bettor, the "wrong" or "don't" player is called a back line player. He is betting on the back line of the number, when he bets against the dice. The space above the number is where the "don't" wagers are put, when you come through the Don't Come, or when you lay against the number.

The following illustration will give you an idea of where the Don't Come bets are placed, and the players who lay against the number have their chips positioned in the same section.

X NO FOUR ✓ NO NINE

X				✓	
		PLACE	BETS		
4	5	SIX	8	NINE	10
		PLACE	BETS		

Naturally, you can place a lay bet any time you wish, and take it down whenever you want. In chapter 17, I explained the basic rules of laying against the number, where the house calls for you to wager enough money to win four $5 units. You must lay the true odds for that number, plus the 5% vig. These figures cause a little trepidation in the hearts of the people who have scared bankrolls, or short amounts of chips, since two or three losses will put them out of action.

Following is the chart for laying against the number: (minimum amounts)

NUMBER	TRUE ODDS	AMOUNT LAID	PAYOFF
4, 10	2-1	$41	$19
5, 9	3-2	$31	$19
6, 8	6-5	$25	$19

It's very simple to figure out. You merely lay the correct odds of the number you wish to bet against, for an amount that allows you to win four units, and then tag on 5% of the amount you would win.

Memorize these figures, as the Don't systems in later chapters will include use of these plays. If you would like to lay higher amounts, merely multiply the payoff by the true odds, and add 5% of the win amount.

To win $60 on betting No Nine, you must lay $90, plus $3 vig, for a total of $93. Simply drop your chips on the lay-out and tell the dealer, "No Nine, please." He will place your chips behind the 9, and they are affected only by a 7 or a 9, and can be removed, for no charge, any time you desire. They may also be put in action on the come-out roll, but you must so state your wish to the dealer. He will acknowledge the action by telling the boxman, "Action on the come-out."

21 KNOWLEDGE OF THE GAME

Field Bets

Let's put to sleep a theory that's been handed down for years and years, about people who play the field being dumb players. I vehemently disagree with this mode of thinking.

Now, I'm not telling you to go and play the field, that will be your choice. What I am trying to do is let you know the comparative risk of playing the field, as opposed to some other bets that are available on the table.

The Field section is not hard to spot on the lay-out. It is situated in such a way that you can not miss it. It's staring you right in the face. It's a one roll action bet, meaning that the very next roll of the dice provides a decision of win or lose.

There's no mystery to the bet either. If the shooter rolls a 2, 3, 4, 9, 10, 11, or 12, you win. If he rolls 5, 6, 7, or 8, you lose. Some lay-outs have the 2 and 12 paying double, and still others offer a 3-1 payoff for the 12.

First examine the ways you can make the numbers that provide a win. In the case of the 2 and 12, the 2-1 payoff adds a winning roll, since all odds are based against something happening, if everything falls according to the laws of probability. The following chart shows the winning numbers, and the ways that number can be made.

NUMBER	WAYS IT CAN BE MADE	TOTAL
2 (paying double)	1-1	2 ways
3	1-2, 2-1	2 ways
4	1-3, 3-1, 2-2	3 ways
9	4-5, 5-4, 3-6, 6-3	4 ways
10	4-6, 6-4, 5-5	3 ways
11	5-6, 6-5	2 ways
12 (paying double)	6-6	2 ways

That's eighteen ways of winning. If the 12 pays 3-1, you have nineteen ways of winning. Let's go to the possible losing rolls.

NUMBER	WAYS IT CAN BE MADE	TOTAL
5	1-4, 4-1, 2-3, 3-2	4 ways
6	1-5, 5-1, 2-4, 4-2, 3-3	5 ways
7	1-6, 6-1, 2-5, 5-2, 3-4, 4-3	6 ways
8	2-6, 6-2, 3-5, 5-3, 4-4	5 ways

That's twenty ways of losing. Naturally, the house has more going for them. The vigorish comes to 5.55% against you, when you have eighteen ways of winning, and 2.77% against you, when there are nineteen ways of losing, as in the case of the 3-1 payoff for the 12.

Since these are one roll bets, the 2.77% could be banging against you on roll after roll, even with the 3-1 payoff on the 12. On the other hand, 2.77% is not at all that devastating, when compared with the dope who plays blackjack, with no knowledge of basic strategy, and is fighting vigs in the 20-40% range.

What gets me is the scorn that the habitual craps shooter has for the field player. Manny Esdumm stands at the table placing the 4 and 10 (vig is 6.67%), playing all the hard ways (vig is 11.1% on hard 4 and 10, vig 9.09% on hard 6 and 8), and constantly betting the "Yo" (11 to you novices), and fighting a vig of 11.1%.

Along comes some quiet guy who drops a chip into the field, where the house percentage is only 2.77%. Right away, Manny Esdumm starts telling his buddy how stupid the field player is. Manny's bets all carry higher vigs, and his "Yo" bets are one roll deals, with over four times the amount of percentage working against him.

On a bet to bet basis, Manny has to get shelled before the field player.

There are better bets at the craps table than the field bet. But there are also worse bets, and the self proclaimed dice expert can be seen making these jerky bets over and over and over and over, etc.

22 KNOWLEDGE OF THE GAME

Big 6 and Big 8

This bet is not found on the Atlantic City lay-outs, but stands out boldly on the Las Vegas tables. It surprises me that the Vegas casinos have offered this bet for so many years. It is located on each side of the table and, like the proposition bets, carry a heavy house vig.

Is it a bad bet? It's a rotten one, my friend, a down and out stupid bet, and anyone making this wager is a dope. Owing to the fact that the same type bet can be made only a few inches away, for a better payoff, and with a lower vig against you, this by comparison stands out as the dumbest, stupidest, most idiotic play in the casino.

Yet, dumb, stupid, idiotic people make this bet day after day. Come to think of it, maybe that's why the Vegas casinos make the bet available.

It is called the Big 6, and/or the Big 8. You put your money on either number and if that number shows, you are paid even money. The bet is affected by only that particular number showing, or the 7. Seems simple enough, but the rub is this. The payoff is even money.

Since your chances of making a 6 or 8 are five ways, as compared to the 7, which can be made six ways, the chances against you are 6-5, yet you receive only even money. The vigorish against you is a whopping 9.09%.

Yet, only a couple of inches away, you have the chance of making the same bet, by placing either the 6 or 8, and getting a payoff of 7-6. The vig on placing the 6 and 8 is only 1.52%, a terrific move.

So, how the devil can people be so ignorant of the vast

differences in these two identical moves, where there is such a tremendous difference in the payoff? You already know the answer, besides stupidity. It's intimidation. They are too scared to ask the dealer to place their 6 or 8, so they suffer this sure fire drain on their money, because they don't understand the damage that vigorish can cause.

Do you realize the difference between these two bets? They're taking one of the best plays in the casino, and turning it into one of the worst.

Go back to intimidation. A guy who punishes his kid in public, beats his wife, doesn't brush his teeth, hasn't the brains to take a bath more than twice a month, and dresses like a left over special from a Saturday garage sale, is scared to look stupid in front of a casino dealer.

He doesn't want to bother the dealer, with placing the 6 or 8, and then taking it down after two or three rolls, because he "feels" a 7 is due. You see, this particular boob likes the fun of taking his bets on and off the Big 6 and Big 8 at random. He tries to outguess the dice, and only likes to leave his bets in action for two or three rolls.

And he's too scared to ask the dealer to get involved in his style of play, by constantly taking his bets off and on. He'd rather go broke, than look bad in the casino. Forget about the fool he makes of himself outside the casino.

Other players like to move their bets back and forth between the two numbers, and think the dealer will get mad at them for giving him extra work. This is absolutely not true. If you want to place the 6 or 8, and leave it there for only two or three rolls, do it. The dealer won't bite you. And you'll save yourself a lot of money.

Of course, you still have the absolute novices, who honestly don't understand the difference, but that's no excuse either. They shouldn't be at the table in the first place. Even when a friendly dealer suggests to these people that it is better to place the 6 or 8, than play Big 6 or Big 8, these jerks give him a cold stare. Like "Who's this dealer to question my play? It's my money ain't it?" If they keep playing like boobs, the money will soon belong to the casino.

Bottom line—never play the Big 6 or Big 8. It is better to place those numbers and the dealers will not mind handling the bets. That's what they are there for. And a sharp dealer will have more respect for you.

23 KNOWLEDGE OF THE GAME

Proposition Bets

In the center of the table lie a multitude of possible wagers, which are referred to as proposition bets. These bets face the stickman, who can easily handle all of these side wagers, which come from players on either end of the table.

Whenever you wish to make such a bet, toss it in front of the stickman, and announce your preference, such as, "Hard eight, please," or "Any craps, please." If he doesn't hear your request, the dealer closest to you will acknowledge your wager by simply saying: "Bet."

Keep your eyes on your chips. Make sure your bet is acknowledged, as the stickman will look to see whose chips they are, and put them on that particular part of the lay-out, in a place that coincides with where you are standing at the table.

I see guys throw a $5 chip into the center of the table, for a bet on the hard 8. Instead of watching his money, he orders a drink, counts his chips, checks out the cocktail waitress at the far blackjack table, lights a cigarette, yells at his wife, says hello to two friends passing by, asks the pit boss for a complimentary lunch and the dealer for the right time. Then he looks up and finds there's no bet on the hard 8.

The poor boob is so wrapped up in other things, he forgets to concentrate on the main reason for his being there. All of that other nonsense should be put out of your mind. You're there to win, not to conduct a popularity program. If you can't concentrate long enough on the things it takes to win, get the hell out of the casino and take up something that your pea brain can take seriously, but certainly not gambling, which requires maximum effort, full concentration, and total desire to win—just to have a 50-50 chance.

You go to the supermarket with a computer, to make sure you don't over spend sixteen cents, and make the checkout girl account for every penny. Then you go to a casino like a big shot and act like money doesn't mean a thing—because that's the way you think you're *supposed* to act. A sharp casino pit boss or floor person immediately reads you for what you are—a phony!!!!!

Most proposition bets are one roll action, which means they work on the next roll of the dice, where a decision, either for or against you, will occur. Most of these bets have high vigs and should be avoided.

However, since my theory of gambling has to do with minimizing losses, you will see how to get some of these bets to work for you, not to win money, but to lessen your chances of losing, on the other wagers you will be making. Maybe it sounds a little confusing right now, but just bear with the tide. The pieces will fall in line.

The thing to remember right now about proposition bets is to forget about playing them as a source of getting a quick win. You're not smart enough to "guess" when something is going to happen, and throw out your gut feelings, too.

Each proposition bet will be covered separately in the next couple of chapters, and in this way you will be able to refer to them, when we reach the Money Management section.

KNOWLEDGE OF THE GAME 24

Any Seven

Let's get this one over with—right away. This betting opportunity sits smack in the middle of the lay-out, and means you are betting that a 7 will show on the next roll of the dice.

There are six ways of winning and thirty ways of losing, a 5-1 ratio working against you. The house pays 4-1. The vig is 16.67%, a real bummer.

This is the worst bet on the table, bar none. You'd be in the same win–lose situation as those people that play the Big Wheel.

There is absolutely no reason to make this bet, ever.

25 KNOWLEDGE OF THE GAME

Any Craps

It's self explanatory. You are betting that a craps (1-1, 6-6, 1-2, or 2-1) will occur on the next roll. Here you have four chances of winning, and thirty-two chances of losing, an 8-1 shot against you.

The house pays 7-1, holding an 11.1% edge over the player. That's pretty heavy. Craps players make this bet for different reasons. See if you can locate yourself in the following:

1. Hunch bet, and your hunches *always* come in.
2. Craps is *due* to come.
3. It *only* costs $1.
4. You're behind, and need a high payoff. (NOTE: If this is an example of your gambling theory, than you really are a behind.)
5. Makes you look like you know what you're doing. Gives you character.
6. You're leaving for the day, have only $3 left, not enough for a Pass Line bet, and you want to *get rid* of your chips.
7. All of the above.

Any of the above classifies you as a boob. A pit boss, boxman, or dealer does not get impressed by the guy who makes a bet like this, yet the dealers are instructed to "hype" these wagers, by the stickman constantly yelling, "Anybody for the Hard Ways?" "Anyone like the Craps bet?" "Get your Yo bet in early."

They know that some people figure if the dealer tells them to make a bet, it must be a good idea. What if they told you to jump off the closest bridge, to clear your sinuses? Would you do it??

To keep track of which bet belongs to which player, there are the initials (C) and (E) shown on both sides of the proposition bets' boxes. They stand for Craps and Eleven.

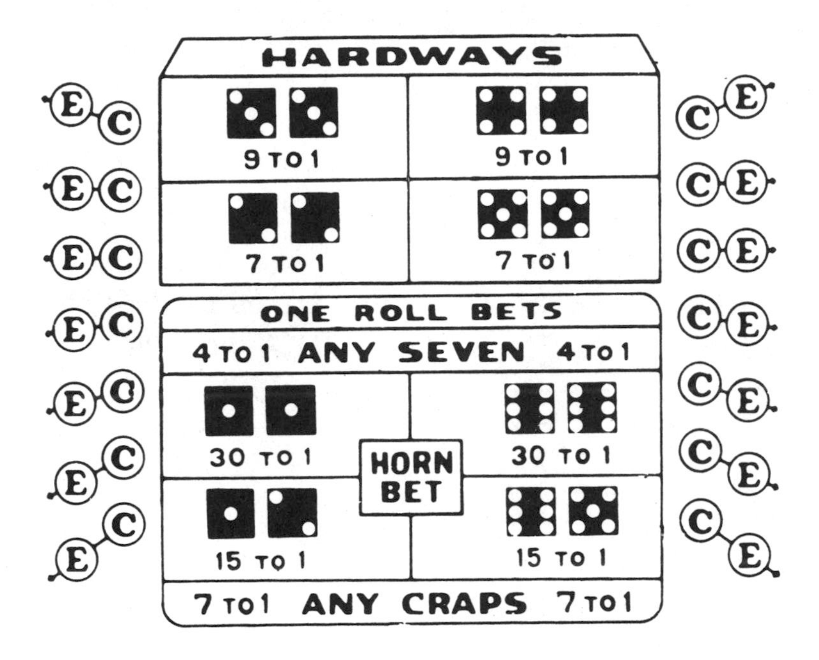

When an Any Craps bet is tossed into the center of the table, it is placed on the (C) which has the arrow pointing to the position where that particular player is standing. This way, the stickman can easily ascertain which bet belongs to each player.

I do not use the Any Craps bet, unless it is to hedge a multiple chip bet on the Pass Line. For instance, if I put $15 on the Pass Line, I will make an "any craps" bet for $2, not because I think it will show, but because I want to reduce my chances of losing that Pass Line wager.

If the 7 (or 11) shows, I win $15 and lose the $2 "any craps" bet. If a craps appears, for example the 6-6, I lose the $15 Pass Line bet, but pick up my Any Craps side bet, in this case, $14. I make my craps bet coincide with the Pass Line amount, but only when it reaches a total of $15, and higher.

Even on $5, $10, and $25 minimum tables, you are allowed to wager only $1 on the side bets, like Any Craps, or the Yo.

This theory is disagreed with in many other books on Craps. But you lose four or five Pass Line wagers of $15, $20, or $25, and you'll welcome the chance to hedge your bet. However, like I've said before, you decide which theory of play suits your own temperament. Mine is overwhelmingly in favor of minimizing losses, and accepting small, but consistent wins.

What's yours?

KNOWLEDGE OF THE GAME

26

Three-Way Craps

The previous chapter dealt with Any Craps, which encompasses the four ways of making them (1-1, 1-2, 2-1, 6-6). The payoff is 7-1, and the chances of it occurring is 8-1 against you, based on thirty-two versus four possibilities.

It is also possible for you to bet any of these combinations, separately, with the house of course, always retaining an edge. You could bet, for instance, "snake eyes." That means you are betting that on the next roll of the dice, two Aces will show. There is one way for this to occur, and thirty-five ways to lose. The house pays you 30-1, which comes to a 13.9% shot in the bread basket, or pocket book. You could also bet "box cars" (6-6), and the vigorish would be the same.

The last possible way for craps to show is 1-2, and 2-1, which can be made two ways versus thirty-four possible losing combinations. That's 17-1 against you and the house pays only 15-1, holding an 11.1% hammer.

The reason I'm going over this breakdown is to give you an option, in the event you wish to protect your Pass Line wager.

Suppose you bet $15 on the Pass Line, and wish to hedge against a craps knocking down that bet. By tossing two $1 chips into the stickman, and asking for Any Craps, you reduce your profit to $13, if the 7 or 11 shows. Any other number becomes a point. If craps show, you lose $15, but pick up $14 (7-1), for "any craps."

By throwing three $1 chips to the stickman and telling him, "Three-way craps, please," you are changing your possible payoff—if a craps should show—to the following:

1. 7 or 11 give off a $15 win on Pass Line, and $3 loss on three-way craps.
2. 4, 5, 6, 8, 9, 10 result in $3 loss on three-way craps, and that number becoming the point.
3. Two aces (1-1), paying off at 30-1, show a $17 craps and Pass Line loss, with a $30 three-way craps win, for a $13 net win.
4. Box cars (6-6) have $17 craps and Pass Line loss, $30 craps win, and a $13 net win.
5. Three (1-2, 2-1) will give off a $17 craps and Pass Line loss, $15 craps win, and a net loss of $2.

Remember, this is based on a $15 Pass Line bet and $3 three-way craps bet, which means you have $1 on each separate craps possibility, and not an "any craps" bet.

I am giving you different options, in the event you wish to hedge your Pass Line bet. Following are those options, all based on a $15 line bet:

1. Bet $2 Any Craps, and lose total of $1 if any one of the craps combinations shows, which is about a wash.
2. Bet $3 on three-way craps, and get a $12 profit with a 7 or 11, and a profit of $13 if either Aces or box cars come in. If the 1-2 or 2-1 combo shows, you have a net loss of $2.

If you decide to hedge your Pass Line bet, you have these two options, either Any Craps or three-way craps. Or, you can decide no to hedge at all, and just let the $15 Pass Line bet stand on its own.

One final comparison, before you make a decision, still based on the $15 Pass Line bet.

1. 11 can be made two ways, as can the 3, which, in effect is a standoff.
2. 7 can be made six ways, and Aces and box cars one way each.

If you decide to just let the Pass Line bet stand alone, not counting the point numbers that could appear, or the 11-3, which is a standoff, you have six ways of winning versus two ways of losing.

The decision is yours, whichever way you choose. Stay with it all the time. Don't start bouncing your decisions all over the place. My humble opinion on what to do? Hedge against a $15 Pass Line bet, and higher, with the three-way craps.

KNOWLEDGE OF THE GAME 27

Yo

This is the outlet bet for the right bettor. The chance to let off steam, to make a bet and sound like a big shot. This is the one roll bet on the 11. But it sounds so dorky to say 11, so you toss your chip into the center of the table and promptly yell: "Yo!" The dealer places your chip on the 11.

And then of course you have the more advanced yeller, with a variation of "Yo!" He throws in his chip and screams: "Yo-lev!"

Wow, does this ever catch on. All of a sudden, the other bettors at the table start emulating the calls with their own "Yo's" and "Yo-lev's." Why? I can't for the life of me figure this out.

It goes back to the list of reasons I gave you in the Any Craps chapter. The chance of an 11 coming is: two ways to make it, and thirty-four ways to lose. Chances are 17-1 against you, and the house pays 15-1. This is 11.1% vig against you.

You know, I see a guy put a $10 bet on the Pass Line, and then throw $1 on the 11. Why? He wins anyway on his Pass Line bet, if the 7 or 11 shows. Why go back and make that extra wager on 11? I'll never understand that.

I was playing Craps the other night, and there was a gorgeous girl at the same table. Everyone had his eyes on her. She made only a few bets on the field and a constant number of $5 bets on the 11. When she won, she collected $75 (15-1), and this kept her going for several more bets.

Everytime she neglected to bet on the 11, the stickman would remind her, and she'd toss a $5 chip to him to place on the 11. Eventually, she went broke and left the table. What a disappointment!

The next morning, I was playing Craps and lo and behold,

she showed up and played the exact same way. A new stickman kept reminding her of the "any eleven" bet, and she kept complying. Eventually, whacko, again she went broke, and left the table.

A few hours later I spotted her playing the slots and went over to talk to her. Her husband was with her, and they told me they were on their honeymoon, had come up from Georgia, and were almost out of money. I asked her why she kept playing the 11. Her answer was that it was the only bet she knew—without looking stupid, and she said the dealers were so nice to keep reminding her to make that bet, when she forgot. We spoke for awhile, and I told them to stay completely away from the craps table—due to their lack of knowledge. Another case of people taking a bath, making stupid bets, and then being "talked" into making more dumb bets, just because the dealer is doing what he is supposed to do, hype the proposition bets. Ever hear a stickman yell out to the players: "OK, all you right bettors, be sure and take your free odds" . . . Of course not, but they sure as heck keep pumping you to bet the hard ways.

The story I've related is not an isolated case. At a craps table, about 90% of the players know about 10% of the game—not only the odds but HOW TO BET WHEN THEY WIN, HOW TO BET WHEN THEY LOSE. Well, you'd better learn how to play this game, if you have any intention of risking your money.

When you bet the 11, your bet is placed by the stickman, on the table, much like the Any Craps wager. It is placed on one of the (E) sections with the arrow pointing in the direction of where you are standing at the table.

From my own personal standpoint, I use the 11 as a hedge against a $15 bet, or higher, on the Don't Pass or Don't Come. Cuts down my chances of losing on the come-out. Along with the chance of winning with the 1-1, 1-2, or 2-1, on that come-out, this hedge with the 11 should be taken.

However, one thing I never learned to say was "Yo." I still say, "Eleven, please." Maybe that's what's wrong with my game.

So it behooves you to learn how to say "Yo," or "Yo-lev." But say it real loud, so they know you're a big shot, and maybe even the dice will hear you and oblige. Sure they will.

KNOWLEDGE OF THE GAME 28

Horn Bet

Some genius (working for the house no doubt) came up with this beauty. It is the chance to bet on four of the one-roll bets at the same time. By saying "Horn, please," you toss four $1 chips in front of the stickman and he places them on the part of the lay-out that indicates "Horn," and, again positioning them to coincide with where you are standing. You automatically get the following.

1. $1 on the two Aces.................................. vig 11.1%
2. $1 on the two 6's .... vig 11.1%
3. $1 on the 1-2, 2-1 .... vig 11.1%
4. $1 on the 5-6, 6-5 .... vig 11.1%

The payoff is exactly the same as was explained in the previous chapters, minus the amount placed on the ones that did not win.

For example, the 11 shows. You win $15 for the bet, minus the three chips you lose for the other three parts of the Horn. Your net win is $12.

Then, to go one step further, the house tries to avoid having to give you $1 change when you toss a $5 chip on the table to cover the Horn bet. So, they allow you to bet the extra dollar on one of the four parts of the Horn. You could say, "Horn, high Aces." That means you have $2 on the Aces, and $1 on each of the other three. All it does is increase the amount of proposition bets from $4 to $5, and increase the number of times you fight that 11.1% vig.

Like I've said, whoever invented this gem of a bet did a great service for the casino. Yet, any time you pass a craps table and check out the action, invariably you'll hear the players screaming out this bet.

This type bet has no logical reason for being. Players make it strictly on feelings and hunches, and neither of those emotions have any right being at a table. Should you bet the Horn? N-O!!! Period.

KNOWLEDGE OF THE GAME

29

Hopping

This is a variation of a proposition bet, but is not offered in all the casinos. Some Vegas houses offer this play, but so far, Atlantic City has not made it available.

In fact, it is not even shown on the Vegas lay-outs, you must ask for the bet. In this case, you could make a bet on any one single combination showing up, much like two Aces, or box cars.

You could ask for the 5 and 3. Since that combo could be made two ways, the payoff would be 15-1, for a vig of 11.1%. The same would apply for any combination you desired, and the applicable vigorish, based on the payoff, would apply.

It's simply not a good percentage play, and should never be made.

30 KNOWLEDGE OF THE GAME

Hard Way Bets

You've heard this term, and the explanation is as simple as the words themselves. The distinction "hard" refers to the even point numbers of 4, 6, 8, and 10. If you throw double two, it is called a Hard Four. If you throw a 1-3, or 3-1, it is called an Easy Four. That's it! The same rule applies for the other three even numbers.

In the case of the 5 and 9, they cannot be made by any two similar numbers, hence there is no "hard" designation given to those two numbers.

Hard way bets are merely another opportunity, in the game of Bank Craps, where the house can take a good shot at your money. These bets, however, are not one-roll action bets. They stay in play for as long as you want them to, and are affected only by that particular number showing, or the 7 rearing it's ugly head. It is a bet that has the following set of rules:

1. Located in center of table
2. Handled by stickman
3. Can be made for as low as $1 and in Vegas clubs, you may bet even less
4. Is affected by only that number (any combination) or a 7
5. Can be taken down at any time
6. Off on the come-out roll, unless you tell dealer, "Hard ways work, please"

The bet is made by tossing a chip into the center of the table and telling the stickman which bet you desire. For instance, you want the Hard Eight:

HARD EIGHT (X)

Assume you are standing to the right of the stickman, directly in the corner of the table. The chip will be placed right in the corner of the Hard Eight box. Keep your eye on it.

The payoffs are easy to understand. On the Hard Six and Hard Eight, the payoff is 9-1. There is one way to make Hard Eight . . . (4-4). There are ten ways to lose . . . any 7 will beat you, and the four ways to make an Easy Eight (2-6, 6-2, 3-5, 5-3). That's a total of ten possible losing combinations against the one possible way to win. The chances are 10-1 against you, and the house pays 9-1. Vig is 9.09% in favor of house. The same percentages apply to the Hard Six.

On the Hard Four (or Hard Ten), there is one way to make that number (2-2). You can lose with any combination of 7, which is six ways, and the Easy Four (1-3, 3-1), for a total of eight possible losing rolls versus one winning possibility. Odds are 8-1 against you and house pays 7-1. Vig is 11.1% against you.

A lot of players will use this bet to tip the dealers. Merely throw a chip into the center of the table and state, "Boys play on the Hard Six," and stickman will place the chip at the top of the hard way box, and now you've got the attention of all of the dealers, but tipping will be elaborated upon in a future chapter.

If you want to play one of the hard numbers yourself, and also include the dealer, throw two chips into the center of the table and state, "Two way Hard Six." That means $1 for yourself on the Hard Six, and $1 for the boys.

Suppose you threw two $5 chips to the stickman, and said: "All the hard ways, $2 each, and boys play on the 6 and 8." That means you have $2 each on the Hard Four, Six, Eight, and Ten, and the dealers have $1 each on the Hard Six and Eight. I'm not telling you big spenders to run out and start making these bets, but at least you'll know what the other players are saying, during the course of a game.

When I play "right," I never bet the hard ways. Why should I? If I've got a bet on the 6 or 8, for instance, I'm going to win if the 6 or 8 shows. I hate it when I win a place bet on the

6, and lose my hard way bet, because it showed 5 and 1. A move like that cuts into that excellent 1.52% which I am fighting, when placing the 6. The hard way vig cuts into that percent.

Now to theory. A lot of craps experts tell you never to play the hard ways. I throw it out to you as a way of reducing your chances of losing, but only when you bet on the Don't side.

Suppose you had a $15 bet on the Don't Pass, and 4 became the point? You have six ways of winning with the 7, and three ways of losing, if the 4 shows (1-3, 3-1, 2-2). Why not a $2 bet on the Hard Four? This reduces your chances of losing, from three ways, down to two (1-3, 3-1), because if the 4 showed hard, you'd lose your $15 Don't bet, but pick up $14 for the 2-2.

It's an option, not a rule written in stone. It emphasizes my theory of reducing your chance of losing. Sure, if the 7 shows, you win $15 on the Don't, and have to surrender the $2 you had on the Hard Four. You could also argue that playing the Hard Four, cut into the edge you had going for you, when the point became the 4. But that put the edge so heavy in your favor, wherein you had six ways to win with the 7, and only three ways to lose with the 4, that there was ample room to reduce your chances of losing, while still maintaining a great chance of winning your bet. Go back and read this last sentence over and over. In effect, it is my whole theory of gambling, wrapped into a neat little package. You have the house against the wall, with a potential even money payoff coming to you, and the odds are 2-1 in your favor that you will win. Why not further protect that bet, by reducing the chances of the 4 beating you. You're still sitting with a gun to the casino's head, but instead of having six bullets in the gun, you have five. Wouldn't you agree that you're still in a fairly good position?

My good friends, this is what gambling is all about. Not the super amounts that lift you to the stratosphere of great feelings, but the constant small wins that keep you going, and the overall prospect of minimizing your losses. The sick, helpless feelings that we all go through when we get wiped out, can be eliminated, by sensibly attacking the gambling industry, in a smart, sophisticated, calculated, percentage wise method. Get that stupid theory out of your head that your wild, uncontrolled, bigshot way of gambling will kick off constant super winnings. Yeah, you'll hit it big on those days when the "trends" (Little 3) are clicking for you. But most of the time, when the 50-50 chances of winning are running in streaks against you—your jerky lack of Money Management will give you more losing days than your bankroll can stand.

Again and again and again I state: I am not knocking the casinos, or the lottery, or the bingo halls, or the bookies, or the track. They open their doors, give you a chance to bet on the game of your choice, and don't stop you from quitting when you're ahead. The casinos, especially, make a trip to their tables an exercise in super entertainment. The free drinks, great shows, terrific food, and lavish decor all add to the allure. But the best part is that they offer games with very, very low house edges going for them, and still the boobs go down and get whacked. Look at the following games and the small percentage the house has in its favor.

Craps, Pass line and Don't Pass	1.41%
Craps, Odds on Pass and Don't Pass	0.00%
Craps, combination on the above	0.8%
Craps, Double odds on the above	0.6%
Craps, placing the 6 or 8	1.52%
Blackjack, with basic strategy	1.50%
Blackjack, with card counting	+2.00% (in your favor)
Roulette, outside bets	2.63%
Baccarat, playing Player	1.38%
Baccarat, playing Bank	1.17%

I've mentioned these facts in other parts of this book, in the hopes I'll get your attention. These are fabulous games to play, and offer you a good chance to win, if you're perfect at the game. Yet the casino wipes the floor with the boobs who attack these games with their uncontrolled method of play. The games are there, the chances of losing are reduced, if you concentrate on these particular sections of the casino, and you can win quite often, if you follow the Big 4. Will you do it? Nah!!!!! You'll still play like a novice, get whacked, and then say the games are fixed. And they'll still be building more casinos, as you make your ascent into the Great Casino in the Sky, with your final words being: "I know I can still beat 'em." But, have faith, my friend. When you reach that Super craps game in Heaven, be aware that the stickman in that game, God Himself loves everybody . . . even losers, so you oughta be right at home.

All right, enough preaching. I wanted to get to a hedge bet, in this case the hedge with the hard ways against the Don't Pass and Don't Come bets, to expound on my overall theory of minimizing losses.

Notice that the payoff reads like this on the Hard Eight or Six: PAYS 9-1. That means $9 to every $1 you wagered. Suppose you put $1 on the Hard Eight and it showed. The stickman will tap the space in front of you and say, "Hard Eight pays $9, and still up." He is telling the dealer, on your side of the table, to give you $9, and then in a mumbled monotone, he is also telling you that the $1 bet on the Hard Eight is still up. They do not pull it down and give it back to you. If you want that dollar back, merely say to the dealer, "And down." You're simply telling him to take that bet down. When I hedge against a Don't 4, 6, 8, or 10, and the result is in, I always ask for my hard bet to be returned, since the only reason I made it was to act as a hedge. If the number showed hard, and I lost my Don't bet, but got paid for the hard way, I ask for my chips back.

Naturally, if you've made a bet for the dealers on that wager, their bet is automatically paid off, and the dollar taken off the lay-out. It does not remain in action.

You'll notice some lay-outs use the work 10 for 1, instead of 9 to 1. It means the same payoff, but a different method. On the lay-outs that say 10 for 1, they give you the $9 payoff and also give you your dollar back. If you want it back up on the hard way, you must have it replaced. But it makes that particular casino look like they're giving a higher payoff. It's exactly the same.

Maybe you think I'm trying to take the joy out of craps play, by denouncing the guy playing these window dressing bets. No, I'm not. But I am trying to make you aware of the fact that each bet you make must have a distinct method in mind, and not a sudden feeling that comes over you, and drives you to "take a chance." Hedge betting is simply a means of offsetting total wipeouts.

This hedge against the even numbers can be adjusted, according to your own personal feelings. It could be a partial hedge, or no hedge at all. You come up with your own theory, and stick to it.

I vehemently disagree with the authors of books who tell you to never play those proposition bets. Yeah, they carry high vigs, but added in with the low vigs of the basic bets, you can manipulate your play to reduce losses, as you become more and more prolific in your knowledge of gambling in general, and Craps in this case. You will learn how to take advantage of these side bets; make them work for you.

Do I use the hedge? Does a craps game require dice? You can bet your Aunt Tilley's last set of falsies I do. Should you use them? (The hedge systems, not the falsies.) That's up to you.

Maybe you won't feel comfortable using them. (The hedge plays, not the falsies.) Then don't use them, but keep them in the back of your mind, because some day you may realize how powerful they are. (The hedge system, not the—but you already know what I mean.)

31 KNOWLEDGE OF THE GAME

Wrapping Up Proposition Bets

I want you to approach Bank Craps with a new, clear, different outlook as to the various bets on the table. Craps is a game, where knowledge is based on your understanding the multiple number of ways you can use most of the plays on the table. It is called hedge betting, and based on my theory of play, hedge betting is a method of reducing losses.

I repeat a message here that I gave you before, and will continue to drive the thought home in future chapters. Winning is the ultimate goal in gambling. Not playing. The boob, who plays to play, absolutely sickens me. If you think you cannot win at gambling, then close the book and take up something easier, like diving off buildings.

I will teach you how to win, but you have to want to win. And the amount you want to win should be based on your bankroll. If you've heard me say this before—good—it is the major obstacle that separates the dope from the pro.

Hedge betting will be elaborated upon in the Money Management section, but first you must have an awareness of the flexibility of these prop bets. As separate wagers, based only on your inclination to make a bet, they are absolutely worthless. But, used as an intelligent hedge, to lessen your chances of losing your basic bet, they become powerful tools.

Memorize the variations of uses for the prop bets, and eventually your own set of moves will become a part of your attack plan.

1. Any Seven..Never to be used
2. Any Craps
   a. To protect Pass Line bet of $15 or higher
   b. To protect Come Line bet of $15 or higher
   c. 7-1 payoff can be used as either a partial or full hedge for right bettors.
3. Three Way Craps
   a. Option off of an any Craps bet, and can be used same way, especially on Pass and Come bets of $25 or higher. This is a better hedge on those bigger plays, *if* you prefer this method.
4. Eleven
   a. To protect $15 or higher, bet on the Don't Pass or Don't Come, and with 15-1 payoff, hedge should reflect amount of base bet: ($1 for $15, $2 for $30, $3 for $45, etc.)
5. Horn ....Never to be used
6. Hopping Bet ....Never to be used
7. Hard Ways
   a. To protect against $15 Don't bets on the even-numbered points. As amount of the Don't bets increase, proportionately increase the size of your hedge. For example, a $40 No Eight could be hedged with a $4 Hard Eight, etc.

Remember, I am not telling you that these are great bets, and should always be made. But they are available, and when used properly, can be pretty beneficial. But only you, yourself, know how aggressively you wish to play. If you do not like to hedge, don't do it.

Personally, I believe hedging is very effective, and have had great success with it. But then again—my bag is consistent, though smaller wins, and a preference towards holding losses to a minimum.

KNOWLEDGE OF THE GAME

32

Summary on Knowledge

I've just covered the various parts of the table, their use, the vig, and the way they become a part of the overall game of Bank Craps.

If you understand the entire table, that's good, but it's no big deal. You're supposed to understand it. I see guys with enormous bankrolls playing Craps, and making ridiculous bets, every other roll of the dice. Many times you'll hear them ask the dealer which bets are theirs. Are they blind? The chips are right there in front of them, and it was they who made the bets. I can never figure out why they have to ask the dealer this question, and I've narrowed it down to the following possibilities.

1. They forgot what bets they made
2. They're too stupid to know how to read the position of the chips
3. They are looking to make conversation with the dealer
4. They enjoy the sound of their own voices
5. All of the above

He'll ask the boxman what a $15 payoff on the placed 9 will be. He asks the guy next to him if a certain bet can be made. He'd ask the cocktail waitress for advice, if he got the chance. He flounders through two hours, loses $1,400, displays an incredible lack of understanding of what's going on, and then curses his luck when he gets destroyed.

He's a typical boob. The tough part is that he doesn't even realize that he knows nothing about the game. He calls himself a craps expert, because he's been playing the game for ten years.

If you don't understand every single part of that lay-out, then get the heck away from the table until you do. What right do you have, wasting money at a table, where you lack a 100% knowledge of that game?

You craps players have it easier then the Blackjack fanatic. The amount of knowledge that he must have is much greater than any other casino game. Craps is a snap to play.

Suppose Ivan Losenmunny is playing Blackjack, and has memorized only half of his Basic Strategy chart. He plunks $5 on the table, and makes the wrong decision. It costs him the hand. The $5 he loses, and the $5 he would have won. That's a $10 swing. Try blowing seven or eight $10 swings an hour. Or two hours, or three. You think you can offset a constant $70 loss, per hour, because of dumb moves? You must be some player!!!!!

Since Blackjack is a game that requires a knowledge of every percentage move in your favor, Ivan cannot hope to stay in the game, if he continues to make plays that buck the Basic Strategy moves. There are a lot of Ivan Losenmunnys in gambling, and they are losing money because of this lack of knowledge.

In Craps, you should know how to manage your money, and you should know every play that is available on the table. But once those dice begin their fight across the lay-out, a new force comes into play, and that is called CHANCE.

Since you have no way of knowing which of the thirty-six combinations will show, your knowledge of betting the various parts of the table will come into play. But before you can bet them, you gotta understand what they are. That is why you should know every part of that lay-out.

I'm not saying knowledge is the most important part of gambling, as it is only 25% of the Big 4, but you must have that 25%. In the next section we move into Money Management. If you haven't digested the information in this section, go back over the areas that are hazy. Eventually, the whole picture will become very clear, and your game will improve a hundred fold.

MONEY MANAGEMENT

1

Money Management—What Is It?

Now we get to the meat of gambling. Money Management. This part of the Big 4 is needed whenever you gamble, whether tossing pennies, playing Bingo, attacking the slots, penny-ante poker, or the lottery. Name the game, and you need Money Management.

Along comes a higher stakes game, like Bank Craps, and these same people, who can't manage the few dollars they invest in the lottery each month, are completely lost when they enter a casino.

I give lectures to senior citizen groups on Money Management in Bingo, lotteries and slot machines. They are controlled systems, and minimize losses until the streak or trend appears, for that particular player. When the hot streak finally ends, the player will drop all the way back to minimum outlays of money, waiting for another trend to occur. It's a very logical approach to all games.

If you think Money Management only applies to high stakes games, you're eight miles off the road. Without Money Management, it is absolutely impossible to win at gambling.

Money Management is the art of handling your starting bankroll. It is knowing when to bet in higher or lower amounts than the first bet of your series. Every single solitary bet you make—should be a predetermined amount, based on your starting bankroll, and the outcome of the previous bet. The previous sentence must be repeated ten times—before you enter a game.

A lot of people think Money Management comes into play only at the end of the day. No way! Every bet is a systematic predetermined amount. Nothing is assumed, or taken for granted. No hunches, gut feelings, choice curse words, or silent prayers will help you at that table. Only the Big 4 will keep you afloat.

You think people don't pray in a casino? Man, if prayers were bricks, you could build a stairway right up to the Pearly Gates, and talk to God in person. And God hears all of your prayers. It's just that sometimes he says No. So you have to revert to Money Management. Something most of you don't have.

The systems I show you will work. They will minimize your losses, get you to bet small when you're losing and to bet high when things are going in your favor. They will provide consistent wins and show you how to abide by Loss Limits and Win Goals. They will change your entire approach to gambling. They will show you how to win.

Will you follow these few simple rules? Nah! I'll be lucky to convert some people over, but the stubborn ones will fight Money Management. But, the day will come when you will be engulfed with control. What a beautiful player you will be, not to mention successful.

MONEY MANAGEMENT

2

Sessions

You know what a bankroll is. It's the amount of money that you take to a casino. There's no specific amount what a bankroll must be. Economic fortunes determine what each person can bring to a casino. Whatever amount you take—that's your bankroll. Now how do you handle it?

The foremost thing is being aware of one of the points of the Little 3: trends. The dominance of trends in gambling, is something no one has ever been able to understand, much less explain. But trends do dominate.

Just as sure as you want to get caught up in a hot trend that is going your way, it is as important to avoid cold streaks running against you. To avoid these bad trends, you should split your bankroll into sessions. I suggest three of them. These sessions are, in reality, three different tables, and is always comprised of one third of your total starting bankroll. This way, you can never lose your whole cache at one table.

Naturally, if you bring $300 to a casino, you would have three sessions of $100 apiece. Just divide your money into thirds, regardless of the amount, and each third will then become a session. Once you get over $450 you may divide the bankroll into breakdowns that will allow additional sessions.

Following is the list of items that determine your initial approach to each session:

1. In Blackjack, you should have forty times the amount of the minimum for that table. (A $5 table requires $200 for each session.) The least you should have is thirty times the amount of the table minimum. That would be $150

per session, and $450 total starting bankroll.

2. In Baccarat, thirty times the minimum, preferably forty times.
3. In Roulette, twenty times the amount of your first bet. If your first wager is $3, you must have $60 per session, and $180 for your bankroll. However, in Roulette, the minimum may vary, depending on which system you use.
4. In Craps, the theory is the same. If you are a right bettor, with a $5 Pass Line bet, and $5 free odds, and you place the 6 and 8, you would have $22 at risk for that first shooter. You must have ten times the amount of what your wager on that first shooter, or $220 per session. That's a $660 bankroll.
    a. If you just bet the 6 and 8, that's an outlay of $12 at risk, so you should have $120 per session, and a $360 bankroll.

This is the theory behind the using of ten times the amount of the initial outlay. Since everything pertaining to gambling should have a logical explanation, and every game is based on Money Management and Discipline, the crapshooter must be aware of this when he gets to a table.

Assume you are a right bettor, with the basic play system (explained in detail later). That would be $5 bet on the Pass Line, with single odds, and placing the 6 and 8 for $6 each. You would have $22 at risk. Since this is the method you chose to play for this session, you must give the dice a chance to reach a favorable trend. Since it takes an average of one shooter in ten to get a hot roll, you must have ten times the amount of what you are risking on the first shooter, for ten players around the table. If $22 is that amount, you'd darn well better have $220 for that session. It usually takes that long for a trend to develop.

Many players don't have the patience to play this control type of game. They start making bets all over the table, and if that particular group of four or five shooters are cold, the guy with itchy pants can go broke pretty quick.

A session is approached with a tight rein on emotions, and with a burning desire to win. The sessions will last until you win a certain amount, or until you lose a certain amount.

These controls are called "Win Goals" and "Loss Limits." In the Bankroll and Discipline sections of this book, these two phases of the game are discussed in great detail. It is the most important part of your game.

Without the "Win Goal" or "Loss Limit" controls, you are just tossing in the wind, until the vigorish or your own stupid play annihilates you. For now, get to understand that a session is one third of your bankroll, or you can set your own number of sessions, *if* you have enough money to meet the requirements of each session, based on the minimum of each table you attack.

The length of that session is not based on a certain amount of time. It is affected simply and strictly by the aforementioned Win Goals and Loss Limits.

I've heard guys say, "I'm going to play for two hours, win or lose." Does this jerk mean that even if he is losing at that table, he is going to stay there, fighting cold dice, just because his time to leave hasn't come? At the same time, am I to believe that this wooden-brained boob is going to be in a hot streak, knocking the socks off the house, and will suddenly pack it in when the aforementioned allotted time to play has expired?

Of all the idiotic illusions that some people have toward gambling, this one is right up there with the dumbest. It's very hard to catch a table with an extended winning trend, and when you're fortunate to find one, you sure as heck don't want to leave it.

I see people look at their watches and say, "Oh my God, it's almost seven o'clock and we haven't eaten yet. We'd better leave." And right in the middle of a very successful session. They could be up $800 and suddenly take off. Me? I'd wet my pants before I'd leave a winning session for any reason. By now you should have the idea that my main concern in gambling is winning. What's yours?

Sessions are one third of your bankroll, or whatever breakdown you desire, as long as you have the proper amount of units to play the number of sessions you decide.

Your Win Goals and Loss Limits will determine the length of these sessions. When you leave a table, that particular session is over. Take a break, collect your thoughts, settle down until you can intelligently concentrate on the next session. If the prior table produced a plus factor, set the amount you now need to reach your original Win Goal for that day.

If the prior session was a losing one, just put it out of your mind, and don't go around complaining to everyone who'll listen what rotten luck you encountered. It's over, and all the bellyaching in the world isn't going to change a thing. If you lost in any previous sessions, absolutely do *not* try and make that money back in the upcoming session. The amount you are down for the first two sessions should have no bearing on the goals and limits for this new table. Over the long run, this method of play will get you ahead, but anyone who tries to recoup past losses in a short period is courting danger.

In football, the quarterback who faces a second and twenty-five situation doesn't try to get it all back in one play. The smart field general will try and get his first down by grabbing eight to ten yards a play for the next three downs. That type quarterback usually stays around many years. Smart management of your money will keep you competitive long after the wild plungers have been wiped out.

Nobody likes to lose, but if you do, don't act like it's the end of the world.

Sessions. Periods of play, based on your starting bankroll, and governed by Win Goals and Loss Limits. A very simple exercise in control. Let's see you follow the rules. It'll be tough to walk away when you must, win or lose, but it's a start.

MONEY MANAGEMENT 3

The Series

The third and final monetary approach to gambling is the series. This is the portion of the game that is based strictly on the amount you bet, and when to increase or decrease your wager.

1. **BANKROLL:** Part one of the Big 4 is the total amount of money you bring to a casino. This sets the guidelines for the amount you will win or lose.

2. **SESSION:** A designated portion of your bankroll, which is equal to other sessions, and guided by predetermined Win Goals and Loss Limits.

3. **SERIES:** The first bet you make at a table begins a series. The first bet you make after a losing bet is a series. A series continues until a loss occurs.

You get the picture. A series could continue for eight hands, as long as each bet produces a win, or push (tie). A series ends when a loss occurs. That series is then over, and a new one begins with the next bet.

In Craps, when a shooter picks up the dice for the first roll of his first come-out, the bet you place on the table starts that series. For as long as that shooter holds the dice, making numbers and points, that series is alive. Once he sevens out, that series is over. A craps on the come-out roll does not constitute the end of a series. Since the shooter retains the dice, your series remains intact.

I want you to concentrate on looking for winning series, regardless of the amount. Each player who picks up the dice will start a new series. If you could learn to accept small wins, per shooter, the larger hits will come, because your starting bankroll will increase, your session money will become larger, and your series bets will naturally begin with extra chips.

The theory is so easy to comprehend, but the actual doing of it is hard. That's because all you big wheeler dealers think you're nothing—unless you bet the family jewels on every roll.

OK, your preliminary approach to the table is completed. Just remember the pattern:

1. Bankroll
2. Sessions
3. Series

Now comes the application of these three items.

4 MONEY MANAGEMENT

Systems in Craps

Of course there are systems in Craps. Or you could call them methods. Whatever the name you apply, it is an approach that a player uses, to try and beat the table. Trouble is, the crapshooter is a unique individual, and finds it hard to stick to a given method of play.

It's funny, the person interested in Blackjack will also play Baccarat and then learn Craps. Buy the dyed-in-the-wool crapshooter is type cast. He sees nothing but those six-sided monsters. He looks with scorn upon the unemotional Blackjack player. He mocks the Roulette player, and absolutely detests the low key Baccarat participants.

A crapshooter is a crapshooter is a crapshooter. One of the things that stirs the crapshooter's blood is the fact that fortunes can be won in the matter of three or four hotrollers. And when a table becomes hot, you can hear the screaming nine miles away.

Now, the professional craps player has a theory about playing Craps, a system of play. It's not written in stone, but it is a controlled method of play. I'll explain it in the chapter called "Basic Right Betting." Every crapshooter should have a system of play, and not just leap back and forth making bets all over the board. I am going to list basic and exotic systems. They'll all work at some point during the day, you just have to hope it's working the way you're playing on that particular table.

A lot of crapshooters can't control their desire to bet and bet and bet. There are many different wagers that can be made, and the crapshooter, an impulsive person to begin with, has a hard time resisting the urge to make multiple wagers.

Whatever system appeals to you, master it, come up with your own variations, and try it. But this is the important part. If you pick a system, and buy in at a table to play that method, you must stay with it throughout that particular session. If it isn't working, you can't just switch over to another method of play. Oh no, if the system you started with is not working, you must kill that session. Pick up your chips and leave that table.

The next table, or session, can then be attacked with the same method, or a new one. But no jumping back and forth, trying different ideas. Everything is disciplined.

MONEY MANAGEMENT 5

Basic Right Betting

I call this the Basic Right Betting method, for the simple reason that most professional craps players use this same approach to the game. It's a good strong method of play, and if you have the proper bankroll, it may end up being your primary course of action.

In Craps, you should have three numbers working for you at all times. This is the theory followed by most craps experts. One number, naturally, is the Pass Line bet, which you have no control over picking. Then comes the placing of two additional numbers.

After the point is established, there is an average of three numbers thrown before the point is made, or the 7 shows. For that reason, I like this method much better than betting the Come. This basic approach calls for you to place two numbers, after the point is established, giving you three working numbers, from which to build this series.

Let's look at the logical choice of numbers that should be placed:

PLACE NUMBER	WAYS CAN BE MADE	HOUSE VIG
4 or 10	3	6.67%
5 or 9	4	4.00%
6 or 8	5	1.52%

The least edge to the house is the 6 and 8, and the numbers that can be made the most ways are also the 6 and 8. Then why not place these two numbers, instead of fighting house vigs, that are over double the bite that the 6 and 8 have?

If your point is 4, 5, 9, or 10, take your odds on the point, then place the 6 and 8. Check out the following place betting rules:

IF POINT IS	PLACE
4	6 and 8
5	6 and 8
6	5 and 8
8	6 and 9
9	6 and 8
10	6 and 8

There should not be one deviation from this method. You'll always have the 6 and 8 working for you, plus the point number. Always place the 5 and 8 when 6 is the point, not because the 5 has a better chance of showing than the 9, but because of the discipline factor.

I never second guess myself when playing this method. If the 6 is the point, without hesitation I drop $11 on the lay-out and tell the dealer, "Five and eight, please." He places my chips, and I wait for a hot run. Going home that night, I never second guess myself that sometimes I placed the 5 and sometimes the 9, when the point was 6.

Same is true for a point of 8. Immediately place the 6 and 9. This form of discipline will become a strong point in your approach to gambling.

Notice I do not place the 4 or 10. This ought to bring howls of complaints from the wheeler dealer craps player. He just loves that 9-5 payoff. Wow, almost twice what you're risking. Imagine, you get paid $18 for only $10 that you risked. What a great deal. Baloney! That $1 charge that the casino retains is just too steep to fight. You should be paid $10 on a $5 place on the 4 or 10, but the house pays $9, and that's a 6.67% bite into your payoff. I'd rather see you play the slots at the Vegas casinos, where they offer a 95% return.

This is a good method of play, but it is a very expensive shot for the craps player who brings only a couple of hundred dollars to battle. If you can't cut the required bankroll, don't play this method, regardless of how well you like it. I'm trying to keep you away from high vigs, like placing the 4 or 10, and keep you in the game.

I've told you that the theory of right bettors is to have three numbers in action all the time. Well, with a $5 bet on the Pass Line, and $5 odds (assume the point is 10), you place the 6 and 8 for $6 each. That's $22 at risk for that first shooter.

Now remember, when the shooter throws those dice across the table, no matter what number shows on either one of those dice, you are halfway to a 7, and a wipe-out of all your bets. The shooter can't make all three numbers at once, but he sure as heck is constantly in danger of throwing a 7. I just want you to be aware of this and not keep wondering why the 7 keeps showing so much. Simple answer is that no matter what one dice shows—it is halfway to disaster for the right bettor.

With an average of only one shooter in ten liable to throw what is considered a hot roll, you'd better have the right session money to be able to compete. And that means $220 per table, for the $5 bettor.

If you have less than the $220 for your session, you might start pulling back after two or three shooters, and only placing one number. Bango—right away you're playing scared, because of your weak bankroll. You've allowed the lack of one part of the Big 4 to affect the other parts.

In the Discipline section, you'll see that 50% is the Loss Limit for Craps. But don't try to soften your possible loss at a session, by buying in for less, and then having to keep reaching into your pocket for more money. Rules are rules, and if you can't follow the entire process of the Big 4, you're on a self destruct course.

I'll continuously harp on the matter of proper bankroll, which allows proper Money Management, until you realize how each part of the Big 4 relies on the others. I'll give you one tiny option play for right now, that will hedge a little on the Knowledge section, regarding the "always taking of odds" statement. That is, if you play this system.

The vig on Pass Line betting, with odds, is .8%, and this option has to do with bypassing the odds on the 4 and 10, and keeping the vig at 1.41%, which in itself is not too shabby.

With this option, if the point becomes 4 or 10, instead of taking your free odds, merely place the 6 and 8. This leaves the hammer against you at 1.41%, but lessens your total lay-out for this shooter. Now, your money at risk is reduced to $17 per shooter, but gives you the chance of taking the odds on that 4 or 10, after you get a hit on the 6 and/or 8.

Remember, this is strictly an optional move, and if you feel comfortable NOT taking odds at all on the 4 or 10, that is up to you, as long as you understand the consequences. Naturally, the free odds bet is the best move in the casino, since the house has absolutely no edge on it.

But, in my years of talking to various casino players, I find that the greatest majority enter the battlefield with short bankrolls. For that reason, I defy some moves, to try and keep these people solvent, and believe me, when I say the majority of people who gamble have short bankrolls, I'm talking 80%, and nothing less.

You think your lousy $500 bankroll allows you to go to a craps table and play like a bored millionaire? Well, you're nuts, if that's your thinking.

The option of not taking odds, when the point is 4 or 10, is adjusted when you get a hit on the 6 and/or 8. If you decide to shun the taking of odds on those numbers, and the shooter bangs out a 6 and 8 on subsequent rolls, you'll have an opportunity to then take the odds on your Pass Line bet.

If you do not have the bread to take odds on the other numbers, this system is not for you. They'll be others down the line that will suit you. The next chapter covers the betting progression for this system.

MONEY MANAGEMENT

Betting Progression for Place Numbers

This is one of those chapters that you should read, re-read, memorize and absorb completely. It is the betting progression for the place numbers. This chapter is in the category of one of the ten most important in the whole book. It covers the proper betting method that the right bettor uses in his money management—or lack of same, when those numbers start popping up.

It's no secret that 95% of the people who gamble have no hard and fast rules as to what to bet, either following a win or a loss on the previous decision. With all due respect to you high rollers at the craps table, get a load of what you sound like, during a typical roll:

Imus Pressit is a degenerate craps player. He loves the game, the action, the fast pace of the whole scene. He has a decent bankroll, a fair knowledge of the game (which isn't enough), and a predetermined desire to pick up a modest profit. But, and this is his problem. Once that game begins, Imus is no longer interested in a small profit. His need turns to greed.

Imus has $5 on the Pass Line, $5 odds, and 4 is the point. He places $5 on both the 5 and 9, and $6 on both the 6 and 8: The 8 hits. The dealer glances at Imus, who immediately tells him, "Press it" (increase the $6 placed 8 up to $12 and give him the extra dollar profit). Again the 8 shows, for a $14 profit. "Press it." This time the dealer increases the place bet on the 8 up to $24 and slides the extra $2 over to Imus.

Next the 6 shows. "Press it," retorts the grinning Imus, and the procedure is carried out by the dealer. Now the 9 comes, and the dealer knows what Imus will request. He presses the 9 up to a $10 bet, and gives the extra $2 to Imus.

Now our hero is impressed that the dealer takes him for a swinger. He tosses a couple of chips on the table and yells loud enough for the guys parking cars in the yard down the street to hear: "Boys play on the hard ways." Then he looks around to see if the pit boss has observed his freewheeling style.

The dice again come to rest with a 5 showing and again the bet is pressed. Next comes a 10, giving Imus a $9 profit. He drops a handful of chips on the table and says, "Buy the ten." His placed 10 is converted to a "Buy ten," when he increases the action up to $25 (discussed fully in chapter on "Buying the Number").

By now, it's apparent that this shooter is just swinging into high gear. For over forty minutes he bangs out both point numbers and place numbers, both hard and easy, and each time Imus grinningly instructs the dealer to "press it." Eventually he has worked his bets up to $100 on the line, with double odds, $100 on the 10, $180 on both the 6 and 8, and $125 on both the 5 and 9. He has all the hard ways covered, four side bets for the dealers and $20 on the "Yo."

Mentally, he envisions walking away from the table with a little over $2,000, give or take a few hundred dollars. He has hardly sipped on his third gin and tonic (where he flipped the cocktail waitress a $25 chip), when the stickman declares the words that are dreaded by all right bettors from the time they threw the dice for Christ's garments—"Out, seven, line away. Take the Do's and pay the Don'ts."

Imus's first impulse is to bite the glass, to stop from crying, but the lump in his throat is too big to allow him to open his mouth. Forty-five minutes the shooter held the dice. It was the hottest roll of the day, and Imus Pressit was in on it. His net for the roll? He lost $148.

Of all the blankety-blank boobs that frequent a casino, the crapshooter who blows the chance to take advantage of a hot roll is right up there with the boobiest. Oh, sure, his retort is always the same: "Yeah, but I gave it a good shot. While that roll was on, I was pouring it in. I was in a position to whack that casino. I had them shaking in their boots. I had their respect. I had them worried, I—I—I—" You dope. You had nothing, and your nothing brain caused you to end up with nothing. And if you can live on self-proclaimed ego trips, then you'll forever remain a dope.

Imus wants to look cool about it, but the spectre of the dealer pulling off "his" chips, puts an ice cold chilling feeling throughout his body. His legs go limp as he calculates the amount of money that went down with that 7. Over $1,000!!! And he didn't garner even a dollar's worth of profit. In fact, the $148 he laid out wasn't even recovered.

He looks sheepishly at the guy standing next to him and says, "I was just gonna pull my bets down." Sure he was.

How about you? Do you have a little bit of Imus Pressit running through your body? I think most crapshooters do. The only words they know are "Press it—press it—press it." There *is* another way, and yet you'll still be able to take advantage of hot rolls.

In the past few years, it has been my pleasure to meet many interesting people. Men and women who have been gambling for years and have fixed theories on their favorite games. Of all of them, the craps player is the wildest. I have had hundreds of them tell me that my betting progression on the place numbers is the best they have ever seen. They reiterate that it has completely changed their way of betting those numbers. The reason I mention this is that people who have played Craps for years are strong-willed players, and getting them to alter their way of playing is, in itself, a minor miracle.

The system is akin to my Regression System, which is used at Blackjack, Baccarat, and the outside bets of Roulette. In my humble opinion, it is the greatest method ever, ever, ever put in use against an "even chance play." If you don't know what it is—please learn it, the method works. The basic reasoning on both the Regression System and the Place betting method is that you lock up a win, before you start increasing your bets.

There is nothing wrong with increasing your bets, by

pressing up the chips, as you continue to win. But this accelerated action should not take place until after you wrap up a guaranteed profit.

The Imus Pressits of the world can't accept a disciplined approach to gambling. Each shooter is looked upon as a potential bearer of a hot roll. The point number is established, and then a few numbers are thrown and right away, the buzzing picks up in volume, as the right bettors anticipate a long run. Invariably they are creamed by that 7, but the worst part is that a lot of times the shooter will pop out a few place numbers before that 7 shows, and the Imus Pressits do not take advantage of them.

Most craps players start pressing their bets right from the go, and it's only a matter of time before their bankroll, or lack of some does them in. Using the basic betting method of Pass Line bet, single odds, and placing of two numbers, is the way to handle a roll. We'll assume 9 is the point, and you placed $6 on both the 6 and 8:

1. If 6 shows.......................................Same bet (take $7)
2. If 6 shows again..................Press it up to $12 (take $1)
3. If 6 shows third time.....................Make it look like $6
   a. On this third hit, you would take the $14 profit, decrease your place bet back down to $6, and receive that other $6 back.
4. If 6 shows fourth time, you have these options:
   a. Same bet
   b. Press the 6 up to $12
   c. Place the 5
5. Assume you pressed the 6 up to $12 (2), and 6 showed again. More options:
   a. Press the 6 up to $24
   b. Press the 6 up to $18
   c. Press the 6 up to $18, and press the 8 up to $12
   d. Same bet

Notice that every hit in a winning series is subject to a new set of options, depending on each players own personal conservative or aggressive method of play. But the initial, basic three moves should never deviate:

1. First hit ....Same bet
   a. You've guaranteed yourself a no-lose situation for the number,
2. Second hit ....Press it (now you may start going up)
   a. A note to the conservative player. On this second hit of a particular number—you may, if you like, again say "Same bet." That's up to you.
3. Third hit ....Make it look like 6
   a. At this point you grab a $14 profit, take back $6 of your bet, but remain in action with a $6 place on the same number.

This last move will not sit well with the Imus Pressits of the world. They feel that they're being deprived of getting on this hot roll. Not so. I'm merely trying to wrap up a winning series, that will keep you in the game. And incidentally, how do you know that it is a hot roll? You never know that, until it's over. But remember, you're still on that number and can now take your best shot—but only because you've pocketed a profit for that series. The following tables will give you various betting progressions. Pick your favorite—or come up with your own.

Variations for Place Betting Series

(HIT)	(A)	(B)	(C)	(D)
First:	Same bet	Same bet	Same bet	Same bet
Second:	Press it up to $12	Press it up to $12	Same bet	Same bet
Third:	Make it look like $6	Make it look like $6	Press it up to $12	Press it up to $12
Fourth:	Press it up to $12	Press it up to $12	Make it look like $6	Make it look like $6
Fifth:	Place the 5 Press the 6 up to $18	Press it up to $18	Press it up to $12	Place the 5
Sixth:	Same bet	Press it up to $24. Press the 8 up to $12	Press it up to $18	Press up the 8 to $12
Seventh:	Press it up to $30	Press it up to $30. Place the 5	Press it up to $30	Same bet

You get the idea, but the two main parts of this method never change:

1. First hit is always same bet
2. You must regress on the winning bet after the first press.

If you intend to make Craps the game you will play in the casino, then you'd better learn how to handle the place bets. It is the key to the game. The theory is laid out for you, and your job is to pick a system that is comfortable for you. Set it up—and follow it. You might even find Imus Pressit looking over your shoulder for a few tips.

MONEY MANAGEMENT 7

Aggressive Place Betting

I use the word aggressive, but actually I am talking to the players who do not start their place bets with $6, but make their first outlay on the numbers a little higher. Maybe they start with $12, or $18, or $24. I will go over the way to handle your bets for the various starting amounts, but in most cases, these players are NUTS.

In a definite attempt to sound repetitive, I again, for the seventy-eighth time, tell you that what you bet, in the amount of chips, is not your decision. It is based on your bankroll, only your bankroll, and nothing else but your bankroll. I don't care if it bores you to make $6 bets, big shot. Get the right amount of playing capital, or go play with Monopoly money in order to satisfy your over-inflated ego.

Since it takes an average of one shooter in ten to come up with a hot roll, you need ten times the amount of what your initial lay-out for the first shooter is to cover you for ten shooters around the table.

So if you have $10 on the Pass Line, and $10 odds, and place the 6 and 8 for $12 each, that's $44 at risk. You need $440 per session, and over $1,300 bankroll. Go back to the chapter on required session money and memorize it.

This example is based on how you would handle just one number being hit. Suppose you placed both the 6 and 8, and we'll say the 8 gets hot:

$12 Place Bet on Both the 6 and 8:

1. First hit........................Same bet (take your $14 profit)
2. Second hit ....Press it (increase your place bet)
   a. Press it to $18 or
   b. Press it to $24

(The option of the amount is up to you. My suggestion is (a).)

3. Third hit..........................Make it look like $6 or $12

You absolutely must go down on the third hit. The amount is up to you, based on what your move on the second hit was. If you pressed your second hit up to $18, you should go down to $6 when the third score shows. If you pressed your second hit up to $24, your next play should be to drop your place bet down to either $6 or $12. I suggest $6, but a more aggressive player might want to just drop to $12. The superaggressive player might opt for dropping to $18 if he pressed up to $24 on the second hit. My suggestion would be either $6 or $12, but if I can just reach the superaggressive player and get him to at least drop down a little bit, it sure beats his old method of Press—Press—Press—.

Let's say you followed my suggestions and did the following:

> Same bet—Press it up to $18—Make it look like $6.

You are now sitting pretty. Even if your bet goes down on the next sequence, you're still guaranteed a profit of $31 for that number. But suppose your trend continues, and the 8 shows again. You have the following options:

1. Same bet
2. Press it up to $12
3. Place the 9
4. Press up the 6 to $18

You've got to have these decisions firmly entrenched in your mind. In this case, I narrow my choices to either (1) or (3), with an edge to (3). You've got another number working for you. Now you bang the 8 for the fifth time. At this point, I would place the 5, if it is not covered by the point, or revert to either (2) or (4). My suggestion would be (2), where I would start back up the ladder with the 8.

I'm going to briefly list three different methods you might like to choose from (based on 8 as the example): ($12 Place bet)

(HIT)	(A)	(B)	(C)
First:	Same bet	Same bet	Same bet
Second:	Press it up to $18	Press it up to $18	Press it up to $24
Third:	Make it look like $6	Make it look like $12	Make it look like $12
Fourth:	Place the 5 (or 9)	Place the 5 and 9	Press it up to $18
Fifth:	Press it up to $12	Press it up to $18	Press it up to $24 and place the 5
Sixth:	Press it up to $24	Press it up to $30 and press the 6 up to $18	Press it up to $30 and press the 6 up to $18

Look over all of the examples shown. Pick one of them, or come up with your own. But make it simple, and above all, include a regression on the third hit, no exceptions.

Let's go to the player who starts with a place bet of $18 on the numbers. Again, the 8 is our example number.

(HIT)	(A)	(B)	(C)
First:	Same bet	Same bet	Same bet
Second:	Press it up to $24	Press it up to $30	Press it up to $30
Third:	Make it look like $12	Make it look like $12	Make it look like $18
Fourth:	Place the 5 (or 9)	Same bet	Place the 5 and 9
Fifth:	Press it up to $18	Press it up to $18 and place the 5 and 9	Press it up to $30
Sixth:	Press it up to $24	Press it up to $30	Make it look like $12 and press the 6 up to $18

You've got enough examples to either follow them, or else come up with your own run. Look at all the possibilities for variations. They're innumerable. Grab a pen and piece of paper and put together a couple of examples that will suit you. Two things *must* remain constant:

1. The first hit is always same bet
2. The third hit is always regressed (the amount you reduce is up to the player)

There are no exceptions for the above. If you can't regress your bets, the eventual 7 will gain an insurmountable edge off your aggressive play. You have absolutely no idea how many crapshooters I speak with, who tell me that they get the hot roll, but end up losing. When I show them these methods, almost to a man, they admit that the power of the system is in the first and third hits.

My friends, this is one of the most powerful chapters in this book, as it deals with one of the most important parts of the game of Craps . . . place betting.

If you must read any chapter over, this one should be in the top five.

8
MONEY MANAGEMENT

Superaggressive

I can feel the rocks swooshing past my head, from the hands of the high roller. They don't wanna hear this nonsense. They want no part of disciplined play, or Money Management at a table. Okay, don't listen to it then. Keep going for the big kill.

Amuse the guys at the local bar of the time you banged the casino for $8,700 at the craps table in Vegas, or the hot time you had in Atlantic City, when you ran a handful of chips into a $5,600 bonanza.

But how many trips to the casino cost you your $2,500 bankroll, plus another $2,000 in markers. You forget the bad times, cause you just love the adulation that comes from the big score.

Notice in my books, that every example of gambling, is based on the single-unit bet. That's because the breakdown of the bankroll into sessions, and then into series, covers the majority of people who enter a casino.

I know you love to bet the green $25 chips, and I know you NEED that big score to take care of some pressing money problems. I know that you saved $1,000 to take a great shot at the table, win or lose, and I know that you consider it beneath you to win only 20% or 30% or 40% of your starting bankroll. I know you go to the casinos only twice a month and the thrill is worth it. I know you have a lot of money in the bank, a good job, and dropping a couple of thousand dollars doesn't really hurt you. ("Not much," "Well, not too much," "Well, maybe a little," "Well, maybe you're right, it does begin to hurt.") You bet your dirty socks it hurts, and everyone who says it doesn't is a *jerk.*

I know you only bring an amount of money to the casino that you can afford to lose. (Show me this boob that can afford to lose money, and I'll show you a constant loser.) Tell the truth—have you ever told anyone that you only lose *what you can afford to lose?* Doesn't that sound stupid? You cannot *afford* to lose money—nobody can. If a person is convinced that he can afford to lose, he will take the losing for granted, and never have the desire to win. He'll never know that it *is* possible to win.

If you fit into any of the categories I've listed, and I know that some of you do, you had better take another vote as to whether you want to gamble. And this is especially aimed at the high roller, who believes every winning amount at a table has to have three zeroes on the end.

If you're a wheeler dealer at the craps table, good. Live it up. But only if you have the bread to bet along the lines of your desires. Based on my examples for the single-unit bettor, you can multiply the chip outlay to coincide with your session money.

However, I'll lay out the amount of money you need, per bankroll, per session, to bet the higher amounts. This chart, for use at a $5 table, is for a $5 bet on the Pass Line, with odds, and a place bet on two additional numbers, but always to include the 6 and 8.

TYPE OF BET		APPROXIMATE INITIAL OUTLAY	NEEDED SESSION MONEY	BANKROLL
a.	One-unit Pass Line, odds, place two numbers	$21	$210	$600
b.	One-unit Pass Line, double odds, two numbers placed	$26	$260	$750
c.	One-unit Pass Line, odds, place three numbers	$26	$260	$750
d.	One-unit Pass Line, double odds, three numbers placed	$31	$310	$900

This chart shows you how much you should have to play the various methods. Take for instance (b) above. It's a simple little system of placing $5 on the Pass Line, taking double odds, and placing two numbers, exactly the way you should play, and maybe even the way you've been playing for years. But do you have the proper amount of money??? Tell the truth, do you take at least $750 with you, when you play this way. You should. In fact you *must.*

I don't advise placing the 4 or 10 as an initial bet, but if that is what you decide to do, you must increase the basic bet by $10, base it on ten shooters around the table, and then multiply it by three, to arrive at your needed starting bankroll. That comes to over $300 per session. Go to a table and observe some of the players. A lot of them play this way, and do you know how much they buy in with? Sometimes $100. Terrible!!

Do you see the amount of money you need, just to make a Pass Line bet, with odds, and place two numbers? Oh sure, you can saunter up to a table with $100 and pick any one of the aforementioned types of bets. But even three shooters, sevening right out (and it will happen), will bang your session money for about $66, two thirds of what you started with, and panic begins to set in. You hold back the odds, neglect placing a certain number, or start trying to create something, by making the ill advised proposition bets, based simply on a hunch—or panic.

Your starting session money of $100 is almost gone, along with your planned method of play. You'd better realize how quickly three or four bad rolls can eat into your session money, even when placing only two numbers, along with the point.

OK, let's get back to you high rollers who wish to make two-, three-, and five-unit bets on the Pass Line, including odds, and a couple of place numbers. This is the required session money for those various bets. (See Chart)

Incidentally, this same advice goes for the Blackjack player who goes up to a table, buys in for $20, and makes his first bet $10. He's got enough for two bets. Reason he does it is he honestly believes he is holding onto his money longer by shelling out only a small amount at a time. To this type bettor I can only say, "My friend, it's only a matter of time before you get whacked! But whacked you will get. You're a scared player, waiting to be beaten."

Be honest now, have you ever played Craps and engaged in any of the methods shown, with less than the required amount of money??? Of course you have. Yet you laugh at the amounts I propose you start with. You laugh at Money Management. I can just feel the heat waves from the five-unit bettor who feels these figures are too high. Again, I remind you of the Loss Limit of 50%.

But even if you cut the required bankroll and session money in half, you'd be in trouble. Take method (c) for instance, and you'd still need $650 per session, and a starting bankroll of $1,950. And this is just to take a $25 bet on the Pass Line, single odds, and playing three inside numbers at a quarter apiece.

Get with it. Either straighten out your finances, or drop to a level of play that is within the confines of your economic situation.

Required Session Money for Higher Bets:

TYPE OF BET		APPROXIMATE OUTLAY	SESSION MONEY	BANKROLL
a.	Two units on Pass Line, Single odds, two place numbers, two units each	$42	$420	$1,200
b.	Two units on Pass Line, Double odds, two place numbers, two units each	$52	$520	$1,500
c.	Two units on Pass Line, single odds, three place numbers, two units each	$52	$520	$1,500
d.	Two units on Pass Line, double odds, three place numbers, two units each	$62	$620	$1,800

Come on now, how many times have you played this way, with a lousy $200 in your kick. You figure one good roll will protect you. Baloney, you better have this amount to play the multiple numbers, and double bets. Again, your Loss Limits will protect you, and eliminate your losing more than 50% of any session, but even cutting it in half, you're in need of a decent starting bankroll. Next we go the three-unit bet:

TYPE OF BET		APPROXIMATE OUTLAY	SESSION MONEY	BANKROLL
a.	Three units on Pass Line, single odds, place two numbers, two units each	$57	$570	$1,700
b.	Three units on Pass Line, double odds, place two numbers, three units each	$83	$830	$2,400
c.	Three units on Pass Line, single odds, place three numbers, two units each	$67	$670	$2,000
d.	Three units on Pass Line, double odds, place three numbers, three units each	$93	$930	$2,700

Yet, I see guys come up to a craps table, buy in for $100 and make (b) bet above. One bad roll and he's gone. Then you see him shaking his head in frustration, anger, despair. You want to play any of the above methods, have the bankroll that's shown. And now I reluctantly give the table for the green chip ($25) player:

	TYPE OF BET	APPROXIMATE OUTLAY	SESSION MONEY	BANKROLL
a.	Five units on Pass Line, single odds, place two numbers, five units each	$105	$1,050	$3,000
b.	Five units on Pass Line, double odds, place two numbers, five units each	$135	$1,350	$4,000
c.	Five units on Pass Line, single odds, place three numbers, five units each	$130	$1,300	$3,900
d.	Five units on Pass Line, double odds, place three numbers, five units each	$155	$1,500	$4,600
e.	Five units on Pass Line, double odds, place four numbers, five units each	$185	$1,850	$5,500

The reason I say "reluctantly" give this method is that, based on my Money Management system of bankroll, session, series, the $25 bettor should be in the minority in a casino. Yet, there they stand, pouring out those $25 chips. Ninety-nine percent of the craps players in a casino have nowhere near the required session money or bankroll required. Will you follow these guidelines? No! Absolutely not—but you should.

MONEY MANAGEMENT

Comment on Right Betting Method

As you leaf through this book, you will find some systems that will catch your fancy, and others that will not appeal to you. In the end, it all comes down to Money Management and Discipline, but you don't realize that yet. But you will . . . you will. Until that time comes, the Basic Right Betting Method is your best approach to betting from the "right" side. You have your three numbers working for you, and a hot roll, if managed properly, will give you some decent returns.

Later on in the book you will find the Patrick System, which will tickle your fancy, and allow you the most multiple set of variations imaginable. But until that system is perfected, use this previously explained approach.

Someday you will realize the enormous effect that the 7 has on the game of Craps, and you'll wonder why they didn't name the game "Seven." Each single dice is one half of that 7. All the other numbers are based on their sister number being similar in odds, payoffs and ways of showing.

Hold a set of dice facing you. If 5 shows, check the other side, it'll be a 9. A 10 facing you will be 4 on the opposite side, and the 6 will have the 8 on the reverse side. Everything concerning these sister numbers are the same. For example, the payoff on the 4 and 10 is both 2-1, the ways that each of those numbers can be made is 3, and the vigorish when placing them is 6.67%.

If you have a 7 facing you, on a set of dice, all the others sides will total 7. I bring this up to stress a point. When you bet "right," even using the Basic Right Betting Method, which is a very good way of playing, you're still vulnerable to that all powerful 7 rearing its ugly head. That's why subsequent chapters on hedging and buying the 4 and 10, which can be made only three ways, is a good way of nullifying that 7, with its crushing six ways of showing.

Finally, give some serious thought to placing only the 6 and 8 as your working numbers, instead of trying to look for returns from the 4, 5, 9, or 10. The vig is better with the 6 and 8, the payoffs better, based on outlay, and the number of ways that the 6 and 8 can be made are better than the other four place numbers.

Then what the devil are you waiting for? All things point to the powerful 6 and 8 as the choice of place numbers, yet many crapshooters keep looking for reasons to drift to the other numbers.

Minimize your losses, and give yourself the best chance of winning. Get smart!!! Try a sensible approach to playing Craps and see if the results aren't more profitable. The Basic Right Betting Method is sensible and effective. Think about it!

MONEY MANAGEMENT 10

Come System

I do not play this system. I teach it in seminars, and I put it in this book for two reasons. One, practically every book ever written on Craps adheres to this method of play. Secondly, a lot of knowledgeable craps players use this method. So, I'll go over it for the purpose of making you aware of it, but I still don't like it.

First of all, go back to the chapter on Come bets, found in Section 3, Knowledge of the Game, Chapter 11. It explains the whole method of this type play, which is exactly the same as the Pass Line, except the Pass Line bet affects only the first roll by a player. The bets can be made time after time, and while it affects the "next" throw of the dice, the basic rules do not differ from the Pass Line wager.

The theory of this system is the same as the place bets. Make a Pass Line bet, take the free odds, and have two numbers working for you. Only in this case, instead of placing the two additional numbers, you make two successive bets in the Come, and both those bets are then moved to the appropriate number box, and you take your free odds, by tossing an amount of chips to the dealer and telling him, "Odds on my Come, please."

There is no Money Management method needed, as with the place bets, because as soon as a Come number scores, they pay you off—even money for the basic Come bet, and true odds for the odds bet, just like the Pass Line. Then, to reestablish your wagers, you just go back through the Come box, when one of your numbers shows. That way, you always have the Pass Line bet, and two additional numbers working for you.

There are a couple of plus factors for this method:

1. If the 7 or 11 does happen to show with your chip in the Come, you automatically win, for the Come bet, even though the 7 would kill your Pass Line bet and any other Come bets that have been established
2. The Come bet, with odds, has only an .8% edge for the house, while none of the place bets offer that low a vig.

But, there are also minus factors with the Come bet:

1. You do not get to pick the Come bets (numbers) that you end up with. It could be a constant run of 4's and 10's
2. You must make that number twice, to get paid. Once, to establish the Come bet, and the second time to get a payoff
3. Come bets work on the come-out, and this restricts the possibility of a long, long roll to materialize, as a hot shooter is *bound* to throw at least one 7 on his subsequent come-outs, and down go all those Come bets (not the odds on them)
4. Place betting allows a more flexible amount of decisions, as to increasing or decreasing wagers on the placed numbers.

It is my humble opinion that the minuses far, far out-weigh the pluses for the Come betting players. Especially (3), dealing with the Come bets working on the come-out. Even though your odds do not work, you could have some shooter in the middle of a scorching roll, where he's just made his fifth straight Pass Line number, kill you with a "winning" roll. You've reeled in a considerable amount of chips, have $25 on the Pass Line for the next come-out, and $15, with odds, on the 6, the 8, and the 10 (all Come bets). The shooter launches his dice, and each player holds his breath. The dealer shouts out: "Seven, seven, winner on the front line." Yahoo!!! You pick up a five-unit payoff on the Pass Line. But down goes your 6, down goes your 8, and down goes your 10. A $45 bath, offsetting the $25 you won with your Pass Line bet.

Naturally, the place bettors are in no trouble at all, as their place bets are off on the come-out. Now you must start climbing back up the Come Line ladder again, just to reestablish your bets.

No, I do not condone the Come bet, regardless of the slight edge in your favor on the low vig, and the plus factor of winning on the 7 that shows on the Come roll. It all goes down the drain when your Come bets are wiped out with a subsequent 7 on a future come-out roll, while a certain shooter is in the midst of a hot streak. But, if you want to play that way—go ahead. Some day I'll win you over.

Incidentally, I can hear your whispers regarding why should you even play the Pass Line, if the Come bet is exactly the same. The difference is the Pass Line wager does not offset any bets on the initial come-out, so that powerful 7 can only help you.

But, don't go getting all wrapped up in the Pass Line bet, as there are offshoots and variations, to even this move, and I'll get to that in due time. For now, you decide on your like or dislike for the Come bet. You know where I stand on it.

11

MONEY MANAGEMENT

Single Bet

If you like to bet "right," but lack the proper bankroll, this method will keep you in the game, and while your wins may not be high, your losses will not be excessive. It is the simple Pass Line bet, with odds. That's it, no other bets, no extra numbers, no placing the 6 and 8, no Come bets.

You put a $5 chip on the Pass Line, and have the 7 and 11 going for you, and craps laying off in the bushes. Once the point is established, you take single odds, and wait. If the point is made, you win. If not, you lose, but your loss is never more than $11. This way, a $100 session amount gives you the needed money for ten players around the table.

Since you wish to risk only $11 per shooter, there are a couple of options to this play. When the point is established, you should always take the odds, thereby reducing the house edge from 1.41% to .8%, although I showed you options on the 4 and 10.

The same is true here. If the point is 4 and 10, instead of taking odds, you could place either the 6 or 8, and stay within the allotted $11 per shooter. You could also do this with the other numbers of 5, 6, 8, and 9, by waiting for one of them to show as the point, and then placing the 6 or 8.

Remember, this is totally contrary to proper play, as you are letting your small bankroll prohibit you from taking the best bet in the house—free odds. On this bet, the house has no edge. But I know—I know—I know—so many people do not have the proper bankroll, and I'm trying to give you paths to follow, that will help you reach the promised land—minimizing losses and winning.

In Vegas, where you can find many $1, $2, and $3 tables, you should never, ever play this way. In Atlantic City, where the tables are mostly $5 minimums, the crusher for the small bettor, you can allow yourself some deviation.

Suppose your $5 bet on the Pass Line produced a point of 6. Instead of taking $5 odds on the 6, you could place the 8. Now you have two numbers working for you, instead of just the 6, that can be made five ways each, bucking the 7 that can be made six ways. On the next roll, you have ten ways of winning, six chances to lose.

Assume the 8 shows. Here are the options:

1. Same bet
2. Take odds behind the 6, which is the point, and pocket $2
3. Place the 5, and now have three numbers working for you

Answer: Naturally, number one, take your $7 profit. Now, if the 7 shows, you are out only $4 for that shooter. You could also accept your $7 profit, take down your place 8, and just sit with the $5 bet on the 6. If you win, that shooter gave you a $12 profit. If the 6 goes down, you still show a $2 profit for that roll.

Don't laugh at these conservative options. There's nothing wrong with winning $2 from every shooter, all around the table. Then, as your session money begins to build you can start taking odds, and placing additional numbers.

One final note. Suppose, after the 8 showed the first time, you took your $7 profit and called for the same bet. The same options would apply, if the 8 showed again:

1. Same bet (leave the 8 placed)
2. Same bet, and put the odds behind the 6
3. Take your $7 payoff and come down off the 8, and just wait for a decision on the point.

If this is the way you will play, based on your bankroll, be sure to pick one of these methods and follow it religiously for the duration of that session—no jumping back and forth with different option decisions.

MONEY MANAGEMENT 12

Pass Line Control

Probably the most impulsive gambler in America today is the crapshooter. He's certainly the noisiest. As soon as a table starts to warm up, so do the players. The noise level reaches screeching points. Most crapshooters are right bettors, and when those numbers start showing, the whole casino is alerted.

The bets become higher and wilder. This is it!! This is the roll!! The longer it lasts, the louder the players become. When the shooter finally does 7 out, after a very long roll, he gets an ovation from his peers. I've seen the Baccarat player dealing the bank, turn over twenty-two straight winnng hands, and not a person at the table even gives evidence that they're alive.

I've dealt Blackjack games, where I lost something like sixteen or seventeen hands in a row, and I wanted to poke the players with a fork to see if they were breathing. But let the crapshooters uncork seven or eight numbers in a row, and you need earmuffs to lessen the noise. And as the noise level rises, so do the bets. It's contagious, and it's constant.

A player drops a $5 chip on the table and the shooter pops a 7—instant winner. What does our hero do? Why, he lets it ride. Some garbage about it being the house's money, or, this could be the start of something big. Two ridiculous assumptions.

If you are a Pass Line player, you *never* increase that initial bet, until two point numbers are made. This does not include 7's and 11's on the come-out roll, which are instant winners. That means you must win twice with a point number, plus odds.

After the shooter makes two points, you then increase your

Pass Line bet by one unit. I know the temptation is to let it all ride. But remember, as soon as a point is established, you also have to take odds, thereby doubling your wager.

I've seen players hit two straight come out 7's and a point number of 6, have a profit of $21, and put $25 on the Pass Line. Nine becomes the new point, and he takes $30 odds. Up pops the 7 and down goes the bet, showing a net loss of $34. This dope won three decisions from the house and lost only one. Yet his result was a minus $34. This guy must love to lose, with a Money Management system like that. But there are many, many players that follow the same pattern.

If you are a $5 bettor, you must make two points, before starting the next come-out with a $10 bet. Then, you must win two wagers with a $10 basic bet, with odds, before going up on the Pass Line. From there, you can go to a $15 bet, wait to score on one point, and then up to $20, and so on, escalating your bets as shown:

1. **Five Dollar Bettor** (Betting sequence, as you win)
    a. 5-5-10-10-15-20-25-25-35-50
    (For a $5 bettor, $50 base bet, with odds, is high enough)
2. **Ten dollar bettor**
    a. 10-10-15-15-20-25-45-60-75-100
    (All of these examples include *single* odds)

With the three-unit bet, the amount of increased odds is permitted. For example, $15 Pass Line bet, point of 6 or 8 allows $25 free odds. Take it.

3. **Twenty-five dollar bettor**
    a. 25-25-45-45-60-75-100-125

With double odds, I suggest lower Pass Line bets, as the amounts can be made up with the double odds availability. Following is progression with double odds:

1. **Five dollar bettor**
    a. 5-5-10-10-15-15-20-20-25-25
2. **Ten dollar bettor**
    a. 10-10-15-15-20-20-25-25-35-50

3. **Twenty-five dollar bettor**
   a. 25-25-40-40-50-50-60-75-100

Hey, don't forget, there are two different factions frequenting the casinos: those with conservative approaches and those who are aggressive. The above will sound great to some, and they'll go diving right into this pattern. But you *MUST* have a strong stomach, not to mention bankroll, to play this way. It always looks good on paper, but the trick of standing at the table and dropping out $50 on the Pass Line, and $100 odds, should cause more than one $5 bettor to check his shorts. Naturally, if you ever get to that point, using this system, you really have no problem, as the profits derived by this progression will have already guaranteed you some solid wins for this shooter.

Then, there is the other side of the coin. The super-aggressive player won't want to be so controlled, as he'll claim he is being restricted from taking advantage of a hot roll. When will these guys ever realize that you don't know it is a hot roll until it is *over*. Or, do you read the dice's mind? This method will unquestionably hold down your losses, provide you with profits on medium hot rolls, and still have you placing decent bets, when you are fortunate enough to be in on a scorcher.

Sevens and elevens on the come-out should be taken as a bonus. Remember that four ways to make a craps, offset the two ways to make 11, plus two of the six ways to bang the 7. So, this four-plus edge doesn't give you the right to think you've got a gun at the casino's head. Go up in degrees. The fall back down won't hurt as much.

I've already explained that I do play "Any Craps," and "three-way craps," to protect my three-unit bets, and higher. When I reach a $30 bet, I increase my Craps bets in the same proportion.

And I never play the 11 (I mean the Yo) on the come out. Never! If it shows, I still win on the Pass Line bet anyway.

Maybe a quick example will put some insight into the damage that could occur, by not waiting for Pass Line victories, before increasing your Pass Line bet.

G.I. Luvtabet drops $5 on the Pass Line and 7 pops right out. He wins a quick $5, and immediately lets $10 ride on the next come-out. Ten becomes the point, and old G.I. takes $10 odds. Bango—out comes the 7, and down goes the Pass Line bet and odds. That series produced a $5 willing roll, and a subsequent losing toss. G.I. ends up with a net loss of $15, yet he won a roll and lost a roll. He played the house even, and got banged for three units.

When he won that $5 for the 7 on the first come-out, he should have pulled back his profit, and bet $5 again. When the 10 became the point, he could take his odds, and then when the 7 beat him, his loss would have been only $5. That's a $10 savings for this particular series. If this same thing happened five times during the course of that session, it could have resulted in a $50 additional loss.

G.I. Luvtabet could argue that if he won, he would have been that much further ahead. Think over how many times that this has happened to you. You pick up a quick win with the 7 or 11 on the come-out, and right away go for the bigger bet. That devastating 7 soon brings you back to earth.

Forget that nonsense about looking for the gigantic kill, right off the bat. Minimize your losses, and build up a neat little profit. The chance for heroics will come.

This is a very big part of Money Management. Do not increase your Pass Line bet until two victories on the point number, with odds, have been safely tucked away. Then you can move your game into second gear.

Patience, my friends. . . . Patience.

MONEY MANAGEMENT 13

1, 2, 3, 4 System

Every week, somebody tells me about a dynamite system that he or she came up with, and after trying it out on the living room rug, they are now ready to give it a shot at the tables. They explain the system to me and ask for comments.

This is one of those brainstorms. It is called the 1, 2, 3, 4 system. I've explained many times my feelings toward the Martingale method of betting, whereby you double your bet after a prior loss, and continue this doubling-up system until a win occurs. At that time, you recover all your past losses, plus a one-unit profit. Well, the system stinks. Laying out a large amount of chips, for a one-unit profit, based on something "due" to happen is an illogical assumption.

This 1, 2, 3, 4 system is not as drastic, but it has the same ridiculous premise that one shooter in four will make a point. Maybe the odds are one in four, but the percentage might be reached by three straight shooters, making three Pass Line numbers, then the next nine shooters sevening out, before making even one pass. The percentage is still one in four, but you only caught the bad streak.

This method calls for you to lay out one chip, with odds, and if you lose, two chips with odds, etc. Four straight losses on the Pass Line, with odds, could add up to a deficit of twenty units in a very quick matter of minutes.

This is just another spin-off of a progression type betting system, based on something "due" to occur. Doubling-up systems don't work in the real world often enough. I know, you've been banging out profits for three years on your living room rug, and you're positive that this type betting scheme will eventually pay large dividends. If you believe that, give me a call, and we'll set up a time to meet. I've got a couple of oil wells in my back yard that I think you'd be interested in. They're due to start paying off, and you can have them cheap.

14 MONEY MANAGEMENT

Follow the Trend

I believe in the Big 4. I honestly believe, that if you have all four of these ingredients to pour into the gambling pan, you will come out cooking more times than you get burned.

Same is true of the Little 3. And this leads me to one of the parts of the Little 3. It's called trends. I've already spent some time explaining how trends dominate in gambling. And it's true. It's a happening that no one seems able to cxplain.

In the game of Craps, the same patterns of streaks seem to emerge. The dice will be hot for long periods, then cold for long periods. Being on the right side at the right time determines whether you win or lose. The chopping table takes its toll on both sides, hence the reason I stress Loss Limits.

But let's get to the matter of trends at a table. I believe that when you begin a session, either as a right bettor, or a wrong bettor, you must stay with that system until you leave that table, no jumping back and forth.

Now I give you a method of play that calls for you to jump back and forth. It is called "Follow the Trend." You're looking for the dice to establish a pattern or streak. Whichever side takes hold first, you will be on it. The idea is getting to it, as quick a you can.

It is simple to apply, and while you do not want to get caught at a chopping table, the truth is, that no system can work at a chopping table. But, your Loss Limit will protect you, just like it does at any session.

You go to a table, buy in, and wait for the first decision to appear. Whatever it is, you follow it. The shooter throws a 6 as his point. After a couple of other numbers have been thrown, he makes his point. The right bettors are happy. Your first bet is on the Pass Line. You continue to bet Pass Line until the shooter sevens out. As soon as that occurs, you will switch over and place the next bet on the Don't Pass, and if that shooter fails to make his point, you continue to bet Don't Pass, as long as the dice stay cold.

The basic right betting method calls for two additional numbers to be placed after the come out. This system is different. You are strictly a Pass Line *and* Don't Pass Line bettor, nothing more. During this session, you will stay in the pattern of following the trend. You'll recall that each session is dedicated to strictly one method of play. It is your choice as to which method you prefer. Right, Wrong, 6/8, Hedge, or in this case, Follow the Trend.

At this point, I re-remind you of the most important thing about gambling—winning. And winning is accomplished only if you stay within the confines of your bankroll. The Basic Right Method calls for outlays of $21 or $22 per shooter, something a lot of players simply just don't have. Why should I try to make like these people don't exist? They are a gigantic percentage of the betting public, so I aim these controlled systems at them.

If you don't have the proper money to bet the Basic Right Method, let me give you some plays that control your money. You'll be unable to take advantage of a red-hot roll, where fifteen or sixteen place numbers in a row are thrown. But, you're also going to hold your losses down, when things go against you.

Let's get to some Money Management for this method. There are numerous variations off of every betting system, including aggressive, semiaggressive, ultra-aggressive, conservative, etc. I'm talking to the single unit bettor. You wanna form your own set of patterns? Perfect. That's what you're supposed to do, after you understand the basic premise of the play.

Wait for the shooter to arrive at a decision. She comes out with a 5, and a few rolls later makes her point. The trend is toward the Pass Line. Your first bet is $5 on the front line.

Take your odds, and stop. That's it. You have two units at risk.

If that shooter makes her point, you come back with a $5 bet on the Pass Line. Suppose the point is a 6. Take your odds and wait. On this roll, she again makes her point of 6. You're paid for your front line and odds bets. She has made three points in a row, but two while you were betting with her. Now you increase your Pass Line wager to two units, and take the odds.

If she throws a craps on the come-out, drop back to one unit, but stay on the Pass Line. On this series, she sevens out. Your next bet is $5 on the Don't Pass, for the next shooter. That's because the previous decision was in favor of the don't.

When betting don't, I do not advise laying the odds, but, of course, that's up to you. Since this is a simple, single unit system, you do not make additional bets in the don't come. If the next two shooters seven out, you may increase your Don't Pass bet to two units.

There's nothing complicated about this method. It is a simple approach for the player with a small bankroll, that allows him to catch a strongly trended table. And it is not restricted to just the $5 player. A heavy heeled player may also desire to play "Follow the Trend." This system is very effective in Baccarat, and the outside bets of Roulette, such as Black/Red, Odd/Even, and High/Low.

Before you sneer, and turn up your snoot at this method, try going to a table and watch trends keep occurring. Whichever way the table is going, you're right with it.

A little later you will find another chapter, called "Trends and the Patrick System." Do not make any commitments to a trend system until you comprehend both of these chapters. There will be variations of plays that you will want to pull from both of these methods.

15 MONEY MANAGEMENT

Variations for the Trend

As in all methods, the variations are unlimited, and I'd like you to establish your own, but only after you completely understand the basic premise. In following the trend, I'll show you some spin-offs that might appeal to your style of play. First of all, you don't have to restrict yourself to the Pass Line bet only, when the trend is toward the "right" bettors. If you have the bankroll, you could also tie in the Basic Right Method, by placing two additional numbers, but always including the 6 and 8 in your three plays. You would then revert to the proper Money Management method for increasing the place numbers.

Now, you say that you could get caught in a chopping table, and find yourself between the gun to the head and the knife to the throat. Yeah, that's right. What do you want, a guaranteed, documented statement, that chopping trends won't come up? You won't get it. But you will become a disciplined player, with a set pattern of play, and definite set goals.

You know, there's an old saying that goes: "A long journey begins with the first step." This method of following the trend is forfeiting your being in on the first decision, because it is absolutely impossible to guess what the first decision will be. But, if you follow the trend, and a shooter makes that first point, you move over to that side, and, if indeed, this turns out to be the roll of the day, you are on it. If a shooter sevens out, you cross over to the Don't betting, and if this signals a cold trend at that table, you will save a heck of a lot of money by not bucking the trend that the table is on. Well, the first step is finding which way the trend is going. The big shot keeps pouring money onto the table, with player after player, hoping that one gets hot. He can't keep doing this, hour after hour. An ice cold table will destroy him, but if he followed the flow of the dice, he'd be able to stay alive at that game until some shooter finally did get hot.

Go a step further. Let's say you have absolutely no intention of betting wrong. OK, that's your prerogative. But watch how the trend method can still help you. Wait for a shooter to make his point. Then, bet on the Pass Line, and follow my suggestions. However, if the first shooter sevened out, instead of following the possible start of a Don't trend, by betting wrong, don't bet at all. Just don't make any bet. This way you are following only the trends toward pass line. It's then called "Following the Right." Your bets will only be made on the Pass Line, following a point being made by the shooter.

This way, you never bet wrong, but when the dice are cold, you're never fighting them, and when that long journey on the right side occurs, you miss only the first step.

Incidentally, I have a few side rules that you might like to follow. I throw out 7's, 11's, or craps on the come-out. I do not let them influence my betting, one way or the other. If a shooter makes a point, and I crossed over to the right side, and the come-out roll produced a craps, I would not swing back to the wrong side. There will be times when a shooter will take five or six rolls to establish a point. Maybe she'll throw 12, 7, 11, 2, 7, 3, in a row. Can you imagine how you would be betting? Wrong, right, right, wrong, right, wrong! You'll drive yourself batty. No, if you stuck with these decisions on the come-out, just swallow your anger, and wait for a point decision.

Well, that's a look at following the trend. Did you ever give it any thought, you die-hard strong willed crapshooters? The design, or intent, is to reduce losses, when the flow is going against you. Realistically, what do you really lose? The first roll of that possible streak. And what if in that first roll, the shooter throws seventy-eight place numbers, before she makes her point? Tough!!! It'll give you something to complain about.

Give this method more than just a ho-hum approach. Variation in betting amounts can be applied, as you see fit.

MONEY MANAGEMENT 16

Forcing the Bet

Let me take a breather, as regards the system of play, to relate a tale or two that you may apply to your own game. This has to do with the persistency of some crapshooters to feel that a certain thing just *has* to happen, because the opposite has occurred.

I was in Atlantic City one night playing Craps, and a cop friend of mine joined me at the table. He was new to the game, and I was showing him some methods on the Don't side. The table was fairly choppy, but not enough to chase us. After about three hours, I was ahead about $400 and my friend Bernie was up about $190. He was glad to be ahead, and since the trend was starting to change, we decided to pack it in. Bernie said he would stay for one more shooter, just to get to the $200 mark. I put my chips in my pocket, but waited with him.

The dice were at the far side of the table, and it was the turn of a redheaded woman, who had been playing for awhile, but never threw the dice. The dealer pushed the dice in front of her, and you'd think he pointed a gun. She jumped back with her arms up. "No, No, I can't throw." A couple of people around her prodded her to take the dice. She still resisted: "No, I don't know how." They told her it was so easy: just pick two dice and toss them to the other end of the table. Finally, and very reluctantly, she chose two dice.

Bernie placed $5 on the Don't Pass. She threw a 7. He lost and placed $10 on Don't. She threw another 7. Again he lost and dropped $20 on the table. I remember telling him he was crazy—that he was fighting the biggest problem that gamblers have: the double-up game. He said, "she just can't keep throwing sevens." He was right. She threw an 11 and he lost again.

Now he was mad, and dropped $50 on the Don't Pass. Whack!!! She threw another 7. The players were in an uproar. The shooter still had only her single $5 chip on the Pass Line, but you could feel the momentum growing.

Bernie reached into his pocket and pulled out two handfuls of chips and dropped them on the table and told the boxlady, "One hundred, on the Don't." She said, "You have a bet." The word had just passed her lips, when the redhead threw her fifth natural, a 7. Bernie couldn't believe it. I told him to get out of there, he was beat.

Would he listen? Nah!!! He took a $100 bill out of his wallet and told the dealer, "All on the Don't." He got a reprieve. She came out with a 6. Bernie still wasn't out of the woods, but he was alive. She threw about five more numbers then banged the 6. My friend was visibly shaken. He couldn't believe it. In a matter of minutes, he had gone from a $190 winner to a $95 loser.

Forget about the fact that it was not a great deal of money. It was a lot to Bernie, and not just the money, but the fact that something that is not *supposed* to happen—happened. The ride home that night was awful. Just like the ride you encounter when you suffer similar fate.

These things happen in gambling. They've happened to you, and your friend, and your neighbor, and your boss, and so on. And they'll continue to happen to anyone who plays this way.

You increase your bets after a win, not after a loss. Remember that, and your losses, when they come, will be minimized. Your wins, when they come, will give out healthy returns. It's called Money Management.

Bernie has managed to live the past four years, despite his experience, but you wanna know something? He still mentions that night. He still remembers. And he has never done it again. Maybe things do work for the best.

MONEY MANAGEMENT 17

Reading the People

I love the people readers, the guys who can tell what will happen, as soon as the shooter picks up the dice. There are table readers in almost every craps game. I love to listen to them.

Years ago, I was working a game out west, and two such players were on my side of the table. They were going through the usual practice of making opinions on each shooter. It reached a time in the afternoon when a certain shooter prompted a heavy bet by the two seers.

The shooter was a tough-looking character, dressed in black, with a smelly cigar and a bankroll big enough to choke an elephant. "Wow, look at this guy, he sure looks like he knows what he's doing."

The two guessers were duly impressed. The shooter looked like a reject from an old "B" gangster movie, scowl and all. My two geniuses popped $50 on the Pass Line and waited to cash in.

The dice came out—"two, craps." They put another $50 on the line. "Two, craps," the stickman shouted. They grumbled a little and hesitantly put another $50 on the line. "Three, craps, line away," again they lost.

"Hey, what is it with this jerk?" they screamed. The two seers were starting to doubt their choice of shooter, and this time put only $25 on the line. Good thing, the "gangster" threw his fourth straight craps, another snake eyes. As per usual, every right shooter at the table was ready to organize a lynch mob for the shooter. Again the dice were coming out. The two fortune-tellers, with an increasingly amount of doubt coming over their predictions, put only $20 on the line. This time 6 became the point.

The hubbub of activity picked up, as all the right bettors made their extra side bets. The dice came sailing across the table, plopped to a stop and showed that devastating 7. My two forecasters were livid. They had increased the $10 bet they were making on the Pass Line all day, up to $50 and $25, just because the shooter "looked" like he was going to throw numbers.

I'm not finished. Even with that disastrous experience, they continued to make their bets, based on the "look" of the shooter.

Anyhow, the dice eventually came to a little old lady that could barely see over the table, even if she stood on her tip-toes. The two experts immediately read her as a wrong bettor. "Look at this—she doesn't even know what table she's at." They put $15 on the Don't Pass. Barely reaching the far end of the table, the shooter popped an 11. Again they bet don't, and again she threw a natural. I don't want to bore you, but you're already aware of the outcome. She threw six naturals and these two dopes refused to back off. They lost $15, $15, $15, $10, $10, and $5.

If it wasn't so pathetic, it would have been hilarious. Eventually, I went on a break and left the two forecasters shaking their heads in disbelief. When I returned, they were gone.

They weren't good craps players, but they were even worse at being forecasters. Don't bet the appearance of the shooter, it doesn't mean a thing. Neither does the nonsense that because the shooter had a prior great roll, he'll repeat the performance.

Get a new outlook on gambling. Base your bets on the Big 4, not assumptions.

But—it's your money. Just don't expect me to come to you to have my palm read.

These stories are true, and I repeat them to make a point. These are intelligent people making illogical moves at gambling, with real money. In isolated instances, some of these wayout moves will pay a small dividend. But in the long run, there is no substantial meat to the silly habit that many people put into play at a table.

MONEY MANAGEMENT

18

Field Place System

Maybe you've heard of this system. It has some good points and some bad ones. I show it here because of the many questions that come up regarding its effectiveness. The intent with this system is to have all the numbers on the board provide you with a possible payoff, except of course, the 7.

I'm amused when I see it written up in an article, or book, where the author says, "It's a great system, all you have to worry about is the 7." It's like telling a soldier, "Don't worry about getting shot, it'll only be a little hole." Or the guy who's scared to fly, "Don't worry about the plane crashing. The only problem is the sudden stop at the end!"

That 7 is devastating. And like all crapshooters before you, the day will come when you realize how potent it is. But, let's get to this method.

By putting a $5 chip in the field, you've covered the numbers: 2, 3, 4, 9, 10, 11, and 12. That leaves only the 5, 6, 7, and 8 uncovered. The next move would be to place one unit on the 5, 6, and 8. You have $22 at risk, and every number on the board is taken care of, except the 7. Since the field is a one-roll action bet, there is a decision reached on every toss of the dice.

This is the possible outcome of each succeeding roll:

1. If 7 shows . . . Loss $22
2. If 5 shows, lose field bet, win place bet on the 5 . . . Win $2
3. If 6 shows, lose field bet, win place bet on the 6 . . . Win $2

4. If 8 shows, lose field bet, win place bet on the 8 . . . Win $2
5. If field number shows, win $5 (2 or 12 pays double) . . . Win $5
   (In this case, there is no decision on place bets.)

Since there are thirty-six possible combinations that could show, this system shows a profit on thirty of them, leaving out only the six ways to make the 7.

On the surface, this sounds great. With every roll of the dice, your chances of winning are thirty against six ways of losing. That's a 5-1 edge in your favor. The drawback is that 7. When that number pops up, you drop $22. It takes a lot of $2 wins to make up for that eventual loss.

One such way you may try is the disciplined three rolls. After leaving your money at risk for three throws of the dice, take down all your bets. If the 7 doesn't show, the worst you get is a $6 profit. It could be more, but $6 is at least guaranteed, based on one-unit wagers. Leaving your money in action for long periods, is flirting with total wipe outs on the 7. I suggest three rolls and down, if you play this system.

There are alternate betting amounts that can be applied, in order to increase the payouts on the 5, 6, and 8. Following is an example:

Field:	$ 7
Place the 5:	$10
Place the 6:	$12
Place the 8:	$12

In this way, if the field shows, you win $7. If the 5, 6, or 8 show, you lose $7 on the field, and win $14 for the place bet, for a net profit of $7. However, you have $41 at risk, when that 7 pops up.

My friend Howie G., an expert card-counter, crapshooter and baccarat player, uses this method quite often. He is in Vegas, and has the opportunity of getting to a casino seven, eight times a day. One thing is, Howie has Discipline. He never gets caught chasing his losses.

He might bring $100 to the table and decide to play this

method. What he's looking for is a quick $14 or $21. He'll chart a table for ten to fifteen minutes, find one that is hot, and go into action. His first move is to wait for a 7, and then go for one or two rolls. As soon as he gets the number of hits he wanted, down come all his bets and he walks. He'll do this several times a day, always waiting until the table is running his way. He has the Discipline to make his score and then leave.

His biggest asset, aside from Discipline, is the availability of the tables. Most people would love to win $100 at the casino, but are there on a bus ride, or junket, or vacation, and feel they must bet all day long. That's your problem. My concern is teaching you how to win.

If you can withstand the possible loss of $41 every time the 7 shows, you could set your goal for one hit every fifteen minutes. That's $28 an hour. Assuming you're in the casino five hours a day, that's $140 per trip. You want more return? Bring more money and play for higher stakes, but be prepared to have some tough days along with the good ones.

One variation to this method has to do with offsetting the 7. It'll put more money at risk, but lessen your chances of losing. The basic approach is the same. We'll use $5 in the field, $5 on the 5 and $6 on both the 6 and 8. That's $22 at risk. The six rolls that can beat you are the ways a 7 can be made.

You then place $41, No Ten. In this way, if the 7 shows, you lose $22 for the initial outlay on the field and place numbers, and pick up $19 for the No Ten. Since a 10 can only be made three ways (6-4, 4-6, 5-5), you've cut your possible loss rolls down from six to three. The kicker is that now you are in a position to lose $41 if that 10 shows.

With this variation, you can lose on only three rolls of the dice, push on three, and win on thirty. This sounds great, and actually it is not all that bad. But you MUST set the amount of rolls, that you leave yourself vulnerable to the number that can beat you. Naturally, it all goes back to the bankroll, and people with strong ones can last a long time playing this way, as they are able to withstand several whacks.

You can come up with your own set of variations off of this

method, based on different amounts of money you can bet on the field and the place numbers. And, like Howie, if you can abide by the restrictive limits, you may grind out a day's pay quite often.

MONEY MANAGEMENT

19

Six and Eight System

I'm talking to all you $5 bettors, who, despite my warnings of need for the strong bankroll, still descend upon the casino, short of cash. This is a nice little system that will keep you in the game, offer you a tremendous opportunity to minimize losses, and still give you the chance of jumping on a hot roll.

You do not bet the Pass Line. You are giving up the four number edge of the seven/eleven over craps. This is to avoid the possibility of having to cover the point, plus odds and placing the 6 and 8. After the point is established, you place the 6 and 8. Twelve dollars will be your total risk, per shooter.

If the shooter sevens out before making a 6 or 8, the worst you have lost is $12. If he makes a 6 or 8, after his point is established, take your $7 profit. If he then sevens out, the worst you have lost is $5 per shooter, and that is asking for only one 6 or 8, before the killer 7.

The theory behind this method, obviously, is minimizing your losses. I believe this is the biggest drawback of 90% of the people who gamble. They refuse to hold down their losses. Let's continue with a typical roll.

It doesn't matter what the point number is, you immediately place the 6 and 8. The Money Management is as follows:

1. First hit with the 6 or 8 ....Same bet
2. Second hit with the 6 or 8 ....Place the 5
3. Next hit on any of the numbers...................Place the 9

You now have the four inside numbers covered. If you seven out, your total loss is only $1. If any of the numbers show on the next roll, pull down all your bets, and wait for the next shooter. Continue with this conservative play until you show a profit of $100. At that time, cut it in half, with $50 going in your pocket and the other $50 kept in play. Keep playing the same way, except now you do not take down your bets after the fourth hit. Instead, start reverting to the correct Money Management method for place numbers: Same bet—Press it—Make it look like 6. Begin to apply that play here, if you so desire. It will allow you to get in on a good roll. But of course I am not telling you that you MUST get aggressive. Play the way you feel the most comfortable.

With this method, you never end up with the 4 or 10 as one of your numbers, and the basis of the system always starts with the 6 or 8. But most of all, the worst loss you can encounter is $12 per shooter, if you place $6 on both the 6 and 8. After your $100 goal is reached, there is nothing wrong with going a little longer with your bets, just as there is nothing wrong with continuing with the play that got you to that $100 profit.

Some of you may not want to spin off onto the 5 and 9, but continue to concentrate on building up the 6 and 8. Great—that's what theory is all about. Work out the play that you feel at ease with.

For a second, go back to the come-out. If 6 or 8 is the point, you still place both numbers. If the point number of 6 or 8 shows, take your profit, and on the next series, start all over with placing only the 6 and 8, after the come-out, and begin the place betting sequence all over again.

Here are the moves for the player who starts his place bets with $12 on both the 6 and 8, for a total outlay of $24. Keep in mind that the moves are always based on one number continuing to show. That's why you must be concentrating on the game, in order to remember the next move for each of the placed numbers.

1. First hit........................Same bet (take your $14 profit)
2. Second hit:...........a. Press it up to $18 (take $8), or
   b. Press it up to $24 (take $2), or
   c. Press both 6 and 8 to $18, or
   d. Same bet (take another $14 profit)

This method is for the conservative player, and even the craps gambler who starts with $12 on both the 6 and 8, can play cautiously. My suggestion would be to decide between either (a), a partial press, or (d) Same bet.

3. Third hit...........Make it look like $6 (Come down to $6). On this third score on the same number, I don't give a rat's tail if you played either (a) or (d), or even if you are aggressive and played (b) or (c), the call is to break your place bet on that number—down to $6.

Since we are still playing a laid-back system for this session, I do not advise going back up if that number hits again. Either place the 5 or 9, or take the same bet. While I strongly advise its use by the player with a short bankroll, the heavy heeled player can also use it by just starting the place bets on the 6 and 8 for two or three units each, depending on your bankroll.

In summary, this is a very simple method to understand, although there are a multitude of variations:

1. No bet on the Pass Line
2. After point is established, place the 6 and 8
3. If either one hits, take your profit
4. Another hit, either place the 5 or 9, or revert to the place betting system, and apply it to the 6 and 8
5. At any time during the roll, don't be afraid to pull everything down, if you are looking for merely a certain amount of win goal—per player.

I know that the initial reaction of the staunchest craps player will be to protest the eliminating of the Pass Line bet. But before you start heaving rocks, take a closer look at the options list. I'm trying to get you away from bucking the tough points of 4 and 10, and keep you consistently on the 6 and 8.

The disadvantage will always be the loss of the edge on the come-out roll. But, when a player has a small bankroll, as is the case with the majority of people, having a Pass Line bet, with odds and two additional numbers calls for that constant $22 outlay, per shooter. This method gives those players two strong numbers at all times and still the chance to place additional bets. But most of all, it cuts the required session money by 50%, and the risk, per shooter, almost 50%.

Take another look at this method.

MONEY MANAGEMENT 20

Regression System

A slightly more conservative offshoot of the place betting system I've just described is what I call the Regression System. It is a powerful tool for the craps player.

It is primarily aimed at "even" bets, such as Blackjack, Baccarat, outside bets of Roulette, Sports Betting, 6 and 8 in Craps and the Don't Pass Line, excluding laying odds.

The basic idea is to bet higher than the minimum, and after a win, regress back down to the minimum, thereby wrapping up a profit.

That means you can win as many hands as the house, yet be guaranteed a profit. The key to the system is the second bet, whereby you regress the next wager.

You must always bet higher than the table minimum, in order to give you room to go down, and the amount of that first bet is based on your own personal bankroll. I'll start by giving you the method as it pertains to $5 increments.

You're at a $5 Blackjack table, so your first bet is $10. If you win, the dealer slides $10 profit to you and you've got $20 in front of you. Here's the key move.

Take back the $10 you started with, plus $5 of the winning payoff, and bet $5. At this point, you're in fat city. You've got your original $10 back, plus a profit of $5, and even if you lose the next bet, your series shows a $5 profit.

Most people, after a win, bet the same amount or go up one unit or even two. If a loss occurs on that second bet, they're in a position where they have won a bet, lost a bet and are either even, or heavens to Betsy, out a unit or two.

Four guys walk up to a table and each bets $10 at a $5 table.

Each wins his bet, yet each has a different Theory as to what the next bet should be:

1. Player A pulls back $10 profit and bets $10
2. Player B pulls back $5 and bets $15
3. Player C pulls back nothing and bets $20
4. Player D pulls back $15 and bets $5

Let's say they all lose the next hand. Look at the results:

1. Player A won a hand, lost a hand, and he's even
2. Player B won a hand, lost a hand, and he's out $5, even though he held the house even
3. Player C won a hand, lost a hand, and is out $10, even though he won as many hands as the house
4. Player D ends up with a $5 profit, although he ended up 1-1 with the house

Once the profit is locked into that series, you can become aggressive with your wagers. For instance, you win that second bet of $5. The dealer slides a $5 chip over to you and you let the whole $10 ride, fully cognizant of the fact that the series is in a profit lock.

Suppose you win that third bet of $10. At this point you revert to Up and Pull, a powerful method of Money Management discussed more fully in the next chapter.

You win the bet at $10 and incorporate the Up and Pull Theory. Raise your bet **Up** to $15 and **Pull** back a profit of $5, which further increases the previous profit for the Series, which was gleaned by regressing after the first win.

If that $15 bet also wins, you now go **Up** to $20 and **Pull** back $10. You could have gone **Up** to $25 and **Pulled** back $5, and that is strictly up to you. Naturally I would have you up only $5, but I like the conservative approach.

But every winning bet must give you a profit, so don't think you can raise the subsequent bet by the full amount of the win unless you've already regressed to the table minimum. Every other winning bet must result in a profit being pulled back!!!

Stop right here my friend and go back over that last

paragraph. It was meant for every single solitary one of you and it should be memorized backwards and forwards.

When you get into your series, be absolutely sure you take back a profit after every winning score. I cannot stress enough the power of this move or the necessity of it. Guys like Imus Pressit and Y.R. Kash, Frank Lee Board, Low N. Shirt, and P. Weebrane will scoff at this theory and claim you can't win serious money by being conservative.

But all I'm asking you to do is give up that second winning bet in a series, lock up a profit, and then go into your aggressive increase in bets.

Besides, what's so hard about taking back a profit after each winning hand or roll. I'm still letting you increase your bets. All I'm asking is that you take back a profit.

As you continue to win, you can raise your bets, as long as each win results in a profit being stashed. Naturally you can also insert another regression into your series and the smarter players will want to do that. It just means you lock up a bigger profit at a specific time in your series and then start back up.

Let's finish that winning series you were in. You won at $15 and had the option of going to either $20 or $25. We'll say you went to $20. Suppose you win again and the dealer slides $20 over to you; this time you get a little more aggressive and raise the bet to $35, while pulling back $5.

Again you get a winning hand and $35 is slid over to you. At this point, you slap another regression bet into your series. Take back the $35 and regress your bet:

1. All the way down to $10
2. Partial regress to $20
3. Partial regress to $25
4. One-unit drop to $30

Choose any of the above and you're not wrong. Then you can start back up. For instance, Connie Conservative drops her next bet all the way to $10 and each subsequent winning hand is increased by $5. I love her!!

Aggie Aggressive likes the regression but drops her next bet to $30 and every succeeding win is pulled back and another $5 lopped off her bet. For instance she wins at $30 and then bets $25. Then wins at $25 and drops to $20 or even a spin-off of that method.

The variations go on and on and on. The next chapter gives you tables to follow, and of course you could come up with your own.

Just remember that after a loss, you revert to the beginning bet of the series and start over.

I might just warn you, or maybe you know already: You won't win forever, so you better think about incorporating additional regressions into your series. It'll soften the blow when that inevitable loss does occur.

Since you should be keyed in on this Regression System right now, swing right into the next chapter and take a look at some series.

21 MONEY MANAGEMENT

Up and Pull

I know, I know, I've covered this before, but while I'm in a groove and have my mind into handling series, there is no reason for me not to take a few minutes and bang away at this method.

Again I'll tell you that the key to winning consistently is to grab a profit after every single winning hand or roll or ball game.

Imus Pressit is addicted to stupidity. How in the name of heaven can he have a $30 6 and 8, get a score of $35, and then drop another $25 on the table and tell the dealer: "All the way up!"

Next hit again will have him having all the profits on the table. Sure he looks like Benny the Brain as the numbers continue to show but he also looks like Dippy the Dope when a 7 shows and bangs down all those profits.

Of course, Imus will then look for someone at the table to blame:

1. One guy hit the dice with his hand
2. The shooter didn't set the dice right
3. He didn't hit both dice against the backboard
4. He threw dice too high
5. He should have only hit one die against the board
6. Shooter used wrong hand
7. Shooter threw too fast
8. Shooter took too long
9. One guy was breathing too hard

Imus has everyone to blame but himself. Yet the answer is in the betting series—nothing else.

When he grabbed that $35 profit with the $30 6 or 8, he could have gone right to Up and Pull. He should:

1. Up both bets to $36 each
2. Pull back $23 profit
3. Up his bet and Pull a profit.

If the 6 or 8 shows again:

1. Up both bets to $42 each
2. Pull back $30 profit
3. He has upped his bets and pulled back a profit

That's why I want you to predetermine your series, incorporating an intelligent Up and Pull sequence.

Notice that the prior example allowed you to increase your wagers by one unit each, while still salting away profits. Every single hit should allow you to pull back something, regardless of the amount.

That's why it is imperative that you learn both of these systems so that you can incorporate both the Up and Pull and Regression in the same series.

Imus is getting a half-baked grin inching its way across his motley puss. Maybe, just maybe, he is beginning to get smart.

Before he can ask the next question, I'll answer it for him. No, no, a thousand times no!!! You cannot go right into the Up and Pull theory after the first hit.

If you place the 6 and 8 for $30 each and an 8 shows, you cannot go up to $36 each and pull back $23. If you lost that $72, you'd be out $49 for that shooter.

First you must regress your bet—then you can go Up and Pull as long as you're in a position where a loss won't eat up all the profits.

By the way, the question that dingdong Imus Pressit was going to ask was: "Can I immediately go to Up and Pull on the first score?"

Here I thought we were finally reaching that dork, but all the time it was just his feeble mind finding a reason for him to press his bet.

The Up and Pull is a super powerful move after you reach

the excess part of your Win Goal and have set up plateaus to handle and take advantage of hot rolls.

This should cover Up and Pull and as we head off towards another system, we leave Watt E. Cey and Imus Pressit trying to explain to each other how to play Craps. There are thousands of players like these two.

—and that's the hell of it!!!!!

MONEY MANAGEMENT 22

Martingale System

Notice I have no system whereby you increase your bet after a loss, and tell you to continue doubling your bet until a winning point is made. That system is called the Martingale, invented, of course, by a man named Martingale.

There are about 4,726 systems on the market, for all types of games, and all with the Martingale theory of doubling up to insure that a win is "sure" to come. Who said it's sure to come? Oh, the system works great on paper, or with buttons on your living room floor. But let's see if you have the money and the guts to continue your progression betting when the losing streak reaches eight plays, and the rules call for you to put out a heavy bet. That's when you'll wish you were back playing with buttons.

You bet $5 and lose, the system calls for a $10 bet on the next roll. If that loses, you go for $20, then $40, $80, $160, $320, etc. Suppose you score with the $320 bet. You recoup the $635 you laid out, plus a $5 profit. That's a lot of bread at risk for a $5 chip.

You can't double up after the $320 bet, by the way, since the casinos have a $500 limit on the table, to restrict the plunger from betting enormous amounts. I know, I know, some of you wise guys say that it's almost impossible to lose six or seven decisions in a row. Oh, no it's not, my friend. It is very easy to lose eight, nine, ten plays in a row. And if you were doubling up, a streak like that would wipe you out.

You do not increase your bets after a loss, to recoup past losses. You should increase your bets only when you get on a hot streak. This is a simple rule, yet one that is broken hour after hour in the casinos. If people would ever adhere to this theory, their losses would drop by gigantic sums.

How about you? Which way do you play? I know you're anxious to get back the money you dropped, and get started on a winning streak. But minimizing losses is just as important to your overall play, as any single necessary facet of the Big 4. It's a part of the all important Money Management.

Bottom line for this chapter? Don't use the Martingale system—never, never, ever, never, ever, never—.

MONEY MANAGEMENT 23

Summarizing the Right Side

I've given you a couple of plays for betting right, and next we'll go over the wrong side of the table. Pick one or two of these methods, master them, and give them a shot at the tables.

The main thing is not to start a session with a certain method, and because it isn't working, swing over to a different system, while at that same session. Suppose you start out with the Basic Right Method, and the table is running cold. Do not swing over and start betting wrong.

You'll knock your loss limit completely out of whack. The Loss Limit is tied in with trends and if you do swing into a different system, because you've lost a few dollars, that means the new method will not have the proper session amount applied to it.

If you are losing at a table, you've got to leave it, and if you want to change systems, it's got to be after you've charted another table, and started off with the proper session money.

After you've reviewed these different right methods, I hope you apply your logical variations to the ones that you like the best. This knowledge of a system will work, if you have the proper starting session money, and follow it up with strict Money Management and Discipline methods.

All systems will work during different periods. Naturally, you'd want the system you pick to work while you're playing it. If it doesn't—then you have the loss limits to protect you, and you wrap up that session and move to another table.

If you're a right bettor, concentrate on these methods. If you're a wrong bettor, start digesting the upcoming chapters.

MONEY MANAGEMENT 24

Simple Don't Pass

Swinging over to the Don't side of the table, I'll list some plays for the wrong bettor. These method will range from very basic to aggressive, and encompass the Hedge betting systems.

Don't betting is a grind. A long, tedious, time consuming grind. Is it the proper or swankiest way to play Craps? There is no hard and fast rule, or proven system, that works all the time.

It still comes down to Money Management and Discipline. Now the hard core crapshooter will disagree with me. He'll swear that it is all a matter of skill, of how you throw those six-headed monsters across the table, that determine whether you win or lose. You'll find these cats juggling the dice, twisting them in all types of positions, stacking them on top of each other, smoothing out the table, blowing on their hands, rubbing their palms, talking to the dice, and then sevening out. So I'll say it again—it all comes down to Money Management, and Discipline.

The difference with wrong bettors is that they have the very dangerous 7 on their side—but only *after* the come-out roll establishes the point. (When you get to my Patrick system later in the book, you'll see how to beat that 7.) The edge swings sharply over to the don't bettor, simply because there are more ways to make the 7, than any other number on the board.

But the wrong bettor still fights that 7 and 11 on the come-out roll, and I've seen 6, 7, 8 in a row thrown by a shooter on a scorching roll. It can happen. But there is a little edge that you, the wrong bettor, can apply. When a trend develops in gambling, it tends to stay that way for awhile. When a shooter gets hot, the wrong bettor will stop betting on that shooter. He won't buck that hot hand. He'll stand back, wait for that shooter to ride out his roll, and pick up his betting against the next shooter.

The right bettor has to keep banging away, always with the idea that the next shooter will light up the board. If you're betting don't, and the shooter makes three points, that's it, don't fight him. Stop betting, until he's through. He can throw fourteen more points, just don't chase, thinking he's "due" to seven out.

I'll start at the beginning. Suppose you like to bet the don't side, have a very short bankroll, but would like to grind out a modest return. Put $5 on the Don't Pass, for the come-out roll. Seven or 11 you lose, craps you win, except for the standoff 12, which gives you a push.

That's it. Just bet the $5 on the Don't Pass, and when the point is established, you don't even lay odds. You're never gonna get rich with this, but it'll take the casinos a long time to wipe you out. When you get ahead, according to your Win Goal, start looking to walk. Of course you're not playing just to stay in the game, but having this very conservative approach to the game, it is very seldom that you will get destroyed in a quick matter of time.

Right now, I'm talking to the small bettor, with perhaps a $50 stake, and an honest intent to quit when he reaches a $15 or $20 profit. For that type person, this is as safe as you can play. If you don't have the bankroll, you're in trouble, but there are thousands of people who, everyday, enter the casinos with a $50 bill as their total stake.

To go a step further, if you desire, you could lay the odds against the point (though I don't recommend it), and that puts us into the option position.

Suppose the point was 6 or 8: these numbers can be made five ways, and many don't bettors fear them, even though they have a 6-5 chance of winning that bet. Here are your options, when 6 or 8 is the point:

1. Just sit with your bet on the Don't Pass, or
2. Lay $6 odds, or

3. Lay $6 odds, and reduce the ways you could lose, from five to four, by placing a $1 bet on the hard 6 (or 8, whichever was the point). On this move, you have reduced your possible losing numbers, because that dollar bet on the hard ways, has covered the 3-3 (or 4-4). Now only an easy 6 (or 8) could beat you.

Suppose the point was 5 or 9:

1. Just sit with your Don't bet, or
2. Lay $9 odds, to win $6 (3-2)

Finally, let's say the point was 4 or 10:

1. Just sit with your bet, or
2. Lay $10 to win $5 (2-1) single odds, or
3. Lay $10 to win $5 single odds, and take one dollar hard 4 (or 10) to reduce your ways of losing from three to two. Now only the easy 4 (or 10) can beat you.

This is the simplest form of don't betting you will find. The amount of units you play depends on your bankroll, and session money.

MONEY MANAGEMENT 25

Three Number Don't

Just as in the Pass Line theory, that calls for the right bettor to have three numbers working for him, the same is true for the wrong bettor. He, too, would like to have three numbers working for him.

However, since the right bettor has the opportunity of placing a number for as little as $5, this is not true in the case of the wrong bettor. The chapter on betting against the numbers elaborates on how the Don't bettor must wager enough to win a four-unit bet, on any of the Place numbers. The player cannot make small bets against any number by simply dropping his chips on the table.

So the wrong bettor is restricted, to a degree, if he does not have a substantial bankroll. To offset the high requirements of betting against the number, the wrong player must reach his two additional Don't numbers by coming through the Don't Come box. This wager can only be made after a point is established. Naturally, you do not have to have a bet on the Don't Pass Line to bet Don't Come. It is a separate wager unto itself. Thc subsequent roll dictates where that chip is placed.

To reach your three-bet goal, place a chip on the Don't Pass. Whatever point number shows, lay single odds against that number, and drop a chip in the Don't Come: By laying against that point number, you are protecting yourself against the 7. If, on the upcoming roll, the 7 shows, you lose the Don't Come chip, but win two chips for your Don't Pass with odds. You've allowed that 7 to work for you.

Assuming the point was 6, you lay $6 odds on your 6, and place a chip in the Don't Come. The 5 shows. Now you have

No Six and No Five. You want another Don't number in your favor.

Merely drop another $5 chip in the Don't Come box and remove your odds from the point number 6. You don't need odds on your 6, because if the 7 shows on the next roll, you lose $5 for your Don't Come bet, but win $5 for your No Six on the backline, and $5 for your $5 chip that is on the No Five.

You're looking to pick up a profit with each shooter, be it $5, $10, or, if possible, the full $15, if the 7 comes before any of the three numbers you have on the Don't—go down. The shooter cannot knock off all of your Don't bets on one roll, but you can win all three, if that 7 shows quickly.

Let's say on that last roll the 7 did not appear. It was the 8. Now you have $5 on the 6 on the backline, and two separate 6, $5 Don't bets; one each on the 5 and 8. You stop betting.

For that shooter to beat you, he has to make all three of these numbers separately. It's not like the right side, where you can get your three numbers placed and one 7 knocks down all of your wagers.

If the shooter hits either the 5 or 8, your two Don't Come numbers come back with a $5 chip in the Don't Come, in order to reestablish three Don'ts for yourself. You still do not have to lay odds, for a 7 will give you a profit of $5 for that roll. However, only replace your Don't Come bets twice. If that shooter knocks off two of your Don't Come numbers, he may be settling in for a red-hot roll, and you don't want to end up chasing. Simply back off. Leave the bets in action that are still alive, but don't make any more Don't Come wagers. Never buck the trend.

Technically, by taking two Don't Come bets, and replacing them twice, if they do go down, that shooter has to repeat five numbers to wipe you out of $25. Oh, it'll happen, and it'll happen many times in your craps career. But if you are a Don't bettor, and like to set up these two additional numbers, it will take a long series of hot shooters to wipe you out. (As you can see—this is a grind.)

Realize that you are fighting that 7 and 11 every time you

come through the Don't Come box, but if you apply the odds in the proper way, the 7 will always be "live" for you.

To tone down this method a notch, you could stop after you get one Don't number, on the Don't Pass Line, plus one Don't Come number, that you got by coming through the Don't Come box. Also, you could stop after you get two "strong" Don't numbers, such as any combination of 4, 5, 9, and 10.

To go all the way down to super conservative, you could place a chip on the Don't Pass, and then, without laying odds against that point, merely drop your next chip in the Don't Come. The 7 will cause a standoff, since you'll lose the Don't Come bet and win the Don't Pass Line wager.

However, if you use this method, my advice would be to:

1. Lay odds against the point for the first Don't Come
2. Take odds off the point while establishing your second Don't Come
3. Only replace two numbers that are hit. And this includes the fact that two Don't Pass Line wagers go down. Merely stop betting the Don't Pass, until that hot shooter is finished.

If, during the course of a particular roll, the shooter makes his point, the two Don't Come numbers stay where they are. For the next come-out roll, place another chip on the Don't Pass.

Since the Don't Come numbers work on the come-out roll, a 7 will gobble up your Don't Pass bet, but allow you to be paid off for your Don't Come bets. Then you come back again with a $5 Don't Pass, which, of course, is now fighting the 7 and 11.

If the shooter, during the course of his roll, makes three passes, stop betting the Don't Come Line, even if he hasn't knocked down any of your Don't Come wagers. Just like you replaced only two Don't Come bets, replace only two Don't Pass bets.

Stay in control, keep tabs on how much you allocate for each shooter. You could put aside a maximum $25 that you will allow to be risked for each shooter, not a chip more. You could also set a goal of $5 profit per shooter. In the case of the larger bettors, your Loss Limit could be $40 per shooter, or $50, but no more. That's plenty to find out if a guy is throwing darts at you.

Betting Don't is a grind. Sometimes you win, sometimes you don't. But when that 7 keeps popping up, proper money management will kick off some consistent wins for the wrong bettor. I can remember playing Don't at tables in Vegas, and staying at that session for over thirty hours. After awhile, you're really playing on habit, but I've always felt that if you have money at risk, you'll keep your eyes open. If you can't—quit the session.

MONEY MANAGEMENT 26

Aggressive Don't Betting

Let's step up the initial bet on two units on the Don't Pass Line. You could still opt for the three number method, but the variations off of this higher initial bet, allow you a more flexible betting scheme. Place $10 on the Don't Pass. Nine becomes the point. Now look at the options:

1. Drop $10 in Don't Come and lay $15 odds on the 9, or
2. Drop $10 in Don't Come, lay $9 odds on the 9 (laying only half of the bet), or
3. Drop $5 in Don't Come. Do not lay any odds on the point.

Here's a quick capsule of reasoning behind each of these options:

1. The $15 odds on the 9 is allowing you to get out on the Don't Come, and guarantees a $10 profit, if the 7 shows on that roll
2. The $9 odds on the 9 allows you to get out on the Don't Come, and guarantees a $6 profit, if the 7 shows on that roll
3. On this option, you don't need to lay odds, to make the 7 work for you. The $5 Don't Come will go down if the 7 shows, but you'd win $10 for your Don't Pass bet, still giving you a net of $5 profit, if the 7 shows.

Notice that each of these are designed to "get you out," on the Don't Come number, giving you two numbers working for you, and still protecting your bet against the 7.

OK, you've got your first Don't Come in position, and you

now wish to go for the second one. Another can of options is opened, and each one will be based on the leverage of the 7 in your favor.

Let's say you chose option (1), and the 6 showed. Remove your odds from the 9. You now have $10 No Nine as the point, and $10 No Six. Your next move would be another $10 in the Don't Come, to get that third number working for you. You're protected by the fact that a 7 would pull down your Don't Come bet, but pay you $20 for your two live Don't numbers, and give you a net profit of $10.

Assume the 4 showed. Now you have $10 on each of the 9, 6, and 4. You stop. No further bets are made, unless one of these numbers are hit, and then you only replace them twice.

At this time, you have the option of taking a $1 Hard Six, and $1 Hard Four. This would reduce your chances of losing on those numbers down to 4 and two ways, respectively, instead of 5 and 3.

Your maximum outlay on this shooter is $50. Incidentally, you've got to include any come-out 7's and 11's, or any subsequent 11's that are thrown when you are on the Don't Come, in your maximum loss, per shooter. Also include your wins on craps that may pop up on these rolls.

I hope you see the theory behind this method, for the options can go right out of the ceiling, and you've got to be prepared to make the moves you predetermined. This method will give you three working Don't numbers, and I'm giving you the options of offsetting that 7 showing up—until you get the three Don'ts in action. By laying either half, or full odds, for that first roll after the come-out number is established, you don't care if the 7 does show, for you'll be sure to get your profit.

Naturally, they could bang the number right back, and your Don't Come would then slide behind that number, but you would go down with your basic bet, plus odds. Sure it'll hurt, but it's all in the game. Besides, whichever number becomes the point, and you decide to lay odds, it is always in your favor that the 7 will show before that number.

Because of the damage that can come when you lay odds, I try to limit the number of rolls that you are exposed to losing your bet, with odds. That is another reason I give you the option of taking the hard way bet on the even numbers. It cuts down your chances of losing.

Are you getting the drift of the Don't side? Don't worry, it'll come.

MONEY MANAGEMENT 27

Advanced Two-Unit Don't

I hope you fully understand the previous chapter, before you attempt to comprehend this one. Actually, it is only an advanced method off of the two Don'ts, but it is imperative that you understand how many variations are open to you. Play goes as follows:

Drop $10 on the Don't Pass. Ten is the point. Lay $20 odds on your bet, and drop $10 in the Don't Come. If you like, take $3 Hard Ten, to soften the possibility of the number repeating.

Next roll is an 8, and the Don't Come bet is moved to the proper position behind that number. OK, the following set of options appear, and you decide which one you like, depending on your type of approach, aggressive or conservative:

1. Remove odds from your 10, and drop $5 in Don't Come
2. Remove odds from your 10, and drop $10 in Don't Come
3. Remove odds from your 10, and drop $15 in Don't Come
4. Leave one half odds on your 10 (10-5), and drop $10 in Don't Come
5. Leave one half odds on your 10 (10-5), and drop $15 in Don't Come
6. Leave one half odds on your 10 (10-5), and drop $20 in Don't Come

(On all bets in the Don't Come, at amounts of $15 or higher, you may take $1 Yo, to reduce chances of that number beating you.)

7. Leave full odds on your 10 and drop $15 in Don't Come
8. Leave full odds on your 10 and drop $20 in Don't Come
9. Leave full odds on your 10 and drop $25 in Don't Come
10. Leave full odds on your 10, plus lay full odds on your Don't Come 8, take $2 hard 8, $3 hard 10, drop either $35, $30, $25, or $20 in the Don't Come. (As long as the amount in the Don't Come is protected from the 7 showing. The working Don't Pass bet, and variables on the odds, give you plenty of room to vary that upcoming Don't Come bet.)

Had enough??? I'm not trying to be a wise guy. I'm not trying to dazzle you with charts or figures. What I am giving you, or at least trying to let you be aware of—is that the variations on this table are innumerable, and change after every decision, and every time a new Don't Come number becomes "live."

Every one of those bets and several other smaller options would protect against the 7 showing, while you are in the Don't Come box. Naturally, you're wide open for the 8 or 10 to repeat, but the play on the hard ways, for those two bets, would soften the blow.

You could stop after one Don't Pass and one Don't Come bet, or you could carry out for two additional numbers. However, once you have three numbers working for you, remove your odds and adjust your hard ways hedge to the money at risk, that's if you use the hard way hedge to lessen your chances of losing.

These variations are very simple to understand, and provide plenty of action, for both the small and large bettor. But, have a complete understanding of the whole method, and your own personal attack plan should be down pat in your head, and no type of deviation from that plan should be used.

Gambling is a serious business. It is not for the weak of heart, weak of pocketbook or weak of disciplined approach. Pick one of these methods of setting up three don't numbers, perfect it, and stick to it. (But abide by the win goal you set for that session. When it is reached, grab your guaranteed profit, before continuing on in that session.)

28 MONEY MANAGEMENT

Choosing a Method

Take a peek back at the previous chapter, where you had $10 Don't Pass, with the 10 as the point, and $10 Don't Come, with the 8 showing. There are lots of choices you could decide upon, but I'll pick one of them to carry out a particular series. Personally, since 8 became one of my Don't numbers, I would like to have another strong Don't.

Actually, there are a lot of good options in that list, and each person will find his or her own reason for choosing one of them. I'll take (4), where I lay one half odds on the 10, and leave the 8 open. With half odds, the 7 will give me a profit of $25, as there are five units open, between my Don't 10, and Don't 8.

So, I'll take advantage of that edge and drop $15 in the Don't Come, and $1 on the 11. We'll say the 5 popped up. Now I have my three Don't numbers, and will just sit and wait for that 7, but first have to make a few adjustments. Remove the half odds from the 10, and place $6 on the 8 (this is a hedge that will be explained later), as I want to lessen my chances of losing with that strong 8. All of my hard way bets are off.

Right now I have $10 on each of the No Ten, No Five, and No Eight, with $6 placed on the 8. If any of these numbers go down, I will replace them with another bet coming through the Don't Come. But, only replace your Don't Come bets twice. It may be the shooter could be getting hot, and I don't want to get caught in any big roll.

But you get the idea of how to set up your Don't bets. Always keep that 7 as your barometer. The amount of the bet you put in the Don't Come to set up your additional two Don't numbers will depend on how much you stand to WIN, if that 7 shows. I suggest you start off slowly, until you understand the method. As you become more proficient with options, you'll see a fantastic number of them opening up.

For the player with the extra heavy bankroll, the use of double odds, on both the Don't Pass bet, and the Don't Come numbers can be utilized. This way, your second Don't Come wager could become very heavy. Be sure and protect it, while it is in the Don't Come box, with a bet on the 11. The 7 can't hurt you, as your Don't Pass number, with odds, will nullify the 7. As your bets become larger and larger, get in the habit of reducing possible losses, by using the hard way hedge. It cuts down one of the ways to make that Don't number.

I'm fully aware of the possibility that these systems seem very deep to the new players to Craps. Don't try to comprehend the entire game with your first trip through this book. Take each part of the game in degrees, and work your way up to this method. The two-, three-, and four-unit Don't bets, with or without odds, and with or without hedging, is very deep. Try to grasp the simpler part of the game, and then this part will become chopped meat.

Associate Craps systems with your trying to understand the female mind. At first it seems very complicated, but as you move along in your feeble attempt to dominate the situation, you find that it really wasn't so complicated after all.

I just hope you guys have more success in conquering the game of Craps, then you have in dominating the members of the fairer sex. When a certain "line," or approach doesn't work, you try another. In Craps, when a certain method is not working, you have many options to go to.

This system has many offshoots, so don't try any of them at a table, until you have your approach perfected. My suggestion would be to grab a set of dice, a handful of chips, and go over each of the plays from the previous chapter, for an extended series of plays. Start off with a very simple system, and then work your way up to the ultimate.

Just like working your way up to . . . ah, but that's another story. You don't want to hear about those things.

29 MONEY MANAGEMENT

Removing Your Bet

I've already touched on this, but a few more words won't hurt you. If you don't want to listen, go get a snack, like you do at commercial time with TV.

A bet on the Pass Line, or Come Line, once it's established, is a contract. You cannot remove it. That's because after a point is in action, the edge is always with the house, since the 7 can be made more ways than any of the possible six Place numbers. The house isn't going to let your remove a bet that has it holding the upper hand.

But, on the Don't side of the ledger, you may remove your bet any time you wish. That's because once a number is working for you on the wrong side, that 7 is now providing you with the hammer. The house is on the short end, so it gives you the option of removing the bet, anytime you want.

Don't remove it—ever—even if the 6 or 8 is the number. I'll show you how to hedge those numbers, but even with them as the point, you still hold a 6-5 margin in your favor.

One-roll action bets and field bets are decided on one flip of the dice, so you have no decision there. Odds, on either the right or wrong side, may be removed or changed whenever you like. That's because the house holds no edge on these wagers.

When betting right or wrong, you can adjust your own odds on the line, but the dealer will take care of all odds moves on the Come and Don't Come wagers. Don't be afraid to adjust your Don't Come odds, as the situation calls for it.

For instance, if you have a chip on the Don't Pass and two separate wagers working on the Don't Come, and the point is made, you have a couple of moves open to you. On the next come-out, you can put $10, or $15 on the Don't Pass, and then lay odds on one or both of your Don't Come wagers, in order to protect against a 7 on the come-out.

After the point is established, don't be afraid to ask the dealer to remove your odds bet from the Don't Come bets. Just say, "Odds off my Don'ts, please."

Guess the commercial is over, the snackers are coming back. (Bet you they sneak a look at this chapter—even if it is a rerun.)

I'm going to get a little more advanced for the rest of the Money Management section. If you feel it getting too far over your head, skip to the Discipline chapters and go back later. I just want to give you advanced players something new to think about. (By the way, all you Don't bettors should at least glance at the Patrick System chapter before moving on.)

MONEY MANAGEMENT 30

Off-Setting the Don't Six and Eight

OK, there are still a handful of wrong bettors who continue to fear that 6 and 8, especially when they have higher than a one-unit bet at risk. I'm one of them. I like to have these two numbers working for me when betting "right," since they have a good chance of showing, so it is only natural I fear them on the "wrong" side, for the same reason.

I'm going to show you a hedge system that will swing the odds around, and have you booking the house, while taking away these two numbers that you fear so much.

Assume you've bet $10 on the Don't Pass and the 6 shows. Your method is to just stay with one bet on the Don't Pass Line, yet you don't like the 6 or 8 as the point, and you don't want to go for an additional number through the Don't Come. (Incidentally, this method may be used any time you have a multiple number of chips on either the Don't 6 or 8, and whether you are on the Don't Pass, or Don't Come.)

Don't remove your $10 bet, like so many people do. Remember my jeweler friend, Charley? The guy who looked for dopes, who removed their No Six and No 8, and he took the action, after they fought the 7 on the come-out?

Merely place the point. Now you've got $10 No Six on the back line, and a $6 place bet on the 6. It's called a hedge bet. You're betting both ways. Let's see what could happen to these bets:

1. If the 7 shows, you lose $6 place bet, and win $10 No Six, for a profit of $4

2. If the 6 shows, you lose $10 for your No Six, and win $7 on your place bet, for a net loss of $3

You are in a position to win $4 if the 7 shows, and lose $3 if the 6 shows. Now the house is risking $4 to win $3, and the chances of a 7 coming before a 6 (or 8), is 6-5 in your favor.

Not only is the house risking more to win less, the chances of winning your bet are decidedly in your favor. Let's carry out a full cycle on the dice, based on the thirty-six possible rolls, after you set up your hedges. If the numbers fall according to the laws of probability, there will be six 7's showing and five 6's. You could expect to win $4 six times, for an overall plus of $24. You could expect to lose $3 on five occasions, for a $15 total loss. You are now the bookie, and the house is on the other side of the coin. You, the player, are risking $15 to win $24, and the chances are a positive 6-5 in your favor. Not bad.

You may also use this method to offset a Don't Come wager on these two numbers. Suppose you want to establish three numbers, and two of them end up as the 6 and 8. Place both of these numbers and come through the Don't Come with a $5 bet, as long as the 7 stays live. That simply means you have enough bets and odds in action to have the showing of the 7 give you a profit.

The same is true on the Don't Pass bet. If 6 or 8 becomes the point, and you wish extra numbers working for you on the Don't side, establish these numbers, before hedging your back line wager. Again, adjust your Don't Come bets to coincide with the hedge bet, but leaving room for the 7 to work for you.

For instance, you have $10 Don't Pass and 8 is the point. You then get a $10 Don't Come wager with the 6 appearing. Drop another $10 in the Don't Come, but you can only hedge either the 6 or the 8, not both. Otherwise, if the 7 shows on that roll, you'll lose $10 in the Don't Come, and $12 on the two place numbers, and pick up only $20 for your two Don't numbers. That would be a net loss of $4. As a wrong bettor, you don't want that.

Once that second Don't Come picks up a number, you can follow through with your second hedge against the open danger number. Now you have a $10 Don't Come on a strong number, and two hedge bets working for you on the 6 and 8.

Whether you sit or follow up with another $5 or $10 wager in the Don't Come is your choice. You are neither right nor wrong in whichever method you choose, although I would advise you to just sit and wait.

I hope all you wrong bettors, who pull off your 6's and 8's, will take a good long look at this optional play. The amount of the hedge for the 6 and 8 may be adjusted, according to the amount of the wager on those numbers.

Examine the possible options: (6 is the Point).

Fifteen-dollar wager:

1. Hedge $6 on the 6, or
2. Hedge $12 on the 6

Twenty-dollar wager:

1. Hedge $6
2. Hedge $12
3. Hedge $18

Twenty-five dollar wager:

1. Hedge $12
2. Hedge $18 (could win $7, but could only lose $4)
3. Hedge $24 (no-lose situation, either win $1 or $3)

The above hedges are done to cut losses on the 6 and 8, two powerful numbers, but this hedging is a billion times better than taking down your bet. In some cases, you are in a no-lose situation, even though it's only a few dollars. Work out the results.

Now I'll give you a few additional ways to soften that Don't 6 or 8:

Fifteen-dollar wager:

1. $6 place, and $1 hard 6

Twenty-dollar wager:

1. $12 place, $1 hard 6

Twenty-five dollar wager:

1. $12 place, and $2 hard 6
2. $18 place, and $1 hard 6

You can come up with your own set or combinations of sets of hedges. The idea is to minimize losses. Get used to hedge betting. We're going deeper into the subject.

MONEY MANAGEMENT 31

Accepting the Small Return

In the previous chapter, I explained how you can put the casino in a position where they are laying you $4 to win $3, and of course this dollar amount changes, as the hedges vary.

For instance, if you had a $15 No Six, and hedged $12, you would be in a position where you could lose $1, and win $3. These numbers aren't going to build your castle in the sky, but it does put you in an advantageous position.

Your response usually goes something like this: "I'm not happy unless I win a thousand dollars." A thousand dollars? You probably started with a bankroll of $75. What right do you have in setting a ridiculous win goal like that for?

The casinos offer you a game, such as Baccarat, where they hold an edge of 1.17% with the bank, and 1.38% with the player. Blackjack can be reduced to about 1.51% with perfect basic strategy, and craps gives them only an edge of .8% with single odds, and .6% with double odds.

If the casinos, with all their money, are content to play with only a 1% possible win factor, then why aren't you? And you can use Money Management and Discipline if you know about them. The casinos can't.

But they win, for the simple fact that greed takes over the players' gambling habits, and the average player actually scorns at small wins. Some of these boobs are heard to utter this gem of a statement, "I'd rather lose $200 trying to win $2,000, than go away a lousy $100 winner." If you know anyone like that, please have them contact me. The casinos would more than welcome this idiot through their portals, but I'd like first crack at him. Something like one born every second...

and I'd like to give this person an opportunity to purchase a diamond mine I have in my cellar. Great return—small investment.

The method I've shown you for handling the 6 and 8 is a good one. Accept these small returns. They'll serve as a good base for when a losing trend comes. Your big paydays will show. You've got to be patient. You've got to build, and then maintain that bankroll. Small, consistent wins will build it.

32 MONEY MANAGEMENT

The Don't Bettor

The Don't bettor is a lonesome breed. Since the players usually bet right, he automatically has a lot of enemies as soon as he makes his first bet. The saying goes that all crapshooters die broke. So what? When you die, it doesn't really make much difference if you're broke or loaded.

I think it's worse to be broke when you're alive. The reason this saying gained momentum is because of the fantastic swing in the fortunes of the crapshooter. A right bettor can win or lose a small fortune, within the space of eight or ten shooters.

The wrong bettor, basically very quiet at the table, plays a very controlled game, limiting his bets and his losses. When the dice get hot, he'll pull back quickly. The right bettor tends to charge ahead.

As I'm writing this chapter, I'm thinking of a right bettor who played next to me in Atlantic City. I was at a craps table, bought in for my session money, and played the Basic Right Method.

The gentleman to my right had about the same money and was betting $30 on the Pass Line, taking double odds, two Come numbers, at $20 each, double odds on the Come numbers, Horn bets, any 7 and hard way bets.

His session fluctuated back and forth, reaching highs of about $2,000, all the way down to $200 at some points. I stayed within a profit of $50 to $150, and was never out more than $75, as the dice stayed choppy.

At one point, the boxman remarked to the Come player that he was getting a lot of mileage out of his money. He was. He continuously had big bets in action.

To my left, was a wrong bettor. He didn't look any which way but down. He'd place his bet and just stand there, staring at his chips. The right bettor would be screaming and yelling when he was winning, and moaning out loud when the dice were cold.

After about two hours, I showed a small profit of about $180. The right bettor was now betting $5 on the line, no odds, and an occasional hard way bet. His once decent bankroll of about $2,000 had dwindled to about $30. He didn't quit when winning, and won't leave the table until his last chip is gone.

The wrong better was still hanging in, grinding out his bets. He had Discipline, for I saw him back off when the numbers were coming. He counted his chips every twenty seconds, and I'll bet he walked from that table, when he got up to a certain win level.

I believe there is more ingrained discipline in the wrong bettor, than the people who bet right. I have absolutely no opinion as to which is the "better" side of the game—right betting or the grinding wrong side. Both will kick off their share of profits. It's up to the player to walk when he's ahead.

The Don't bettor is more susceptible to disciplined systems, because he has it on his mind constantly, that the Don't side is more attuned to smaller returns.

The methods I give you for the Don't side and the hedge bet are not designed for big returns. They never will be. But the Don't bettors may find these systems beneficial to their style of play, due to the multiple amount of variables.

I can't promise you'll die rich, but it may enrich your way of playing while you're still around.

MONEY MANAGEMENT 33

The Hedge Bettor

You already got a taste of the hedge bet. It is the method of taking a certain bet, and cutting down its potential loss factor.

As in the case of a $10 Don't 6 or 8, you place that number with the intent of cutting down your loss from $10 to $3, while still maintaining an element of chance, to show a profit.

I've also mentioned hedging your even numbered Don't bet: 4, 6, 8, or 10. Suppose you had a $15 No Ten. There are only three numbers that could hurt you (4-6, 6-4, 5-5). By taking the Hard Ten, you've reduced your chances of losing to only two numbers. It's not an altogether bad way of playing.

Following is a list of plays, and a possible hedge bet, to offset a total loss, or to reduce your chances of losing.

BET	HEDGE
$15 Pass Line	$2 Any Craps
$20 Pass Line	$3 Three-Way Craps
$15 Don't Pass or Don't Come	$1 Yo
$10 No Six or Eight	$6 Place on 6 (or 8)
$15 No Four or Ten	$2 Hard Four (or Ten)
$15 No Six or Eight	$6 or $12. Place 6 (or 8)
$10 No Six or Eight	$1 Hard Six (or Eight)
$24 No Six or Eight	$12 Place Six (or Eight) plus $1 Hard Six (or Eight)
$41 No Four or Ten	$5 Hard Four (or Ten)

As long as you understand the theory of the hedge—reducing the chance of you losing on that bet, you can work out your own hedges. The ones above are for certain amounts. As the amount of your basic bet increases, naturally the amount of your hedge goes up—as you desire.

The hedge is primarily used by the Don't bettor, and it can encompass every number, not just the 6 and 8. Suppose you had a $25 bet on the Don't Pass, and 10 became the point. You could now place the 10 for $20. This is what the outcome would be. If the 7 shows, you win $25 for the No Ten, lose $20 for the placed 10, for a profit of $5. If the 10 showed, your $25 No Ten goes down, and you win $36 for the $20 place 10, for a profit of $11. You're in a position of winning either $5 or $11.

Again the 10 shows, with a $25 bet on the Don't Pass, but this time you place only $15 on the 10. The 7 gives you a profit of $10, and if the 10 shows, you lose $25 No Ten, but pick up $27 for the place bet, giving off a profit of $2. You stand to win either $2 or $10. After the point is established, you can't lose—if you turn to hedging, and accept small returns.

It would take me seven hundred and sixty-two pages to give you all the hedges and then the combinations with place bet and hard ways, and then for different amounts. It's up to you to put all of the different amounts on a piece of paper, and then list the hedge possibilities.

But, you get the idea. These are only a few examples. Personally, I love to use the hedge. I'll go over some of the basic uses, and you'll be able to apply your own set, after you get going.

Even you high rollers ought to take a second look at some of the plays. For instance, a wrong bettor, with a $30 wager on the Don't Pass. What's so wrong about putting a couple of chips on the Yo? Now the 11 can't hurt you. The 7 can be made six ways, but the 1-1, 1-2, 2-1, craps—picks up three of them right back. Now, there are only three rolls that can grab that come-out wager. You've reduced your chances of losing from 8-3 against you to 6-3. And for only two bucks.

The same is true for the Pass Line bettor. When you get up to a $15 bet on the line, why not get rid of those four pesty possible crap combinations. A $2 Any Craps, or a $3 "three-way craps," eliminates any possible wipeout on the come-out, and further strengthens the 7 and 11.

Personally, I start taking my Any Craps, and "three-way craps" bets as soon as my wagers reach $15, $20, and up.

The three-way craps bet is merely breaking it down to a $1 bet on the 1-1, which pays 30-1, a $1 bet on the 6-6, which pays 30-1, and a $1 bet on the 1-2, 2-1, which pays $15-1. I see guys bet $3 Any Craps, and I think what would their reaction be if they ever heard of the three-way craps bet. The Any Craps payoff is 7-1. Why call for that return, when the three-way craps bet offers you better payoffs on two of the three combinations.

Remember way back in an earlier chapter, I told you that the proposition bets, by themselves, were sucker bets, but if used as a hedge, have a definite plus value? I give into the high vig here, to protect my larger bets, because the low vigorish on these basic bets give me a little room to invest a chip or two, and reduce my overall chances of losing.

As I've said earlier in this chapter, it is a good move to place the 6 and 8, when you are betting Don't, and have at least a two-unit bet in action. If the casino is going to beat me, let them take their best shot when I have No Four or No Five or No Nine or No Ten. With those numbers, I am strong, and if they beat me, at least I held the hammer going into the fight.

If you like hedging, you can also use the method against any of the numbers, as I've shown in the case of the 10. But since you are sitting good with these hard to make numbers, I'd advise just staying with them. At least you know that the opportunity to hedge is available with all the numbers, not just the 6 or 8.

For the sake of my favorite player—the $5 player, let me go over a very simple hedge with a $5 Don't Pass. Four became the point, giving you $5 No Four. You could then place the 4 for $5. If the 4 showed, you lose the bet on the Don't Pass, and win $9 for the Place bet, giving you a profit of $4. If the 7 shows, you lose $5 on the Place, and win $5 for the No Four. It's a wash. You have put yourself in a position where you will either win $4 or break even. It's a no-lose shot. Naturally, it's a grind, but I know of many professionals who play exactly like this. The argument against it is that after going through all the trouble of getting a strong number, why weaken it with a hedge. Answer—because of the no-lose situation it puts you in.

Also, there are many senior citizens that I've taught to play this way. Their starting bankrolls are very, very small, and this method of play has been a super tonic for them. They hedge everything, right down to the 6's and 8's, that have single units on them. If they have $5 No Eight, they'll place the 8 for $6. If the 8 shows, they have a net win of $2. The 7 costs them $1. They are risking $1 to win $2, with the odds only 6-5 against them.

A $5 hedge against the 5 (or 9) results in a net win of $2, if the 5 shows, and a push with the 7. Again it is a guaranteed win situation. The 4 or 10, with a $5 Don't, has a guaranteed $4 win with the 4 (or 10) showing, and a push with the 7.

Naturally, as your Don't bets increase, your hedge becomes more flexible. Again I tell you that this is merely a method of play. After that come-out, you're sitting pretty, but the tedious, grinding requirements of long hours, for small returns, may not be your bag.

On the other hand, my aggressive-minded, win-starved friend, why don't you stifle your snickers, approach this method with an open mind, and give hedge betting a second look. Methinks you will be surprised at the results, that may be small—but successful.

MONEY MANAGEMENT 34

$41 No Ten

You're aware, that to bet against a specific number, you must bet an amount sufficient to return a four-unit profit, plus a $5 charge, or vig, on the profit. Since the 4 and 10 are the hardest numbers to make, they will be the basis of this wager.

Drop $41 on the table and tell the dealer, "No Ten, please." You stand to win $20, less the 5%, or $1, vig. You're looking for a 7. This, in itself, is a wager made by many wrong bettors.

To go a step further, also drop $22 on the table, and tell the dealer, "Twenty-two inside, please." You then get a place bet on each of the 5, 6, 8, and 9. Subsequent rolls of the dice offer you eighteen ways to obtain a $7 payoff, if one of these numbers show. If the 7 shows, you lose the $22 but pick up $19, as the 7 allowed a payoff on the No Ten. Your net loss is $3 if none of the place numbers showed before the 7. The bad part is the possible loss of $41 if that 10 shows, even though there are only three ways to lose. The good part, is that you always have the possibility of winning with eighteen chances, as opposed to the three bad ones.

This is an inside hedge against the 10. You've eliminated the 7 from beating you, and stand in the position of being beat, only by that 10. In the meantime you've given yourself four place numbers, that could return a profit, before a pro or con decision is reached on the No Ten bet.

If you like, you could bet a couple of chips on the Hard Ten, so that your chances of losing have now been reduced to only the 4-6 and 6-4. Based on the amount you bet on Hard Ten, this increases your possible loss with the 7. My advice would be to bet $4 Hard Ten, for as long as that bet stays up.

A further variation would be to bet $52 No Ten, $22 inside, and $5 Hard Ten. The 6-4 combo could hurt you, but the 7 has once again been neutralized.

I've seen the Easy Ten pop up five times in a row, and knock the stuffings out of this method, but I've also seen some days when the Easy Ten doesn't show for roller after roller.

If you do play with the No Ten or No Four, it is imperative that you preset an amount of rolls that you will leave your money in play. Accept either one hit, two hits, or three hits on those inside numbers, and come right down on all bets when that goal has been attained. When that 10 does show, it takes a lot of place numbers to recoup that loss.

If you play this method, the taking of the Hard Ten is strictly optional. I suggest a bankroll of $200 per session, which is a possible loss of five hits on the 10.

I suggest leaving your place bets up for one or no more than two hits. This way, you can pick up a few place numbers, and then take down your inside bets. If you wish to remain up on the No Ten or No Four, and look for the 7 to give you another payoff, it's strictly up to you. Whether you decide to play strictly a No Ten or No Four system, and bank on the 7 showing, is your decision. If you stick with hedging of the inside numbers, against the No Ten—again—that is your option.

I'm going to give you a little system to follow, in the event you decide to get the No Ten. Merely as a form of controlled discipline, walk around the Craps section of the casino until you find either the 4 or 10 as the point. Drop your chips on the table, and tell the dealer, "No Ten, please" (or No Four, whichever was the point). The option is still yours as to whether you want to sit with just the Don't bet, or go for the $22 inside. As soon as a decision is reached, leave that table, and start your search for another game where either the 4 or 10 is the point, and start over. It will put you in action—only where the 10 or 4 is already the point.

And finally, it is not written in stone that you should play the No Ten or No Four. You could bet No Five or No Nine, and lay $31 to win four units. The total risk in terms of money is less, but the chances of losing has been increased, because there are more ways (four) of being beaten.

There are, in all plays on the Don't side, a plethora of options, so it behooves you to give this system of play a little consideration.

MONEY MANAGEMENT 35

The Simple Hedge

The previous chapter called for an outlay of $41 to bet against the 4 or 10, or $31 to bet against the 5 or 9. That left you free to negate the 7, and place either four or three inside numbers. If one of those Place numbers showed, you pick up a $7 profit. The amount of rolls you leave your bets in action is up to you. Personally, I suggest one or two, and then come down.

That's because you're staring at a $41 loss if the 4 or 10 shows, and you need quite a few hits to recover. But, you've offset that dangerous 7. So there are pros and cons to this method—just like there are to every single method of play.

The key will always lie within your own ability to accept a few scores, grab your profit, take down your bets and run. You're still alive to take another shot at another table. And you've still got your bankroll. You need it to compete.

I'll give you a simple hedge that will offset any possible large wipeout. The amount of your first bet is strictly up to your own individual session money. Your first bet could be $5, $10, $15, $20, $25, $50—you decide, after you see the theory of it. Naturally, the basic premise is to thwart the 7.

Drop $5 on the Don't Pass. As soon as a point is established, lay the odds, and place the inside numbers. If the point is:

1. **4 or 10**—place the 5, 6, 8, 9
   a. If the 7 shows, you lose $22, but win $10 for your Don't Pass bet, with odds, for a net loss of $12.
2. **5 or 9**—place the 6, 8, and 5 or 9 (whichever wasn't the point)

   a. If the 7 shows, you lose $17, but win $11 for your Don't Pass bet, with odds, for a net loss of $6
3. **6 or 8**—place the 5, 9, and 6 or 8 (whichever wasn't the point)
   a. If the 7 shows, you lose $16, but win $10 for your Don't Pass bet, with odds, for a net loss of $6

Now, all of the above possible losses apply, only if the 7 comes back right after the point is established. Taking the hard 6, 8, 4, or 10, for $1, is optional. If you score on one of the place numbers, before the 7 shows, or the point is made, naturally your potential loss is reduced.

But, you must predetermine how many scores you are looking for, before the roll begins. When you reach that number, pull off all your place bets, including your odds against the point, and just sit with your initial don't pass bet.

Here I give you a little razzle-dazzle hedge. Assume your Don't Pass bet was $5 and the 8 showed. You laid odds on the 8, placed the 6, 5, and 9, and picked up a hit on the 6, for a win of $7 on that shooter. You could pull down your place bets, and odds against the 8, and then place the 8 for $6. You stand to lose only $1 if the 7 shows, or win $2 if the 8 shows. The idea is that after you scored with the place bet, and hedged the point, there was no way in the world, that this particular shooter was going to give you a profit of anything less than $6. You are going win either $6 or $9, depending on the outcome of that point bet. Think about it.

Let's go over an example of a typical roll. You've set your number of place hits at two, and drop $5 on the Don't Pass. The 6 shows. You lay $6 odds on the 6, and take $16 inside. You also take $1 hard 6. You've reduced your chances of losing on the 6 to four ways.

On the subsequent rolls, you have a combined thirteen ways of winning, the total number of ways that the 5, 8, and 9 can be made, against four possible losing ways.

1. Shooter throws an 8—Same bet. You take $7
2. Shooter throws craps—No decision

3. Shooter throws 4—No decision
4. Shooter throws 9—Down on the bets. You take $7

Dealer takes down your place bets. Tell him to take down your hard 6. You remove your odds from your back-line bet, and leave the $5 bet on the don't 6 stand. If the shooter makes the point, your profit for that shooter is $9. If the shooter sevens out, your profit for that shooter is $19.

The most you could have lost was $12, and that was if the shooter came right back with the point, on the first roll following the come-out. If you decide to take a shot with this method: here are some things to remember.

1. You've got to accept a possible $5 loss on the come-out.
2. You've got to take down your hard way bet, even if it is only $1 once you remove your odds.
3. You absolutely, positively must predetermine the number of hits you want, with your place bets.
4. When you reach that number, you can't say, "Oh, maybe one more hit."
5. If, after you pull your place bets down, the shooter throws seventy-three more winning hits on the aforementioned place numbers, don't start acting like somebody cut your throat. Accept everything that happens—after you make your decision. Don't be a hindsight thinker. You only make a behind of yourself.

This simple hedge is designed to give you small profits, while keeping potential losses at a minimum. I know, if you try this method, the temptation will be to leave your bets in action for five, six, seven scores, before pulling down.

You *can't* do this. The theory behind the hedge is to reduce losses. That's the whole idea of hedging your bets. You're reducing losses. So, if you do pick up a quick two or three wins, why not bring down all of your bets, leaving only the one that has an edge in your favor—the Don't Pass wager.

Your argument will be that you "came to play," and don't want to look like a chicken at the table. My friend—maybe you "came to play," but you should have "came to win" (bad

English, but good advice). There's a difference. And the difference lies in how you approach gambling.

And what's so bad about being a chicken? Instead of laying an egg in the casino, you can leave there with the start of a nest egg, and I guarantee you'll cackle all the way home.

MONEY MANAGEMENT 36

The Double Hedge

Let's get a little more aggressive. Instead of a one-unit bet on the Don't Pass, we'll increase it to two units. When you completely understand the intent of the method, it'll be a snap to work out your variations, starting with three, four, five, or more units.

The more units you use, the more variations that will arise. The three and four starting units will offer untold variations, but you must have your predetermined way of playing firmly laid out before you attack that table, because of the amount of options.

OK, you place $10, or two chips, on the Don't Pass. The point becomes 10:

1. Lay $20 odds against the 10, take $4 hard 10, and place $22 inside, or
2. Lay $10 (half) odds, take $2 hard 10, and place $22 inside

When you get the number of hits you wanted, pull down all your bets, except the $10 Don't Pass, and wait for a decision. Or, you can now place the 10 for $5. This gives you the chance of winning another $5 for only a $1 risk. And, the odds are 6-3 in your favor that you'll win that $5.

Suppose the point was 5 or 9:

1. Lay $15 odds, and place $17 inside, or
2. Lay $9 (half) odds, and place $17 inside

This is strictly optional. Laying half odds holds down the amount you could lose, if the 5 (or 9) is made. Laying full odds gives you full protection against the 7. You decide which method makes you most comfortable.

If the point is 6 or 8:

1. Lay $12 odds, take $2 hard way, and place $16 inside, or
2. Lay $6 (half) odds, take $1 hard way, and place $16 inside.

Since the 6 and 8 are strong place numbers, you don't want to fight them. After you hit your one or two scores with the place bets, remove all of your wagers, then hedge the point, all the time.

To go even further, if 6 or 8 becomes the point, immediately come through the Don't Come with a two-unit wager. This way, you have a chance of picking up a better don't bet. If you get for instance, a 5, immediately hedge the point of 6 (or 8). Now you've got one-and-a-half Don't working for you.

This double hedge will allow you to remove your odds from the point number, thereby reducing the chances of one number taking a big bite into your session money. If that Don't Come became another strong right number, you've now got both No Six and No Eight. I'd hedge both of them, and just wait for a decision on that shooter. Don't place the 5 and 9.

I'll go over a typical roll, and you'll see the different variations arise. Don't forget, I could fill sixty-four pages of probable happenings, so you're going to have to grasp the theory, to see the different avenues you can take.

1. Start with two-unit Don't Pass. Nine becomes the point,
2. Place $17 inside, lay the odds on the 9, and drop one unit in the Don't Come. This is what could happen:
   a. If 7 shows you lose Don't Come and three Place bets ($22), and win $20 Don't Pass with odds. Net: minus $2
   b. If 9 shows, you lose Don't Pass bet with odds, and Don't Come moves behind the 9, to be "live" on next sequence come-out
   c. If 5, 6, or 8 show, you win $7, the Don't Come moves behind that number (let's say it's 8), and now you may remove the odds from your 9.

At this time, you have $10 No Nine, $5 No Eight with the 5 and 6 still placed, and a $7 profit. Your option here is to take down your 5 and 6 Place bets, and stay with the No Eight and No Nine, or, wait for one hit on the 5 or 6. I would opt for taking down my place bets, and waiting for the 7 to show. Additionally, you can now hedge the 9.

Now, if that Don't Come number became 4 or 10, I'd leave my Place bets sit, and merely remove my odds from the 9. I like to have the 6 and 8 working for me. Finally, when that Don't Come number showed, regardless of whether it was 5, 6, or 8, you could have taken the profit, and removed all the Place bets. That would leave you with the No Nine as the point, and the No bet that was the Don't Come.

This system attempts to get two Don't numbers working for you, while picking up at least one hit on the place numbers. In effect, this type hedge has you betting both right and wrong. Like I say, the options are innumerable, and if you take on the double hedge, I warn you, have your game plan systematically laid out.

The roughest part of the play is when you have your odds on your Don't Pass, leaving yourself open for a big loss on one roll. This will occur when the shooter establishes a point and comes right back with the point. After that, you've nullified the 7, which is the main purpose of craps playing. A red-hot roll can't hurt you, as in the interim, you'll pick up a couple of place bets, which will soften any lengthy roll by some shooter.

I try to keep the 6 and 8 open for as long as I can. When the 4, 5, 9, and 10 become the Don't Pass and Don't Come numbers, I leave the 6 and 8 in action for an extra hit. With the 6 and/or 8 becoming my Don't numbers, I hedge the two-unit bet, and then pull in my horns, and try to get away from that shooter with as little damage as possible. That's what I'm trying to get across to you.

If or when you ever get to the point where you can learn to accept a certain win amount per shooter, you will have conquered the game of Craps. These are the types of players at a table:

1. **Right bettor:** All he wants is a hot roll, after hot roll

after hot roll (he ends up losing his bread).

2. **Wrong bettor:** All he wants is point, 7, point, 7, point, 7.
3. **Hedge bettor:** All he wants is a certain win amount, per shooter. No big killing, but a grinding type attack, that takes advantage of the flow of the dice, either right or wrong.

All of the above are tough—as evidenced by the fact that dice tables still operate in every casino in the country. Isn't it time for you to approach it in a different vein?

Let's go over another example of a double hedge roll, and you can simulate your own variations, as you see fit.

1. Drop $10 on the Don't Pass; 8 becomes the point.
2. This time you lay one half odds, take $1 hard 8, $17 inside, and drop $10 in the Don't Come.
3. Six comes. Take odds off your 8, and down on the hard 8. You've got a $7 profit, but two tough numbers to fight. Remove Place bets on the 5 and 9; 6 and 8 are placed, as a hedge and forfeit the roll. (No matter what happens, you're guaranteed $1 profit, even if the shooter belts both the 6 and 8 before he pops a 7.)

One more time:

1. Drop $10 on the Don't Pass; 4 becomes the point.
2. Place $22 inside, lay full odds against the 4, take $4 hard 4, and drop $10 in the Don't Come.
3. Five shows. You win $7, and Don't Come moves behind the 5. Take odds off the 4, and down on your hard 4. You have several options:
   a. Just sit with No Five and No Four, plus Place bets on 6, 8, and 9.
   b. Come out with another $10 Don't Come, figuring you can establish another Don't number, while still picking up a payoff on the 6, 8, or 9.
   c. Leave Place bets on the 6, 8, and 9, and drop $5 in Don't Come.
   d. Remove all Place bets and wait for a 7.

There are some beautiful options open to you, and none of them is a bad decision. Your responsibility is to pick the one you like, and stick with it. My opinion would be (c), until I reached my win goal in a session. This way, I still win on the 6, 8, or 9 showing, the 7 wouldn't destroy me, and I'd still have a shot at establishing another $5 Don't. When your Win Goal is tucked away, you can get a little more aggressive.

By now you've got the idea, and maybe even some variations of your own. The idea of hedge betting is to win a couple of dollars per shooter, and still keep the 7 in your corner.

Maybe that's not your game. OK, don't do it. I'm only giving you different approaches to this very rough game. Remember, the dice won't stay hot forever, and they won't stay cold forever. Maybe you've lost some small fortunes trying to get a big roll going. This will keep you in the game.

This chapter touched on the double hedge. I could go over more variations on the double, triple, and quintuple hedge. There is no limit to what you can do with hedge betting. How strong you are able to play, will always depend on how much you are able to "get out" with on the Don't Pass. And the amount is based on your session money, and that amount is based on your bankroll. And so on, and so on. But I've told you all this before. Were you listening????? Nah!!!!!

But I'll reach you someday.

MONEY MANAGEMENT 37

Extended Hedges

After reading the previous chapter on the double hedge, I know your head is spinning, and well it should. Craps is not just a game of either looking for a hot table, or a cold table. I preach an altogether different way of gambling.

The emphasis is on winning, and not just gigantic sums. You wanna play crazy, you'll get only pity from me. My only regret is that I cannot lay out the hundreds of plays that are available with Craps.

I don't give a pig's ear if you play right, wrong, or hedge, as long as you have Money Management and Discipline. Every bet on the table, if you go for hedge betting, opens up a tremendous number of moves.

If I kept going, with hedges off of the Don't Pass and Don't Come wagers, with units of four and five chips each, you'd be simply overwhelmed. By going over the single and double hedges, and grasping the theory, you will slide right into your own mode of playing.

This chapter is merely to let you know that there is NO end to these various ways of playing. By my writing chapter after chapter, showing you advanced and super advanced methods, would only become boring by its nature and might completely confuse you.

There is one very important message that I would like to give you a this time. If you do grasp the theory behind the hedge systems that I've given you for single and double units, then by all means explore the aforementioned three-, four-, and five-unit wagers. You can tie in my Regression system, that is explained in detail in my Blackjack book, and also the power of hedge betting, and the powerful Patrick System, which kills any chance of the 7 beating you on the come-out.

You will not be stereotyped as either a right or wrong bettor, but the use of all of these methods will allow you to take advantage of the dice, regardless of whether they are hot or cold.

The main problem is that you must have the proper bankroll, along with a complete understanding of all the variations of these three methods. The Regression system, which is used on the games of Blackjack, Baccarat, and the outside bets at the Roulette table, can be incorporated into the game of Craps, only if your starting bets begin with at least two units on the Pass and Don't Pass Lines, plus two units apiece on the inside place numbers.

That would call for an initial layout of $64 per shooter, and based on the needed session money of ten times the amount wagered on the first shooter, calls for $640 per session, and a bankroll of $1,920.

So as not to discourage the $5 bettor, who just doesn't have this kind of operating capital, I refuse to tempt them with the enormity of this play. But, if you understand the double hedge, and have the bankroll, the use of multiple units, with a combination of all of my systems, will make you die-hard crapshooters the strongest players in the casino, right on a par with the card counter in Blackjack, who enjoys a 2% edge on his wagers.

Believe me, there is NO limit to these variations, and when you conquer the system, armed with the Discipline percentage I give you—even your best friends won't recognize your play.

They'll be saying: "I remember him when he was a dopey player"....

MONEY MANAGEMENT 38

The Patrick System

This system of play has been given my name, and I do it for a good reason. It is very conservative—just like I play, and it has an enormous number of variations, both for the right and wrong bettor. There must be spin-offs, that become an offset of the basic play of a system. This allows you to take advantage of the flow of the dice.

Basically, this method is strictly for the Don't bettor, so any of you right bettors who hate the grinding requirements of the wrong bettor, can just skip this chapter. But you'll miss what I consider a new approach to wrong betting, and a powerful one.

This is a grinding method, and an exercise in total control by the bettor, but it is my opinion that it provides the player with a superb way of playing on the Don't side.

One of the most important things to understand about gambling is that you should play only the games that have low vigs. Games that offer you the least chance of losing. At the craps table, the vig against betting right or wrong is 1.41%, and by laying or taking odds, you can reduce it even further.

But look at the poor wrong bettor. By placing his chip on the Don't Pass, he is trying to "get out" with a point working for him. It's no secret that once the point is established, the odds swing drastically in favor of the Don't bettor, since there are more ways that he can win, with the 7 working for him, than his chances of losing, with any of the point numbers. The problem is bucking that 7 on the come-out.

The Patrick system takes care of that. Merely place a $5 chip on the Pass Line, for the come-out roll, and at the same time, place a $5 chip on the Don't Pass. Now the 7 can't beat you.

Normally, if you bet Don't, you'd win on the 3, but lose on the 11, so those two numbers are considered a wash. It still is. Snake-eyes would give you a $5 profit but it could only be made one way, and the six ways a 7 could show would leave you a minus five ways to lose, on the come-out. The 12 is a push.

That's because the 7 and 11, which can be made a total of eight ways, overshadow the 2 and 3, which combined can only be made three ways. And that's always been the problem with the Don't bettor—getting beat on the come-out by that deadly 7.

The Patrick system nullifies the 7 and gets you out. You will now lose only on the showing of a 12 on the come-out. That's because your Pass Line bet would go down with box cars. By average, that should show up—one out of every thirty-six come-outs. Of course the odds are based on millions of rolls, but the true percentages have to be based on the number of happenings that could occur, based on the thirty-six numbers that could show.

On the come-out, a 7, 11, 2, or 3 would result in a stand-off. When a number shows, the Don't bettor is ready to swing into action.

You will concentrate just on the Don't Pass bet. At this point, merely lay odds against the number, and stop. There is now no vig attached to your play. The vigorish on the come-out, is based on the possibility of the 12 showing.

That should occur once in every thirty-six come-outs, which gives the house an edge of one win out of every thirty-six rolls, or a percentage of 2.8%, for the come-out roll. And since the laying of odds cover no vig, this is the best move the player can get.

The casino offers the player an excellent chance to stay in the game, due to the small vigs. This one even beats the .8% that the Don't player now fights on the playing of the wrong side. This system has only .3% vig. Go ahead—beat that.

At this time, I refer you back to my chapter on laying odds, contained in the Knowledge section of this book. I do not like to lay odds, and except for isolated instances, where I lay them for one roll, to protect a Don't Pass bet, I stay away from them. The reason I do not like to lay odds is that I don't want to weaken the edge I have over the house, by fighting off the 7 on the come-out roll and establishing a bet which will pay me even money—even though the chances of my winning are either 6-3, 6-4, or 6-5 in my favor. I don't want to give an inch—not after I had to go to such pains to get in a good position. I hope you are just as vicious a player.

With the Patrick system, I bet both ways, until the point is established, since the object is to beat the 7, and then I'm in an advantageous position. How I handle it from there on is what we'll discuss. The odds I lay have no edge for the house, since they're free, so my vig on this play is still miniscule.

At this point, you have options, but the basic play is STOP. Just stand there with the odds against the point, and wait for a decision. Naturally, no matter what the point is, the odds are in favor of you winning. The tough part for the Don't better has always been, is, and always will be—getting out.

OK, this method gets you out, and shuts that 7 off. Now, you have it working for you. The theory of this system is based on its power to offset the biggest obstacle in the path of the Don't bettor.

I think I've got your attention.

39 MONEY MANAGEMENT

The Patrick System—Step Two

With every method of play there are variations, and this one is no exception. If you're content to just sit with your laying odds against the point, that's OK. That's your decision. You are not fighting any vig with those true odds.

There are many ways to play this system. For instance, place a chip in both the Don't Pass and on the Pass Line to receive a point. Then lay double odds against that point and place a $5 chip in the Don't Come. The 7 is protected by the odds bet. If another number appears, reduce your point bet to single odds. Now you have odds against the point, and a $5 Don't Come bet.

Look at your options now. You can come through the Don't Come with another $5 chip, since the 7 can't hurt you, or you can simply remove the odds off of your Don't Pass bet, and accept a wash for the point number. You still have that Don't Come bet working, and you were never in trouble, as to the 7 beating you, until you reached that position. Suppose the point was a 6, and the Don't Come was a 9. You feel a little shaky laying odds against that 6, so just nullify the bet, and sit with the strong Don't 9 as your bet for this player. You'll receive even money, and you're holding the hammer.

It didn't cost you anything to establish the Don't Come. The decision to remove the odds off the Don't Pass bet is up to you. Make the point the deciding factor if you like. If it is 6 or 8, accept a push. If it is 4, 5, 9, or 10, lay the odds, and on the even numbers, drop a dollar on the hard way. Cuts down chances of losing.

Finally, you have the option of coming through the Don't Come with still another bet, thereby trying to establish three Don't bets. The number of Don't Come bets you opt for is up to you.

I have a certain way of using this method. The decision to go for Don't Come bets and to leave odds in action is based on what that original point number was. As I explained above, I'll put a bet on both the Don't Pass and Pass Line. If 6 or 8 is the point, I'll lay the odds against the point and drop a bet in the Don't Come. If it is the sister number of the 6 or 8, I'll come through again, and we'll say I get a 9. I'll take my odds off the point (6) and accept a wash on that decision.

I'll sit with the Don't Come bets (No Eight and No Nine), since I have the edge in my favor, and I'm not laying any odds.

I'll then revert to basic Don't, and replace a number only twice before backing off of a hot shooter. Since I have two Don'ts working for me, I'll simply come through the Don't Come, in order to establish the third, before sitting back and waiting for that lucky old 7 to shine.

If, on that opening come-out roll, I got a good Don't number, such as 4, 5, 9, or 10. I'll just lay the odds, forget the Don't Come, and just wait to have that 7 show. Ten dollar wagers and up call for a hard way hedge with the even numbers.

I think you get the idea. The options, after a point is established, are strictly yours. Just understand the power of this method, for the wrong bettor. You never have to fight the 7 on the come-out. There are more options coming up, but the $5 Don't bettor should give this system a second look. You'll find things that will really help you—a lot.

MONEY MANAGEMENT 40

Theory of the Patrick System

Theory, as explained earlier, is part of the Little 3. It is the reasoning, or approach to an endeavor, that a person will take. In my system, I will give you my theory behind the play, as relates to the Don't bettor.

The chapters on playing the Don't Come, and the ones on buying against the number, explain why you cannot lay single-unit bets behind the numbers. You may place a number any time you wish for $5, as in the case of the 4, 5, 9, or 10, and $6 for the 6 and 8.

However, you cannot lay a $5 unit against these numbers. The house says you must bet an amount that calls for a four-unit payoff, such as $40, to win $20 against the 4 or 10, $30 to win $20 against the 5 and 9, and $24 to win $20 against the 6 and 8.

Besides that, you must pay a vig of 5%, whether you win or lose. So, if you bet against any of these numbers, you must lay out amounts of $41, $31, or $25. Well, whether you believe it or not, that is a lot of money to a great many people. Not many Don't bettors will lay $41 to win $20, even though they'd love to. It's just too much money for them, and the house knows it. If it was $10 to win $5 on the 4 and 10, they'd be standing in line around the block, to get their bets down. Just like I've said seven hundred and sixty-three times, you must have the bankroll to play.

OK, let's look at the theory behind the Patrick system. It gives the wrong bettor, who has only a small starting bankroll, the chances to risk much smaller amounts, still bet Don't, and get the pesky 7 out of the way on the come-out.

Let's say you play the system, and 10 appears as the point. Lay $10 odds on your Don't Pass bet and stop. Do nothing else. The worst you have at risk is $10 to win $5. There is no charge to make that bet, other than the 2.8% you were fighting on the come-out, based on the possibility of the 12 getting that Pass Line chip. This allows the $5 bettor to make smaller outlays against the numbers.

What you could do is base your bet on what number showed on the come-out, as I explained earlier. The 4, 5, 9, or 10 would call for odds, and then sit.

If the point was 6 or 8, here are the options:

1. Lay odds, and go through Don't Come to get a strong Don't number. Then remove your odds on that 6 or 8, and just sit with the strong Don't Come.
2. Take odds on the Pass Line point of 8, and place the 6.
   a. With this option, you've become a right bettor for this shooter, and have the 6 and 8 working for you, much like the 6 and 8 System, which was explained earlier. But, this way, you are a right bettor with the strong right numbers, and a wrong bettor with the strong wrong numbers.

OK, let's clarify it:

1. If come-out is 4, 5, 9, or 10, you have a strong Don't number. Lay the odds, and become a wrong bettor.
2. If come-out is 6 or 8, take the odds, place the sister number, giving you the two most powerful right numbers, and you become a right bettor, for this roll.

At no time will you lose with the 7 on the come-out, and you'll always be fighting only the 4, 5, 9, or 10 on the Don't. But, you'll cross over to the right side with the powerful 6 and 8 as your numbers.

If you have played Craps for one day, or one hundred years, you are aware of the 7. It is an all-powerful, all-devastating enemy, regardless of which method you use. All players are in constant fear of that number. This system nullifies it—if you like to play Don't.

Does this system work all the time? No, of course not. No system ever invented, or ever to be invented, will work all the time. It can't, because of the fact you are never in a better than 50-50 chance of winning and losing. But, my methods reduce the chances of losing. After you perfect the method—read, reread, and again read the Discipline techniques of Win Goals and Loss Limits. All tied together, you will become a very, very strong disciplined player.

41 MONEY MANAGEMENT

Two and Three Unit Bets (Patrick System)

You know, you're not restricted to just single unit bets on the Pass and Don't Pass Lines. By increasing your bets to two units, you now have a new set of options open to you.

First, you can follow the same methods outlined in the previous chapters, but for higher amounts. That means that the players with larger bankrolls can "get out" with higher units, whatever you like, on both sides. The only thing that can hurt you is the 12 on that come-out, and if that bothers you, drop $1 on the 12, for that roll.

After the number is established, you have the option of laying against any portion of the Don't, or taking odds on any part, or all, of the point.

Suppose you have two units on both sides, and 5 becomes the point. You can do any of the following:

1. Lay full odds of $15 against the 5, and drop $5 in the Don't Come
2. Lay double odds against the 5, and drop $10 in the Don't Come
3. Lay half odds against the 5 (9-6), and sit
4. Lay full or double odds, and place the 6 and 8
   a. You can revert to the correct betting method for place numbers
   b. You can take one hit on the 6 or 8 and take down place numbers
   c. You can take two hits on the place numbers, then come down off the 6 and 8, and either leave odds

against the point, or even remove the odds, accept the wash, and end up with the profit you gained by hitting the place numbers.

There is no end to the options you can derive from this method. You could increase the original bets to four and five units, and the options you then have at your fingertips are innumerable.

Grasp the theory—nullifying the 7 on the come-out, and then stay strictly Don't, or become a hedge bettor, or make your decision based on what the point number becomes. The system you choose must not be changed once you reach the table. After you decide on which way you will play, that session can only be played with that particular method. You wanna change—kill the session and go to another table.

42 MONEY MANAGEMENT

Using the 7 Both Ways

This method will make the 7 work for you all day long. You will never lose with the 7. You will win with 7 on the come-out, and then win with 7 if you swing over and bet Don't.

Instead of betting one unit on both the Pass and Don't Pass Lines, this system calls for you to bet $15 on the Pass Line, and $10 on the Don't Pass. Now the 7 is in your corner on the come-out, and of course, the 11 and 3 cancel each other out. Dropping $1 on the 12 is optional.

If the 7 shows on the first roll, you lose $10 on the Don't Pass, and win $15 on the Pass Line, for a profit of $5. Once the point is established, you can then lay odds on the Don't side, and have the 7 working for you again. But there is a minus side to this play.

Assume you have $15 on the Pass Line, and $10 Don't Pass, and 10 shows. You could then lay $20 odds against the 10. If the 10 shows, you lose $30 on the Don't side, and win $15 on the Pass Line, for a loss of $15. If the 7 shows, you lose your $15 Pass Line bet, but win $20 on the Don't Pass, with odds.

Now, the good part is that you have the 7 working all the time, even on the come-out roll, and then it swings over to work for you on the Don't side.

But the problem is the risk against the profit potential. With this system of three units Do, two units Don't, and laying free odds on the point, this is what could happen:

1. If the 4 or 10 shows, and you lay the odds, you could lose $15 or win $5
2. If the 5 or 9 shows, and you lay the odds, you could lose $10 or win $5

3. If the 6 or 8 shows, and you lay the odds, you could lose $7 or win $5
   a. On the 6 and 8, you could have become a right bettor and taken odds.

There you have some plays that make the 7 work for you all day long, but the problem is in having to lay higher amounts to pay for that privilege. Notice in the case of the 4 or 10 becoming the point, you're risking $15 to win $5. I realize you're never fighting that 7, and that you could make up some hits on the come-out roll, but the total at risk, after the point is established, is heavy.

So you're asking the logical question of why would I show you a system, and then warn you against it? That's because if you play my system, you should use it only on the Don't side, and strictly to save your Don't Pass and eventual Don't Come bets. Some of you would have discovered this method of totally neutralizing the 7, and I merely wanted to show you what could happen.

If you decide to play the Patrick System, stay with the aforementioned methods in the preceding chapters, and concentrate on the Don't side. And, of course, you'll start popping off your own methods.

MONEY MANAGEMENT 43

Trends and the Patrick System

I believe in trends and streaks. When things are going a certain way, they tend to stay that way for a period of time. This was all explained in the chapter on the Little 3, so I want you to look for trends and follow them. If they stay in a certain pattern for five or six shooters, you want to be on those rolls, whether they're going with or against the flow of the dice.

Here is the best way to take advantage of the trends at a craps table, and utilize the Patrick system to its fullest.

You want to wait for the dice to head in a certain direction—either hot or cold, and then you want to be on that streak. When you come up to a table, wait for a decision to be reached on either the game in progress or the upcoming one. Whichever way that particular game goes, you bet in that direction.

Incidentally, come-out rolls have absolutely no bearing on how you will bet. A 7 or 11 will not call for you to bet "right," and a craps not signal wrong way pattern. All decisions are based on the point. You then follow that trend.

Suppose the prior game ended with the shooter sevening out. You will now bet "wrong." Place a chip on the Pass Line, and one on the Don't Pass Line. This assures you of a point being established, and not getting beat by a come-out 7.

If the point is 4, 5, 9, or 10, lay the odds and stop. Wait for a decision, and make no further bets in the Don't Come. You're laying single odds against the point, and each of these numbers are considered strong Don't numbers. Back in the chapter on laying odds, I told you that I did not agree with that practice, and I don't. That's because on a regular bet, through the Don't Pass or Don't Come, you go to all the trouble of fighting that 7 on the come-out, and then weaken that possible even money payoff by laying odds and giving back some leverage to the house. With the Patrick system, you are not in any danger of getting beat on the come-out roll by that 7.

So, by laying odds, with this system you have the opportunity of betting lesser amounts, with no vig, and the chance to build up your winnings, before taking a bigger shot against the house.

If, on that come-out roll, the 6 or 8 became the point, your next move would be a little different. Since you don't feel that comfortable with a Don't 6 or 8, you want to pick up another strong number.

Lay the odds against that 6 (or 8) and put a chip in the Don't Come. If the point repeats, you lose only your odds against the point, and the Don't Come bet moves behind that number.

If the point was 6, and 8 showed as the Don't Come number, the chip would be moved behind the 8, and now you have two Don'ts, but they are considered strong right numbers, so you drop another chip in the Don't Come. Do not lay odds against that No Eight.

Suppose the next roll produced a 9. Now, you have No Eight, No Nine, and odds against the point number 6. That's it for this shooter. Three Don'ts are enough. If either of the Don't Come numbers get shot down, replace them, but only twice. You don't want to end up chasing a potential hot roll.

If that shooter sevens out, the dice pass to the next shooter, and you stay betting Don't. Start the next game with a chip on both the Pass Line and Don't Pass Line. If you have the proper bankroll, it is OK to put two units on each line.

Again, if the point is 4, 5, 9, or 10, lay the odds and just sit. If the point is 6 or 8, lay single odds and come through the Don't Come for an additional number. If that first Don't Come produces a 5, stop. You have a Don't Pass (odds against) 6, and a Don't Come 5 (or 4, or 9, or 10, whatever showed).

Wait for a decision, but replace that Don't Come only twice. You're sitting pretty.

Suppose the shooter makes the point. Now you swing over and bet "right," because the trend has shifted in another direction, and if this is going to be a hot roll, you wanna be in on it. All you missed was the first win.

If the shooter made his point, and you swung over and bet on the Pass Line, you might have a bet or two still sitting on the Don't Come numbers. That's OK, just hope he throws a 7 on the subsequent come-out. Then you win on both the Pass Line and existing Don't Come bets.

When you swing over to bet "right," your bet is on the Pass Line. You only bet both sides when you are betting "wrong," and wish to nullify the 7. Now we start to get a little deep, so put on your thinking cap. There will be variations of moves, depending on what that point number becomes.

1. If point is 6, take odds, and place the 8
2. If point is 8, take odds, and place the 6
3. If point is 5 or 9, take odds, and place the 6 and 8
4. If point is 4 or 10, buy the $41 No Four (or No Ten) and place $22 inside
   a. Wait for two hits on the inside numbers and then remove your No Four (or No Ten), and take down your place 5 and 9
   b. Taking odds on your 4 (or 10) after you remove your $41 No bet is strictly up to you.
   c. The amount of hits on your place bets could be one, two, or three, whatever you like. I suggest two, because you want to get that $41 wager down as soon as you can
   d. If you like, you can eliminate betting the $41 No Four or No Ten, and merely take odds on the point, and place the 6 and 8.

NOTE: The option to bet $41 No Four or No Ten when 4 or 10 is the point, is your decision. You could stay strictly as a normal "right" bettor, and leave the bets stand on their own. With this method, I take the No bets for two hits, and then revert back to the normal play.

NOTE: Another option, when 4 or 10 is the point would be to just take odds on the point, and place the 6 and 8 (I prefer (4) above).

Once that No Four or No Ten is taken down, leave your place bets up, on the 6 and 8, and revert to the proper place betting method. When you catch a hot shooter, you're right there with him.

If the shooter makes the point, again come out on the Pass Line with a one-unit bet. Do not increase his Pass Line to two units until you have won two Pass Line numbers. I'm aware that the shooter made two Pass Line numbers, at this juncture, but you weren't on the first one. You were on the Don't side for the first win, and then crossed over. So, you only had the advantage of one score. I want you to personally pick up two wins before upping your Pass Line bet.

As long as he keeps banging out a point, you stay on the Pass Line. If he sevens out, the table now suggests Don't, so you will then swing over and bet Don't for the next shooter. You may bet one or two units on each of the Pass and Don't Pass lines, when you are betting wrong. Two units give you a little more leverage. Your only road-block would be the 12 on the come-out, and that is a one in thirty-six shot.

The only thing that can beat you, with this Follow the Trend system, is a choppy table, where only one decision in a row keeps occurring. If that's the case, leave that table. There will be times that this will occur, so don't go looking for a bridge to leap off of, if it does happen.

Eventually, you'll catch a hot "right" roll, which is what you want, and the Money Management method will allow you to cash in. A consistently cold table will have you sitting on that side of the play, and you won't get hurt.

Down the road, if you decide to use the Patrick system as your primary method of play at Craps, and you follow the strict Money Management and Discipline techniques that I lay out for you, this will probably be the system you will use. So absorb this chapter, and the following one, covering a hedging process, for this Follow the Trend system.

MONEY MANAGEMENT 44

Hedging the Trend (Patrick System)

You've probably already formed his question in your mind, so I'll answer it now to take the pressure off your brain cells. When betting "wrong," with the Patrick system, and the trend is Don't, can I hedge against the strong Don't numbers, if 4, 5, 9, or 10 is the point? The answer is yes—if you want to.

In the previous chapter I told you that if you were betting "wrong," and the come-out produced a strong Don't number, merely lay the odds and sit. The hedge players may do the following (based on the fact that you are betting two or more units on both the Pass Line, and Don't Pass Line, and looking to bet "wrong"):

1. If 4 or 10 shows, place $22 inside, wait for two hits, then take down your Place bets, and lay either full or half odds against the point (hard way hedges are optional at this point)
2. If 5 or 9 shows, place $17 inside, wait for one hit, then remove Place bets, and lay either full or half odds against the point
   a. I prefer two hits against the 4 or 10, and one hit against the 5 or 9
   b. Until you reach your first level Win Goal, I suggest half odds against the 5 and 9, and full odds against the 4 and 10, with $2 hard way hedge.

Since hedging can become very sophisticated, I suggest you revert back to the chapters on Simple and Double Hedges, for additional moves. And don't attack the tables until you have your game plan completely laid out.

This is a powerful way to play Craps. You will be on both hot and cold runs, and you may hedge your Don't bets with many different combinations. But I hesitate to illustrate bets off of three or four or five or more units, so as not to bore the reader with a multiple amount of plays.

With this method of following the trend, you are assured of eventually catching a scorching hot roll, or an ice cold table.

It'll happen.

MONEY MANAGEMENT 45

Synopsis of the Patrick System

There are good and bad sides to everything. Going to school, cleaning your house, taking night courses, having a second job, undergoing an operation, having a big party at your house, getting married—you name it, there are peaks and valleys.

Look over every one of these happenings. Each has something good about it, and then again something bad. For example, an operation—the bad part is that you're scared to death, and know it will hurt, but the good part is that it will cure you of something that is making you miserable.

Having a gigantic party is a tremendous thing to look forward to, and to enjoy while it is going on. But the next day, having to clean up that mess, and with a hangover, you wonder if it was worth it.

The same is true in gambling, as you could win or you could lose. And the same is true with systems that attack gambling. My system is very effective, and will really help the wrong bettor, but I want to list both the good and the bad, so that you'll understand where you stand, if this is the way you'd like to play.

BAD PARTS: (Wrong Betting)

1. You're laying out more money than what you could win, even though the odds are correct, as to your chances of winning (2-1, 3-2, 6-5)
   a. As with the 10, you're laying $10 to win $5, even though your chances of winning are 6-3, in your favor,

2. After the come-out, you'll never have an even money payoff in your favor, since you'll always be laying odds,
   a. You gave up that edge to offset any chance of the 7 beating you,
3. Twelve on the come-out will take down your Pass Line bet.

GOOD PARTS:

1. Seven on come-out can never beat you
2. Seven on come-out can still allow you to win Don't Come bets, if that is the method you use
3. Vigorish on the come-out is reduced to 2.8%
4. After nullifying that 7 on the come-out, you still have it working for you, despite the fact you are laying true odds, which carry no vig for the house
5. The number of variations off of the Don't Pass and Don't Come, can still be used, including the hedge betting

The flexibility of betting right, when the come-out is 6 or 8, and betting wrong, when point is 4, 5, 9, or 10, is a sneaky strong system. Think about it. A lot of people, as explained in the chapter covering betting on the 6 and 8 only, fear getting the other numbers as points. That's why the 6 and 8 place betting method is gaining in popularity.

Well, with this method, you still have the 6 and 8, and on one of them you're getting true odds. (If point was 6, you place the 8, and take free odds behind the 6.) Then, if it is a strong Don't number as the point, you swing over and bet Don't. Maybe you'd like to include the 5 and 9 as right numbers, and just play Don't when 4 or 10 is the point. That's up to you.

Once you've established the point on both sides, you're in control of which way you want to go. Naturally, you could sit with the 6 and 8, take a couple of hits, and then switch to wrong. If the point was 4, 5, 9, or 10, become an immediate Don't bettor. You've got the 7 working for you against the strong Don't numbers, and the strong 6 and 8 working for you on the "right."

There you have a taste of the Patrick system, a method by

which the Don't bettor is saved from that devastating 7 on the come-out. Maybe you'll like it, and maybe you won't.

But if you're a Don't bettor, I suggest a second and third look. And finally, be aware that how you manage your money and when you leave that table are still the determining factors in gambling. They're called Money Management and Discipline.

By all means do not totally disregard the theory behind this system. If you become a complete Craps player, the methods explained in these chapters on the Patrick system will come in handy. One day you will utilize most of these plays and the results will surprise you.

MONEY MANAGEMENT 46

You and Money Management

Almost everyone does some type of gambling. Some people do it to excess and get in trouble. The thrill of victory is so all consuming that the person returns again and again, trying to recapture the gold ring. The lure is so great that people flock to the casinos just to get a taste of gambling, just to become part of the overall glamour.

I've asked people why they go to Atlantic City without knowing anything about the game and they give me the stock answer: "Oh, I only go a couple times a year. I just take a couple hundred dollars, just to have a ball."

Then I see these same people at a table having a "ball." They lose three bets in a row, based on their own lousy play, and you'd think someone smashed their knee caps. They growl, snarl, curse, yell at the dealers, almost squeeze the color off the chips, and display an unbelievable and uncontrollable show of disgust. They say it doesn't bother them to lose, but watch these same people in action. They have absolutely no idea how to bet. They don't know when to increase their bets or when to drop down. There is no set Win Goal or Loss Limit, no idea as to when to leave a table. If you walked up to a table and saw a guy with a stack of chips in front of him, a huge smile on his face and a cocky attitude, you'd know right away he was winning. If you asked him how long he was going to play, he'd look at his watch for an answer. He doesn't base his sessions on a Win Goal, but instead on the time the bus is leaving, or when it's time to eat. In the long run, he'll get whacked.

I've seen people play Blackjack, win fifteen out of twenty hands, and leave the table a loser. Can you imagine? It's a lack of Money Management. I've also seen players drop a $5 chip on the Pass Line, pick up the dice, and throw numbers for an hour. When they finally seven out, they've made eight passes, about fifty-five numbers, get a rousing ovation from the players at the table for a hot roll, and pocket a profit of $45. Isn't that awful? It's because of a lack of Money Management.

A guy betting football games wins six out of nine games on a Sunday and loses money. You think I'm making this up? It happens every weekend. Why??? Lack of Money Management.

Years ago in Vegas, there was a young guy who worked for a local bank. He was an assistant teller, made about $150 a week, and was quite a mathematical whiz.

Five days a week, on his lunch hour, he would enter the casino where I was and put his $40 into action at the craps table. He played a rough, tough game. Never made crazy bets, played close to the vest when he was losing, and really laid it out when he was in a hot spell. I got to know him, and we talked about his approach. He didn't have a lot of money, but he had discipline and determination.

He never lost more than the $40, and occasionally picked up some good scores. One of the pit bosses remarked how hard a player like that was on the casino. They never had a chance to wipe him out. He said that some day that player would get his streak, and win a fortune.

He was right. Several months later, the banker caught a scorching hot table. The roll lasted long over his usual lunch hour, but he stayed on, and shoveled in his bets, back and forth, in a controlled method that enhanced his reputation. He cashed in over $9,000. The next day he was back with a $40 stake. That's a tough player.

The same goes for you, in whatever game you choose. You must have Money Management. You simply must get to realize how important the control of your money at a game must be.

Go to a casino sometime. Not to play, just to observe. Stand for awhile at a table and just watch the different players. See if there is a pattern to their bets, following a win, or after a loss. Usually, they count their chips before making a bet and let the present standing of their money determine the bet. A follow-up win or loss has no set base, and the wagers are made in an alternating scale, with no set reasoning.

These people have absolutely no Money Management, and no right to be playing. It's only a matter of time before they go broke.

I've given you about ten methods to use at a craps table. It doesn't matter which ones appeal to you. They are all based on a strict, controlled hold over your session money. Every winning bet has its own predetermined follow-up bet. Every losing roll reverts back down to the basic bet.

Every system has Money Management built right in. Every system will work at various times during the course of a day. The Loss Limit and Win Goals are there to protect all of these methods.

Sure, you may be a little bored playing like this, but it definitely will minimize your losses. When the wins do come, the Money Management that held your losses down will enable you to roll up some decent returns and get you to win more often. Maybe not the telephone numbers that you dream about, but enough to form a base bankroll, to allow you to go for bigger session percentages.

It's not going to come overnight, and it's not going to be easy, especially for you people who believe you really don't need Money Management.

But if you want to change your approach to gambling in general, and Craps in particular, take note of the following: For years and years and years, the same staid system of Craps has been handed down from generation to generation. A lot of books written on the subject all revert to the same system of Pass Line, two Comes, etc. etc. etc.

Then they tell you that they have something for the "advanced player." It turns out to be the exact same system, but just played with more chips. And this is usually more than the average visitor to a casino can only dream about. The ideas look good on paper, but the real world of crapshooting is at the table, and it is rough, man, it is really rough.

I address the majority of my systems to the $5 bettor, the backbone of the gambling industry. You higher rollers can readily apply your own unit bets, based on your session money. But don't think a couple of thousand dollars gives you the almighty right to go to a $25 table and start betting like every time you blink, a $25 chip pops out of your left ear. You're playing with money that you shouldn't want to lose, and the object is to win. How much you win is unimportant. The main thing is that you leave that game with your starting session money, and a profit, based on that starting amount.

I'm not going to apologize for repeating over and over, the necessity to wise up and learn how to win. If you were so good, you wouldn't have to read a book to learn how to win. The answer is not in just knowing the game. The answer is in following the four requirements of the Big 4. And Money Management is there.

MONEY MANAGEMENT 47

Wrapping up Money Management

In a nutshell, you can't win without Money Management. But, then, you can't win without all parts of the Big 4. Don't let your lack of the ability to make intelligent bets destroy the time you spend in a casino. You know what makes me feel very good? When I give a lecture or seminar at a certain adult school or club or gathering about the power of the Big 4 and how it will minimize your losses. I get a certain number of people who question my theory because it is conservative. Then, maybe a couple of weeks later, I receive letters or phone calls from these same people, actually marveling over the fact that their last three or four trips to the casinos have been either break evens or winning days.

They can hardly believe that you can actually stop losing so much, just by the following of the simple rules I lay out, and by managing your bets, so as to take advantage of hot rolls and back off on cold shooters.

If you don't have the proper amount of bankroll, don't force it by making large bets with small session money. Don't try to force a win by increasing your wager after just losing five hands in a row. Their comment? "Hey, I can't lose forever, and one win will pull me right back into the game." Oh, man, what a dope. Maybe you can't lose forever, but there is no rule that says you can't lose ten, twelve, fourteen, even twenty hands in a row. It's happened before, it's happening every day, and it'll happen again and again. Stop thinking you are due to win.

I've seen crapshooters bet one unit at a time all around the table. When the dice come to them, they drop four units on the Pass Line because they feel they are hot and want to bet more on themselves. I'll never understand what possesses these boobs to bet more on themselves, just on a hunch, and then drop down to lower amounts for everybody else.

The driving urge to recover past losses, in one quick roll, is a nasty habit. It throws caution, logic, and Money Management out the window. Better you follow it out the window. Might turn out to be a lot less expensive move.

I don't know how many of you will take this advice. All I'm suggesting is that you try it. I guarantee you, your whole approach to gambling will change. First off, your losses will be tremendously reduced because of that powerful Loss Limit. It will absolutely prevent you from ever going broke. On the plus side, while the wins might not be gigantic, they will be consistent, because of the Win Goals being intelligently set up ahead of time.

Set up your controlled pattern of bets, never deviating from the play you adopt, or the one you choose from these chapters.

It's called Money Management. And if it doesn't rhyme with winning, at least it goes hand in hand.

DISCIPLINE 1

Discipline—What Is It?

Discipline, it's the bottom line. It's the Discipline factor that determines whether you will win or lose in gambling. Baby, it's the difference. The pro has it. The novice doesn't.

It is my humble opinion that 95% of the people who gamble lack this virtue. It takes guts to walk when you've won a certain amount, and it is the guts to walk when you've lost a certain amount that will teach you how to win.

Is it hard to walk away from a session? You can bet that today is tomorrow's yesterday it's hard to walk, whether you're losing or winning. But the day you acquire this ability is the day your gambling habits change.

Of all of the facets of the Big 4, this one is the most important. They all lend credence to each other, and each relies on the others' input into the total package. But it still comes down to your own parcel of guts, to see if you have nerve to accept the Win Goal you set, and also adhere to the restrictions you placed on your losses.

If you have this Discipline, it is only a matter of time before you will start to win. The bankroll put together is your own decision. But it must be in line with the amounts I've laid out.

Knowledge is consuming all of the information on the game of your choice. You must understand the percentages, methods, and variations, until you are perfect in your knowledge of even the smallest part of the game that you are risking money on.

Money Management is simply following the rules of play, and allocating the proper amount of money after a win or loss. This is the part of the game where you preset your own series of bets and follow them to the letter. No hunches, no assumptions, no gut feelings. Just a smart, logical method of play.

But Discipline comes from within. It takes guts, heart, nerve, and intelligence to walk. It takes an intense desire to want to win, not play. You must preserve as much of your bankroll, on a bad day, as you can. By the same token, if you get ahead on a good day, you've got to be able to leave that casino a winner, and not kick it back in, if the trend starts to go against you.

Did you grab the main part of that sentence? When I get ahead on a given day, I'm looking for that door. Sure, I'd love to win gigantic amounts. But as soon as my Win Goal is reached, and I break those chips in half, there is no way in the world that I cannot end up a winner that day. The 50% I stash away is my guaranteed profit, and I'm gone if the excess goes down the tubes.

That predetermined Win Goal is always set low enough, so that it is easily attainable, and 20% is a decent amount, if you have a decent bankroll. But if you're going to the casino with a handful of singles, and a couple of $5 bills, where the heck do you get the right to expect big returns?

The guy who gets ahead, and starts looking for the door, is going to be tough for the casinos to beat. Personally, I refuse to put back my winnings, and even if the scores come early, it never crosses my mind to stay, just to keep busy. It is imperative that you, too, learn how to win.

I talk to people every day about gambling. You have no idea of how frustrated many of them are. They tell me story after story of what happened to them, and how much they were ahead, and how the dealer kept pulling 21 in Blackjack. They detail gory stories of the craps game where they built mountains, only to have a rotten 7 show, and destroy their day. In fact, I hear more confessions than a priest.

Always I get the question: "How come I can't win? How come my luck is so bad?" I give everyone the same answer. Your luck isn't bad. It's your approach that's rotten. You don't know how to win.

And Discipline is the underlying factor. What is Discipline? You know by now what it is. But knowing it, and practicing it, are two different things.

DISCIPLINE 2

Discipline and the Dentist

Way back in section one are two chapters, that I told you were probably the most important in the whole book. I was wrong. I shouldn't have put in the "probably." The two chapters are "Loss Limits" and "Win Goals."

Hands down, they are unquestionably the two things most players don't set. At this time, after going through the entire section on Money Management, I'd like you to re-read those two chapters. I put them in the Bankroll section, because they apply to your money.

But they should also be included in this section, because of their complete dominance of the word Discipline. So—you must read them again, as you've probably forgotten what was said. If I put a couple of dirty jokes in those chapters, you'd probably read them over, so make believe you've got a good reason to take a second peek.

OK, you've digested the contents, and maybe the theory has more meaning at this time. Now the problem is getting you to apply it to your game.

Ever have a toothache? Hurts, doesn't it? You'd like it to go away, but you know that the only thing that will make it disappear is going to the dentist. And that's gonna hurt, too. Even though you know he will take away that ache, the hurt that he will inflict makes you waver. Sometimes you don't go. You figure the ache will go away.

Well, apply that toothache to gambling. You're in need of a couple of dollars to make a car payment. You have no way of raising that money—but you absolutely must have it. There's that NEED again.

To get this money, you go to a casino and whammo, you pick up $250 in a couple of hours. Just like going to the dentist to have that cavity in your tooth repaired, all you have to do is go home with your profit. That will fill the cavity in your bank account.

But, just as you're scared to go to the dentist to be cured, you're hesitant to walk away from the table, to cure that financial need. And just like the fool who won't go the dentist to correct his pain, the gambler won't walk from the table to cure his problem.

You think this is a bad comparison? It is right on the money, my friend. You don't have the guts to practice Discipline. (And you're probably walking around with craters in your teeth.)

DISCIPLINE 3

How Do You Walk?

It ain't easy! In fact it's the roughest part of gambling. The ability to walk when you've hit your Loss Limit or your Win Goal is self-contained. That's the whole bag of Discipline—being able to control yourself.

I've already gone over the reasons why people won't quit when they're ahead, and won't leave when they're behind. So, the problem is, how do you learn this disciplined approach? How do you learn to walk, when your predetermined goals have been reached?

Simple! Habit! First you've got to get in the habit of winning. You've got to get a taste of what it's like to win. Then you'll be hooked on winning.

Growing up, I had a dog. Her name was Chubby. When she was a puppy, she ate her dog food, without a problem. When she was about three years old, we started feeding her table food. You know, a couple of nights a week she'd have a treat and her dinner consisted of what we had to eat. After awhile, we couldn't get her to go back to dog food. (Not that I blame her, but that's another story.)

She lived eighteen years, so apparently it never hurt her, but the point is, once she got into the habit of the good tasting regular food, the other was a NO-NO. Now, my daughters Lori and Colleen have a dog, Charmaine. She is six, and we keep her on dog food. She loves it, because she never got into the habit of table food, even though occasionally she does get a treat.

Everyone acquires habits. And when they do, they have trouble breaking them. Smoking habits, drinking habits, eating habits, going to the same places, watching the same TV program. Habits are hard to break.

So, once you get into the habit of winning, you will become accustomed to it. How do you acquire that habit? By getting a taste of winning—even a small steady taste. You set intelligent, easy to reach win goals, and when they are reached, run, don't walk to the nearest exit.

Winning should be the primary goal, and even seemingly ridiculous low goals should be set in the beginning, just to get you started. And they should be set as a percentage of your starting bankroll, however small.

Let's suppose you'd like to win $100 on a given day. A player with a $1,000 bankroll should have a fairly easy time accomplishing that goal. It's like winning $10 with $100. But if the player with the $100 bankroll wants that same $100 return, his chances for accomplishment are decidedly weakened. So, if the $1,000 player accepts 10% with that decent starting amount, who the heck is the $100 player trying to kid? Only himself!!!

Oh, it'll happen on occasion, where you'll run a small amount of chips into a decent win, but not often enough to offset the bad times.

If you don't have the discipline to accept the proper percentage return, then wait till you have the bankroll to play properly. In other words, stop playing right now.

At lectures that I give on gambling, there are always a handful of people who decry this theory. They claim that I don't understand how important it is to them that they try for the big windfall.

Those people I'll never reach, and there's no use trying. But for those of you who want to Learn How to Win, try getting into the habit.

DISCIPLINE 4

The Casinos and Discipline

You know, I've been harping on you to practice Discipline. Maybe you'll listen, and maybe you won't. That's up to you. Those of you who won't practice Discipline will object, simply because it's so darn hard to accept the lousy little returns that I call for.

Going to a casino and accepting 25% or 20% or 10% seems like such a waste of time. Almost like not worth the effort. Me? I accept it, 'cause I got beat so many times looking for the big kill that once I learned how to win, the feeling was so great that amounts became unimportant. Only the results count.

A couple of days ago, it was Monday, I drove to Atlantic City for my day's work. The previous two weeks saw me win six out of eight days, so I was in a good streak and actually felt quite comfortable entering the casino.

Since I was winning most of my sessions playing Craps, naturally I headed for the dice tables. I played right, and got whacked. My next session was in Blackjack, but I couldn't get a good foothold. I changed tables (sessions) and could barely stay even.

Finally, I went back to Craps and started another session, again betting right. After nine hours of constant play, I checked my bankroll. I was out $10. Can you imagine?

I couldn't get a streak going, and yet the house couldn't put me away. The day had turned into a standoff. What did I do? Cashed in and walked out. My net was a loss of $10 for nine hours work.

I didn't plunk down a big bet on the table, looking for a decision either way. I accepted the fact that on this day, neither side could overcome the other and I pulled in my horns. That's because I know how hard it is to win. The tables will be there the next day.

Yeah, they'll be there—waiting patiently for the players to take their best shot. And usually that best shot turns out to be a backfire.

The player rushes up to a table, buys in for $100, bets like there's no tomorrow, and never knows when to quit. The more he loses, the higher he bets, figuring he's due to win. He has no Money Management—no control—no Discipline. And he usually loses.

Away he walks, grumbling, cursing, moaning about his rotten luck. And still the tables stand there, unscathed. You know why? Because the house has Discipline.

Yeah, that's right, Discipline. With all its millions, the house shows the greatest display of Discipline imaginable. You go to a craps table, and the minimum is $5. The house is telling you—"You wanna play at this table, it's gonna cost you $5 a pop, minimum, to take me on." It's aware that most people have short bankrolls, and shouldn't be competing at this size table, but that doesn't bother the house—the minimums stand.

Take the tables in Atlantic City, for instance. Holidays and weekends bring an enormous surge of people to the casinos. Up go the minimums. Ten dollar tables, fifteen dollar, twenty-five, it doesn't matter. You wanna play—meet the minimum.

The people balk. They walk away from those tables and look for the $5 ones. The few that there are have lines waiting to play. So, the poor guy walks some more, and more, and more, looking for the lower tables.

The $10 ones are empty. The dealers stand there, arms folded, waiting for action. The house has Discipline. It'll wait out the customers.

Who wins? Who do you think? After awhile, the disgruntled player gets restless, bored. He's got to play. What did he come down for in the first place? To play, naturally. He's talking himself into playing.

Reluctantly, he gives in. Armed with his short bankroll, he heads to the $10 table. Then the next person comes, and the next, and so on. The house held out, and the house won.

Now the patrons are plunking $10 down, taking odds. Or, some of them allow this short bankroll to affect their knowledge, and they don't take the odds at all. If they had the proper bankroll they'd take odds, but now they're playing scared, and try to hold onto their chips. Their entire method of play is affected.

Discipline!!! The house had it—held its ground—and won.

Let's go further. Each table has a minimum bet, and each table has a maximum bet. Suppose you're at a $5 table. Check the rules. It states that the maximum bet allowed at that table is $500.

That's it, $500. The house figures, if it can't beat you over the period of time it takes for you to reach that maximum bet, it'll pull in its horns and wait for another day.

That's its Loss Limit. The house doesn't exceed the Loss Limit at that table. Remember how I told you the most important part of Money Management and Discipline was the Win Goal and the Loss Limit?

Well, the casinos have their own version of that control. And it works. It works so well that it is incorporated in all games, in all casinos. The maximum bet is the house's Loss Limit. Now, if the house can have a Loss Limit and be successful, why can't you have one? Because it's smart and you're—.

Sometimes an extremely high roller will request the maximum be lifted, and the pit boss will make that decision, based on that particular player's reputation and credit standing.

Discipline is a form of control. The controls that the casinos exhibit are their Discipline factor. You'll notice how the casinos will take count of the money at every table, at various times during the day.

They use computers to rate every player who bets a certain amount of chips per hand, or per roll. When they give out comps for dinner or lunch, they restrict the amount of the comp to the size of that particular player's action.

Even the so-called sucker bets on the craps table have maximum limits. You remember how the vigorish against you on a hard way bet could be 11.1%? That's a healthy edge in favor of the casino. Well, the house still has a maximum amount that it will allow you to bet on that proposition. That tells you something—or it should—or don't you notice?

Even though it holds the upper hand, it deals in Discipline, in the manner of minimum and maximum requirements. The house does it, and it's successful. You don't, and you're not. Get the message???

DISCIPLINE 5

The Set Amount

I'll give you the set amount of money you should use as your Loss Limits and Win Goals, and you can apply your own logical percentages. Since we're talking Craps in this book, the figures will apply strictly to Craps and nothing else.

Your overall Loss Limit should be 50%. That's 50% of your bankroll, and 50% of each session. No more. You can adjust your own personal preference to reduce that figure. In other words, you can make it 30% or 35% or 40%, but no higher than 50%.

Suppose you take $3,000 to the casino. Your loss that day can be no more than $1,500. By breaking your bankroll into three sessions, you can lose no more than $500 per session, or a total of $1,500 for the day.

If you broke that bankroll into five sessions of $600 per table, you could lose no more than $300 per table, or a total of $1,500 for that day. And that is the maximum amount—not that you must go that high.

If you broke that $3,000 bankroll into ten sessions of $300 each, you could lose no more than $150 per session, or a total of $1,500 for that day. Get the point? You can set your own personal Loss Limit at whatever you like, 30%, 40%, whatever. You name it, but you must follow it.

By the same token, if you take $300 and play three sessions, the most you lose is $50 per table, or a total of $150. The amounts can differ—but the theory remains the same.

Win Goals are the same. You set an amount and must stick to it. I suggest 20%. That's your goal. When you reach it, break that profit in half, put one half in your pocket, which is your "guarantee" for that session, and then play with the excess.

Every single winning series after that is again broken in half. One half goes with the guarantee, and the other half stays with the excess. You stay at that session until the excess, or at least 70% of it, is gone. Grab what is left, add it to your guaranteed profit, and take a hike. That series is over. This method does the following:

1. Keeps you at a session which is giving off consistent series wins
2. Gets you away from a table that is working against you
3. Has built in Loss Limits and Win Goals
4. Controls the splitting of your Win Goal into two piles: guarantee and excess
5. Controls subsequent series wins, by splitting them between the guarantee and the excess.

You've heard me make this point before, but it bears repeating. It's gonna be doggone hard for you to follow this procedure, but it will work. Again, you can set lower amounts, and then you will be able to accept smaller guaranteed profits. Don't forget, there's nothing that says a good long hot streak couldn't come your way during the excess period.

Some dude might pick up those ivories and throw till wrap-up time. If you follow my Money Management methods for that roll, you'll have all the gravy you need to make that day a stupendous one.

Maybe you'll set 25% or 30% as your Win Goal. That's up to you. But no higher. At least not until you get into the habit of winning. Until you learn how to win. This will seem tough to follow in the beginning. But anything successful usually calls for strict control, strict Discipline, and sometimes only meager returns.

After you realize the tremendous impact that the 7 has on the game of Craps, you'll set realistic goals. Craps is a rough game, and you've got to minimize your losses until your streak comes. Loss Limits and Win Goals, with set amounts, are the answers.

DISCIPLINE 6

The Professional Gambler

I'm not trying to make you a professional gambler. You need a strong stomach for that. You know what it's like to lose, when it is your only source of income?

It's like a good swift kick in the gut. It hurts all the way down to the pit of your stomach. The hurt is real, and it's bitter. And no matter how many times you walk away from a table a loser, it still hurts.

The professional gambler has been through the hurt many times. And when you lose a football game on a fumble with eleven seconds to go, or a baseball game with two out in the bottom of the ninth, or a basketball game with one tick left on the clock, it still hurts, and it always will.

That's why the professional sets his Loss Limits at a realistic, easy to reach figure, so the hurt does not wipe him out. That's also why he doesn't chase that elusive rainbow.

It seems like every ball game I bet on comes down to the last play. And it seems I always lose the close ones, but of course that is not the case. It's just that it is human nature to dwell on the tough losses, and take the wins for granted. I know when I have a bet on a football game, the first three quarters hardly move me. Halfway through the last quarter, the adrenaline starts flowing. The last five minutes of the game, if it is on TV, find me kneeling two inches from the screen. I love the action, the walking on the edge, so to speak, and I especially love the winning. The thrill of victory never loses its feeling of total joy. And then there are the losses. Besides the prospect of spending the rest of the night with sore knees, you also die a little with every losing game. Naturally, there's always tomorrow, but the abrupt finality of a tough loss lingers for several hours. Is it all worth it???

But when you get into a hot streak, I mean a trend that sees you win consistently over a couple of weeks, picking up last second victories and almost impossible wins, it is a new ball game. Not many people can handle this tremendous swing in emotional ups and downs.

Set your bankroll at a decent figure. That's Discipline, but it also lessens the hurt if you do lose. A win—any win—regardless of the amount, by either the novice, and certainly by the professional, is a very relieved feeling.

Just to give some added input from some well-known professional gamblers, I spent some time talking with many of them to get their personal views as to the most important aspects of the game. Most of their comments revolved around the things that I have been repeating over and over. I'm aware that I repeat some of these things, but it is done intentionally. I'll list the things that were mentioned by 90% of these pros:

1. Set your bankroll at a decent amount—no scared money
2. Learn every possible thing about the game you decide to play
3. Play the games that have the least vig. In Craps, play the parts of the table that offer the least chance of losing.
4. Set a logical Win Goal
5. Set an intelligent Loss Limit. (These two, believe it or not, were at the top of every list, bar none.)
6. Have the guts to walk on the days when everything is going bad.

All of these things have been elaborated upon, and it was heartening to hear that the people I spoke to all listed these important facets. The professional follows all of these rules, and while he still suffers the inevitable bad days, the bumpy rides are not disastrous. The boob turns every ride on the gambling roller coaster into a crash over the side of a cliff. No Discipline.

There is a certain oddity about many professional gamblers that doesn't apply to me but is still prevalent in many. That is the fact that most of them concentrate on one game. Naturally, they are expert in the game they choose, but it is the only game they play.

I know of some professional Blackjack players who wouldn't know a Hard Ten on the craps table from a perfect 10 at the local house of ill repute. They simply never go near a craps table—it's not their game. (I don't know of their experiences with the perfect 10's.)

Some professional poker players wouldn't know the horse's ear from his rear. And in the same vein, a professional horse bettor considers the poker player a nonentity in his estimation of a professional player. But all realize the fantastic amount of insight you must have in a game, before you can risk your money.

That's why many of them concentrate on only one outlet. And who's to say they're wrong.

A professional Craps player will spend hours charting a table or tables, and roam from casino to casino, until he locates one that he feels is ready to fall prey to his betting method.

The novice gets out of his car, races pell mell into the casino, grabs the first spot he finds at a table, and immediately buys in. If there's no room at the craps table, he'll play Blackjack, or Roulette, or the slots. Anything that offers him a chance to gamble. He's a professional loser. He's an expert at that.

I, personally, enjoy sports betting. Football, baseball, and basketball offer the greatest interest to me. Maybe it's the challenge of the chase, but it seems I become more "pumped up" for greater periods of time, than with the casino games, which, to me, is like a day at the office.

I'm a card counter in Blackjack, a strong hedge bettor in Craps, and have an excellent nigh perfect method at Baccarat. I also delve into the exciting game of Poker, especially High/Low. But that is unique in gamblers, as most pros concentrate on one game in particular, and occasionally a "minor" interest in another game, just in case their "major" might be running a little bad.

I'd probably bet on the commercials on TV, if they offered a line. But you can be sure my homework would be done before I made an investment. How can anyone invest even one dime in something without knowing the subject inside and out?

And that brings us back to you. Follow the patience and perseverance of the professional. Take a game—say Craps—and perfect it. I mean really conquer it. Learn every single, solitary possible thing that could happen, and its variations. Follow Discipline techniques, and then attack that game. That's the road the professional gambler takes. He wins more than he loses. And so could you. . . .

DISCIPLINE 7

The Big Shot

I just have to use a chapter to talk about the plunger, the big shot. He's in every casino. You can spot him by his bankroll, and also by his mouth.

Now, I'm not talking about the big bettor, the guy who really has the bread to make large wagers. I'm talking about the bettor with only a fair bankroll, but an enormous yen to bet gigantic amounts.

I was at a craps table recently when two such gentlemen walked up. They dropped a fistful of hundred dollar bills on the table, and made sure everyone within six tables knew about it.

They wanted to know the pit boss's first name—probably to hit him up for a free lunch or dinner. But they told him that after they won the casino, he was sure of a permanent job with them. I knew right away they were standing in it—up to their armpits. The dealers were duked $5 chips every other roll, because they were smart enough to call these two jerks by their desired name: "Sir" (which of course they call all the players).

Their buy-in was for $10,000 and the first Pass Line bet was $300, double odds, with $300 placed on each number. They picked up some initial hits, and immediately started pressing the bets.

At one point, they gave a cocktail waitress a black $100 chip for a couple of scotches. The reason I know, is that they proclaimed it to the world, before they deposited the chip between her unmentionables. The girl did a quintuple take, and you knew right then that the service at that table would increase four hundred fold. That move with the cocktail waitress seemed to raise the noise level at that table to a pitch above the first atomic bomb.

At the time, I thought that these two heavy hitters probably hadn't taken their kids to a movie in six months, because it was too expensive, and now they act as if a $100 chip is like so much bother to keep in their rack.

After about an hour of watching them run their stake close to $25,000 with very enormous wagers, and even getting the house to lift the table maximum, the inevitable happened, as it so often does. The trend took a sharp turn against them.

The cooling off period wiped them out, and was followed by another grandstand play of getting a marker for an additional $10,000. They lapped up the attention they got, when play was halted, while their new stake was counted out.

When play resumed, their betting habits and their mouths were functioning at super high levels. In all honestly, I was very amused by their actions. It was so typical of the big shot. I waited for the "difference" to happen. It did. It took a long time, but it finally did, as it always must.

They started to lose again. When they were winning, they poured it in—trying to win bigger. When they lost, they still poured it in, hoping to come back. All they knew was the big bet. Anything less was apparently beneath them.

The two hot shots were soon shot down to reality. The $100 bets dropped to green $25 chips, and finally, one or two red $5 chips represented their bet. The big shot attitude was replaced by the moaning about bad luck, and all the usual griping.

Eventually, these two characters were destroyed. As loud as they were when winning, the sound of their silence was even more penetrating. I watched them. The pain of disappointment was clearly shown on their faces. They cursed every roll, yelled at the other players, ridiculed the ones playing small amounts if they didn't pop out a hot roll, became surly to the dealers, and worst of all, tried to embarrass the waitress who was the beneficiary of the big tips. That's T-I-P-S. At one point, they accused her of looking for another big payoff. Their lack of class showed them for what they really were. If I didn't feel so sorry for them, it would be easy to hate them. But the pathetic part is that there are so many of these types at the tables.

The table remained cold, and the swing in their fortunes was thousands and thousands of dollars. All I could remember was the typical way they played when they had some chips, pouring in stacks of money, acting like it was so unimportant. The craving to be noticed, to be played up to by casino personnel, is always apparent with these types.

Small bets never interest them. This drive to be noticed is the underlying reason why they make these ridiculous bets. Otherwise, why would their actions take such a complete turnaround when they start getting beat. If they're such big shots that they can act like dopes at the table, why should losing a few thousand dollars upset them? The answer is that they are NOT big shots and can't afford the losses. The real jerk in them shows through when party time is over.

The big shots. You see them every day. Different faces, different sizes, different casinos, same style.

I don't know what drives them to play like they do, but the results are usually the same. The casinos recognize the big shot. They give him plenty of rope.

The big shot has his own tree. . . .

DISCIPLINE 8

Charting a Table

It works in Blackjack, when you look for the cold dealer. It works in Baccarat, when you look for the way the trend is going, either bank or player is dominating. It works in sports, when you see which teams play well at certain stadiums or gyms. And it works in Craps.

A shooter picks up the dice to begin his roll: 7, 11, 3, 7, 12, 7, 2, 7, 7, establish a point of 4, and then seven out.

How do you chart that run? You can't. Both right and wrong bettors got whacked. The shooter is neither hot nor cold. That roll cannot be figured either way. And that's not an isolated instance.

Recently, I was playing Craps in Atlantic City, and betting just the 6 and 8, after the come-out, so I wasn't involved in the come-out roll.

A little old man—I swear it—it was funny to me, because I wasn't involved, picked up the dice. He threw 7, craps, 7, craps, 7, craps, 11, 11, craps, before he established the 6. I did not get on that hand. He threw a few more numbers and then sevened out. The looks and comments he got from the right bettors could melt bricks. And this type of thing goes on constantly.

To chart a table, you do not necessarily have to be leaning right or wrong. If you enter the casino, intent on betting the Pass Line that day, you will look only for hot tables. If you've decided to bet wrong, you'll look for cold tables.

If you're looking to follow a trend, or play the system shown in certain chapters which calls for a quick hit and run, you can decide which way to wager after the dice show a definite trend.

You know, if you intend to really practice the art of charting, there may be times when you won't find what you're looking for, until many hours have passed. Maybe there's no room for you at a certain game. Well, don't stand there, wasting your time doing any more charting. You might not be able to even make a bet.

Some days it takes me three hours to find the situation that is geared for my intended type of play. Sometimes I still get beat, but more often than not, the trend will remain for awhile. You call it a waste of time? I call it Discipline.

DISCIPLINE 9

Learning How to Win

I know—I've said it before, but since we're winding down toward the end of the book, there's nothing wrong with one more pointed message on this all-important part of gambling.

Craps is a rough game, where Money Management will dominate any session. The flow of the game is so swift that huge bets can be won or lost in the few seconds it takes for the dice to travel the length of the table.

I know of professional players who have a super conservative method of play that defies some of the theories that I endorse. In their case, in which they agree that trends dominate, they do not wait for a certain winning streak to reach red hot numbers.

This is their theory, and who's to dispute it. They'll chart a craps table and wait for a trend to prevail over a certain period, maybe three shooters.

Let's say the dice are cold. Three successive shooters have established a number and within two more rolls have sevened out. The trend is toward the Don't.

These players will jump in, play against the dice, win their predetermined amount with maybe two shooters, pack it in, and leave that table. They will not wait for the trend to end and possibly eat back into their score.

They are satisfied with small wins, and naturally the Loss Limit is always there to protect them. Suppose a particular table has three consecutive point numbers bite the dust. These players will become involved with a session amount of $300, looking merely to pick up a quick $30. If it covers one shooter—that's it—clear the theater, folks, the fat lady done finished singing—show's over.

They immediately leave that table, $30 to the good, and begin the quest for a definite trend at another game. This hit and run method is not as crazy as it sounds. Sometimes it takes an hour to just find a table heading in one particular direction, over a span of three players, or however many they set in their charting.

After they have won $30 at five different games, they increase the goal to $50, then $75, and so on. A set win amount is put aside as their guarantee, and the excess is used to continue table-hopping.

There's no reason you couldn't apply the same method—if you so desired—to your play, and don't laugh at the suggestion that I'll give you. We'll assume that $200 is your total bankroll, not enough to even divide into $100 sessions. Here's how you could handle it:

1. Divide the $200 into eight sessions of $25 each
2. Chart the table, waiting for a three player swing either way
3. Set Win Goal of $5
4. Set Loss Limit of $15
5. Continue with these sessions until your total net win is $50 regardless of how many sessions it took, then break it in half
6. Accept $25 as your guarantee for the day
7. Continue additional sessions with the $25 excess, and play until another $50 is realized
8. Divide $50 in half, 50% with the previous guarantee of $25 and 50% with your excess
9. Increase session money and Win Goals until you either lose the excess or win another $50
10. The longer you play, the higher your sessions will become, and the higher amount you will want to win with one shooter
11. As you increase the amount you win per session, the normal splitting of each session amount, will keep increasing your guarantee

Nothing fancy about this method: It allows the player with a short bankroll the chance to play within my regular method, but forces him to accept small, quick wins, and then depart that table.

You will learn how to win, and you will love it. Naturally, the hardest part will still entail leaving a table before the trend changes, and after picking up only a $5 score. But, if you can conquer that obstacle, you'll take a big stride in the direction of getting Discipline. You larger heeled players can use the same pattern, and your goal per table can be higher, but only if your starting session money is considerably higher. The variations, naturally, will be up to you, depending on your total bankroll. Set charts for bankrolls of $100, $200, $300, and so on, even $3,000. The people of whom I speak that play this way have a tremendous bankroll, yet this is their method of play. They love it. They work at it. Could it work for you? Of course it can. Will you try it? . . .

Learning How to Win!!! My heavens, if you only realized how important that is.

DISCIPLINE 10

The Author and Discipline

I've been gambling since New York was a prairie, or so it seems. If I owned the state, I wouldn't have sold Manhattan like the Indians; I would have flipped them for it. I enjoy the thrill of the chase, the action, the walking on the edge. A lot of people do.

The professional gamblers are a breed apart. I don't buy that bunk that they are compulsive. I look at it as a business, but a very, very exciting one. It seems that the anticipation of the bet offers a greater thrill than the game itself. And this is true in many, many, many things we undertake. Think about it.

When the session, or game, is over, the winning is very satisfying, but the losing leaves a helpless empty feeling in your gut. Most people can't handle that and start betting more and more, trying to recoup the losses. That's the road to destruction.

The professional does not travel that road. But I believe that at one point in his life, he took his share of lumps. The ones who were able to overcome the bad times and put their act together have made gambling a business.

I've suffered through the bad times and they were rotten. It was always my opinion that knowing all about the games would allow me to win consistently. Well, I did win, and win, and win, but never ended up a winner.

That's not as redundant as it sounds. Years ago, I'd be at a craps table for eight hot shooters in a row, run my $400 session money up to $4,000 and end up washing dishes for a meal that night.

Well, this went on for many years, and I was going no

place. Sure it was a great life, gambling on everything, betting morning, noon and night, but the outcome always had the hero taking the beating. I never lost millions or borrowed money or property. What I did lose was the money I managed to get ahead, and it took a long time to realize I must be doing something wrong.

As you get older, you don't lose your desire to gamble, but the desire to win becomes prevalent. I had to force myself to win small amounts. I mean miniscule returns on my investments. And bingo, the tide done turned.

I acquired Discipline. Sure, I wanted to win bigger amounts, but you know, the thrill of gambling to win replaced the thrill of gambling to gamble.

I've been down that road of false excitement. And my desire to gamble was born of the NEED of which I spoke earlier. I believe my need was the constant excitement which is generated by every form of gambling. I still have the need for the constant pumping of adrenaline that gambling provides. I love it.

I look forward to walking on the edge, but you can bet the mortgage I won't fall off the deep end. In no way, shape or form, under any conditions whatsoever, will I get wiped out. I will never, ever lose more than my Loss Limit. It's absolutely impossible for me to go broke.

I have only the "broke" times to remind me to keep a clear head. And this gives me the right to preach to you. I've been whacked many, many, many, many times, and know what you're going through. I know you are tired of losing and I know you have this "need" that must be satisfied.

I'm showing you how. It is a disciplined approach to an exciting game. And the method works.

You don't have to be a professional gambler to win. But you don't have to play like a dope just because you're not a professional gambler. Take it from a former jerk, and a former loser: the name of the game is winning, and it beats losing, every time.

DISCIPLINE 11

Discipline: The Name of the Game

You get the idea that Discipline is the name of the game. It is, and it isn't.

Discipline is a part of the Big 4, and without all facets of that Big 4, you can't and won't win. All the Discipline in the world isn't gonna help you, if you bring $6.98 to the table.

So you must have a bankroll to compete, and you must know how to play, which is Knowledge of the Game. You also must know how to bet, which is Money Management. Discipline is the final ingredient, and while it may be the most important, it still needs the other three to set up the opportunity to practice Discipline.

One more time, and you don't have to listen to me again: The Big 4!

Bankroll: The amount you bring to a casino, and it should be in line with the figures I've given you. In Craps, a $5 table requires about $150 that you should have available. Each session calls for you to have ten times the amount of what you wager on the first shooter. That session amount is multiplied by three to form your bankroll. Don't play short and don't play scared.

Knowledge of the Game: You gotta be perfect. Being good, or pretty good, or very good is not good enough. And you should know everything about the game you attack. It's money you're risking, baby, and unless you got it to burn, you should treat it with respect. Learn the various plays at a craps table, and which bets offer you the least chance of losing.

Knowledge—the easiest part of the Big 4 to acquire, yet how many of you have it to perfection???

Money Management: Stand at a craps table sometime and watch the different modes of betting. Pick out a couple of people and check the different ways they bet on the same situations. There is no set pattern for their moves. Knowing when to increase your bets and when to decrease them is called Money Management. It is an art—the skill of each player to know what his next wager will be. Yet at the casinos, and in all forms of gambling, Money Management is usually invisible, because the majority of people simply don't have it. Is it important??? It's a must, my friend. Money Management is to gambling what legs are to walking. Do you need legs to walk??? Well, you need Money Management to gamble.

Discipline: We've come to the bottom line. The part of the Big 4 that separates the men from the boys, the winners from the losers, and most people from their money. Discipline is tough to acquire and rough to apply. In simple terms, if you follow my Win Goals and Loss Limits, you will win consistently, and when you lose, the losses will be minimized. If you do not have these controls, you will keep losing. It's as simple as that. If you do not have Discipline, get it or quit gambling.

This concludes my preaching about controls in gambling. Now you must decide if you want to play to play, or play to win. The choice is yours.

Craps is an exciting game, but should not be played for thrills. It should be played for profit, and don't give me that nonsense that you only go to a casino for excitement. You want excitement, get yourself a plane ticket to Russia, and carry an American Flag down the streets of Moscow singing "Three Cheers for the Red, White, and Blue." You'll have all the excitement you can absorb.

But if you want to gamble, play to win. You wouldn't have gotten this far in the book if you weren't looking for ways to win. And win you will.

You can't win all the time, that's impossible. But your losses will be minimized, and when your streak comes, the Money Management systems will get you maximum returns.

It's up to each of you, individually, to accept these words of advice: The fruits of victory taste very sweet. Take a big bite.

DISCIPLINE 12

Wrapping Up Discipline

I think I've covered all the bases on the trip around the craps table. It all begins with your buy-in, which is based on your bankroll. You play the method that suits you best, as long as you have a complete knowledge of that system. By applying proper Money Management to whichever method you play, you'll stay alive until your streak comes.

And if you follow the Discipline that is stressed in this section, you will Learn How to Win. Simple isn't it? It sure is.

After reading these pages, I'm sure you're aware of the importance of Discipline, if you weren't already. You can make all kinds of promises to follow the restrictions to the letter, but the proof comes when you get to the tables and become an accomplished player.

Just for smiles, after you make yourself the perfect player, spend some time watching a typical craps game, and pick up the mistakes made by those players. See if you can spot the "old" you in their play.

In summary:

1. Break bankroll into sessions, preferably three, or more if you have the money.
2. Predetermine your Win Goal, based on session money.
3. Predetermine your Loss Limit, based on session money.
4. Determine which method you will play.
5. Chart the tables, until you find one that is leaning toward your system.
6. Base your goals on dollar amounts, not time limits.
7. Be sure your Win Goal is low enough to be reached

quickly, especially in the beginning, until you conquer the art of winning.

8. When you hit your goal, divide it in half. Put 50% away, and play with the excess.
9. Every succeeding winning series, after the guarantee is reached, should again be divided in half, with 50% going with the guarantee and 50% staying with the excess.
10. You may stay at that table, as long as you do not dip below your Loss Limit.
11. Leave that table if you lose first four series.
12. Leave table when you reach Loss Limit.
13. Stay at table as long as excess stays alive.
14. Do not change systems at a session. You wanna change? Go to another table.
15. Don't take your eyes off your wagers while they're in action.
16. Keep super accurate account of your chips, so that you know when your limits or goals are reached.
17. A series begins with a win and continues as long as you keep winning. When a loss occurs, that series is over. Each shooter is considered a new series.
18. You absolutely, positively must have your predetermined series bets decided upon, before you begin your session.
19. You can never deviate from this predetermined series plan. Once you do, you've commited the cardinal sin of Discipline. It probably means you were losing, and started betting less. If that's the case, you should have left the table.

If you adhere to these rules, your entire game will change. It will take a strong disciplined approach, but that's where they separate the winners from the losers. Beats being separated from your money.

This wraps up Discipline. The chapters are short, the messages seem redundant, but Discipline is the name of the game.

You got it? Flaunt it!!!!!

You don't got it? Get it!!!!!

ODDS AND ENDS 1

Tipping

Let's get right to it. It's a touchy subject and can only be handled with a direct approach. Yet, there is also the fact that since the human element is involved there is always the chance of error.

Why do you tip? For service, for information, for a favor; any of these factors could be the reason. In the casinos, the dealers love to be tipped, or duked, as they call it. And why not? I've never met a dealer yet who said: "No, no, that's OK, sir, I don't like to be tipped."

The tips are the difference in whether the dealers will have a good or bad week, in terms of dollars and cents. The base pay is not fabulous, so the extra money kind of sweetens the pot. The dealers look for these tokes.

In Vegas, the dealers are allowed to keep their tips, as patrons drop the chip in the shirt pocket of the dealer they are tipping. In Atlantic City, the tips collected during a certain shift are divided among the dealers working during those hours.

The way you tip in Blackjack is to simply place a chip, usually $1 for the $5 player, next to your wager, for that hand. That signifies that the dealer is playing that particular hand. If you win, he does too.

Suppose you bet $5 on your hand, and wagered one white chip ($1) for the dealer. You'd place it a few inches away from your $5 chip. First off, you know you have his attention. He sure as heck is rooting for you to win, 'cause it's gravy for him if you do.

You win. He places a $5 winning chip next to your bet.

Then he places $1 winning chip next to the wager you made for him, picks up the $2, and taps the table. This alerts the pit boss that he is placing a winning bet from the player into the plastic box that hangs on the rear end of the table.

Naturally, he'll thank you and he'll remember who you are. In fact, when he leaves the table, for his break, or at the end of his shift, he will point you out to his relief. The signal will usually be: "Good luck to you, sir." Or, "Thanks for the action, sir." Or he'll simply tell the oncoming dealer: "Take care of this lady for me, she's OK." Right off the bat, the new dealer knows that a tipper is at the table. Usually, when one player starts tipping, it wakes up the other combatants, and the dealer can reap in quite a windfall, if he plays it right.

Why do you tip? I've already covered the universal reasoning, but there is also this story that is circulated, whether true or false, no one but the dealers will ever know (and they ain't talking).

Rumor has it that some dealers have been known to make mistakes in paying off bets. But, of course, this could be from human failings, tiredness, whatever. Sometimes those mistakes are in favor of the person making the bets for the dealers, but, of course, that may only seem to be the case.

For instance, if you have been duking some dealer over a period of an hour or so, he sure is hoping you win, for two reasons. One, he now likes you because you've been getting him involved in the action, and two, he wants to keep you at the table.

Let's assume you've been a pretty generous player at this particular table. Eventually you are dealt a hand of A, 2, 2, 10, 3, for a total of 19. Or at least that's the way it looks to the dealer. He's completed his hand with 10, 3, 2, 3 for a total of 18. Maybe he counted his hand as 17, or maybe he counted yours as 19. Who knows? But, instead of tapping the table to signify a tie, or push, he pays off as if you had a winning hand of 19—versus his 18. He scoops up the cards, and proceeds to start another hand.

Of course, it's easy to make a mistake in what is called a string hand. That means the cards are strung out, and sometimes it's difficult to count quickly. Then again, someone watching, who picks up the error, probably thinks he miscounted, since there were so many cards involved, and nothing is said.

Well, how about the pit boss or floor person? Shouldn't these sharp people be able to pick up these errors? Sure they should, but they have several tables to watch, many people to rate, figures to be kept. They can't watch every single hand at every table.

They also understand that occasionally these things happen, and, what the heck, that player who is the recipient of the error will think only good things about that casino, and come back again. Probably, the player will bet that "mistake" back into the coffers of the house.

Finally, that pit boss was once a dealer and realizes that these things could happen. Should you tip? Of course. Why not? But, there are times when you should. I tip all the time, but only when winning. If I'm losing, it may be only a matter of hands before I leave that table, hardly enough time for that dealer to become careless.

I usually start off tipping $1, and repeat it every five or six rolls, as I continue to win. As my bets increase, and the poor dealer suddenly begins getting weary and happens to make a mistake in my favor, I try to reawaken him by jumping up the size of my tips. Works wonders.

However, if that dealer remains a sullen, crabby, uninterested recipient, I figure the heck with him, and stop tipping. Let him fall right across the table in total exhaustion, I no longer try to get his attention. There are people who don't know how to tip or do it in a shabby way:

1. The big mouth who drops a tip for the dealer and proclaims it loud enough so that the pit boss can hear him, three sections down. He's looking for a free meal.
2. The guy who tips $1 once every three hours, and reminds the dealer every other hand that he did so. This guy is just an out and out boob.
3. The hot shot who plays a hand for the dealer, then unashamedly states: "Don't forget to take care of me." He just tied that dealer's hands in knots.

4. The itchy guy who plays at a table, never saying a word, and when he gets up to leave, drops a couple of chips "for the boys." OK, that's great, the dealers like that. But they don't get a chance to help him out while he's at the table. Don't tip when you leave—like it's a restaurant. If you're gonna duke the dealer, do it while you're in action, not at the end of the play.

Another thing, don't just give the tip to the dealer, play it for him. Again, two reasons. First, you take the chance he'll forget you—though that's gotta be a dope of a dealer. The thing is to keep him interested in your play. And second, he stands to win more by having the bet in action.

I've already covered tipping at a Blackjack table. In Roulette, merely place a chip on top of your wager, off to the side, and indicate to the dealer: "For the girls."

In Craps, there are several ways to tip. The most common is the hard way bet. By tossing two chips into the center of the table and saying: "Two-way Hard Six, please," you are telling the stickman to put one chip on the Hard Six for you, and one for the dealers. If the Hard Six shows, you will be paid $9 for your end. The boxman will then take $9 payoff, plus the $1 hard way bet that was for the dealers, tap the table, and deposit $10 into the tip box. Notice that the bet for the dealers does not stay in action after it hits. It must go right down.

Some players make the Any Craps bet for the dealers, and some play the Yo. These are one-roll action plays and don't offer them as good a shot as the hard way move.

Still others will make a play on either the Pass Line, or Don't Pass Line for the dealers. Now, you've really got their attention. When the player makes a $5 bet on the line, and takes the odds, for the dealers, you're giving them a nice shot for a decent return. Sometimes that player will state: ". . . for the boys, and I'll control the bet." He is telling the boxman that if the bet wins, instead of it being paid off and going right into the tip box, the player, usually with the acceptance of one of the dealers, will let it ride on the next roll.

This way, the dealers are caught up in the game, and have a chance to partake in a hot roll. Now they'll remember you.

A while ago, a friend of mine was playing at a casino in Atlantic City and picking up a sizable wad betting Don't. His session lasted for quite some time, and he soon started placing $5 bets on the Don't Pass, and telling the dealer nearest to him: "Boys play on the Don't."

The dealer nearest to him thanked him, as did the stickman, also the oncoming relief dealers, who were quickly alerted to who he was by the dealer that was going on a break, stating: "Take care of my friend, here."

My buddy told me that he was surprised how sometimes the dealers forgot to take off his Don't Come bets when they were hit. Then again, the Don't Come bets, placed as they are on top of the Place numbers, can easily be overlooked by a dealer, during the hustle and bustle of taking and paying off at a crowded table. He figures they forgot to take down at least six of his bets that he lost.

The super fast action at a craps table does tend to cause some things to be overlooked, and mistakes are made because of the swiftness with which money changes hands. The boxman, who was also once a dealer and went through these hectic sessions, naturally doesn't share in the tips, but he too sometimes fails to catch a mistake that a dealer might make in favor of a player. Sometimes he is caught up in the action at another spot on the table, and fails to catch a dealer who forgets to take down a losing bet.

If it appears that the receiver of this good fortune happens to be a tipper, then "bravo," let the good times roll.

So you see, it doesn't hurt to tip, and the dealers do deserve it. Most of them are friendly, decent people, who have absolutely no desire to see you lose. The turn of a card or roll of the dice is not controlled by them, so stop thinking they are to blame—if you do lose.

When you tip, use class, do it in a soft manner, not a boisterous show of your overinflated ego. The dealers will get the message. You're not dealing with idiots.

And the pit bosses will observe and note your generosity. In the long run, a sort of mutual respect will develop. It's how you lay the groundwork. If you are fortunate to find a dealer who becomes very careless, and starts paying you when you push or lose—after you've tipped him a few times, remember what he looks like. And the next time you play, make sure it's at his table.

(And don't forget to send me his name, and the casino he operates out of.)

Should you tip? In a roundabout way, I think I've made my point.

ODDS AND ENDS 2

Comps

Comes from the word complimentary. It is a gift from the casino, in the way of a meal or show. Usually these comps are reserved for the higher roller, the people who have large credit lines, and consistently bet stacks of chips.

The casinos vie for the big bettors, and what better way to keep that person coming to that particular casino, than to offer him meals, rooms, and preferential treatment.

The problem with comps is that the mere idea of them has become somewhat of an obsession with a great many players. I don't know if it's a status symbol or what, but I get asked the same question over and over: "How do you get comps?" The easiest answer is for you to bet higher. Many people have told me how much they bet at a table, just to get a free meal, and some of these plungers are playing with short bankrolls.

Why is it so important that you get comped? Do you think that you've beaten the house out of something? So many times—more than you can imagine—a guy at a $5 craps table, playing the Pass Line, with a couple of place bets, will suddenly ask for a meal.

He might only be in action about a half hour, and right away he thinks the casino owes him something. It doesn't. The house is there to make money. You have a chance to beat it, and are welcome to play as long or as short a period as you like.

When the pit boss sees a high roller, or a lot of action at a table in Vegas, he'll call over the cocktail waitress, and offer everyone free drinks. This has been going on for years. It is the house's way of keeping players at that table, figuring that when the trends go against those contestants, they'll still hang around, as long as they've got a drink to hang onto. There's nothing wrong with that. The comps are also given to the players at the table, to show the gratitude of casinos for you giving them the action. It's their money, and if they want to treat people to drinks, that's their privilege.

When Atlantic City opened, they didn't have to wait for the tables to become full. The casinos are so consistently crowded that they keep the cocktail waitresses hopping all day long. In Atlantic City, the idea is not to hold the players at the table—it is a simple case of good public relations.

Those people are going to be there, drinks or no drinks, but the casinos still offer them, free. A player showing a distinct lack of class starts badgering the dealer, the boxman, and the pit boss, over and over, asking for the cocktail waitress. It's as if they are demanding that they be served immediately. Jerks!!! They act like they never received a free drink before, and that if they don't get it, they're being gyped.

Now, over and above the free drinks that are provided, the casino retains the right to give a free meal, show, room, whatever, to whomever it pleases. It chooses to give them to the high rollers, who understandably do not ask for them, as much as the smaller bettor.

Some players almost resort to begging in an effort to get taken care of. They're pitiful in their direct attempts to be catered to. Many times the pit boss has to out-and-out tell that player that his action is just not heavy enough. You'd think he punched the beggar in the mouth. The jerk is indignant over the fact that the $100 he is betting is not appreciated more, and he's going to take his action elsewhere.

I've been at tables where a guy would walk up, buy in for $100, make a bet, and immediately ask the pit boss where the cocktail waitress is. Who the heck does this boob think he is? Just because he's got his lousy $100 in play, does he think the casino "has" to comp him? Atlantic City spoiled a lot of people who think getting a free drink is all part of the game. It's not. Be thankful you get it, and don't give me that garbage that you're spending your money there and they should take care of you. The reason you are supposed to be there is to try and win the casinos' money. You are trying to beat them, and now you want them to feed you while you're taking your shot. What kinky ideas you have.

While we're on the subject of free drinks, let me touch a little on the matter of class. If you do receive a free drink, it wouldn't hurt you to drop a chip for the waitress. I'm positively not shilling for them, but you are getting something for nothing, and it wouldn't hurt to show appreciation. Sometimes I see a girl bring a round of drinks to a table and the patrons take their treat like it is the casino's obligation to serve them. I'm not telling you to throw $5, or even $1. I am suggesting that you drop "something" on her tray.

Ever see the guy at the table who is offered a free drink during the course of his play? Ivan Dry has been playing Craps for about an hour and suddenly becomes very thirsty. Just about that timc, a waitress takes his order for a drink. He is very happy to be getting the comp. First off, he is dry, and second, he is not doing so well, so he figures the casino "owes him one." However, the girl is a little busy and doesn't get back with Ivan's drink for some time. The poor guy has a bad streak and is getting whacked. He gets belted by four shooters in a row and his buddy starts pulling on his arm to leave. "Are you crazy? I ain't leaving till I get my free drink." The poor dope loses $85 waiting for his lousy $1 drink. A typical novice move. But it is that illogical reasoning that many people think that they are getting something for nothing.

I also hear the nonsense about the casinos trying to get you drunk so that you will play stupid and lose. Let me tell you my friend, a lot of players don't have to get drunk to play stupid. These people have that method of play ingrained in them, without any help from liquor. The casinos don't have to try to get people drunk to get them to bet dumb.

I always have a drink in the casino. If you can't handle the liquor while you're playing, don't drink. I enjoy a cocktail during play, but I know my limit. Many players feel the same way. They don't drink to excess, and know when to stop. If you can't drink and play, don't do it. I'm glad the casinos offer these treats, and you should be, too. Take it as it is meant—a gift, and for none of the other silly reasons that you would like to blame on your own losses.

I'm not shilling for the casinos, but only trying to make you see the other side of the coin. I'm attempting to give you an insight into all of the things that are part of the gambling package, and maybe get you to change your approach a little.

Sometimes, a player has a legitimate gripe against the casinos in the way of comps. Since they opened the Pandora's box, by offering rooms, shows, meals, etc. to bigger rollers, where do they draw the line when handing out these comps?

In the first place, that's none of your business. It's their money and their meals and their rooms, and they can give them to whomever they choose. But, since comps are available, a lot of people have a legitimate gripe that their play is not rewarded.

The way to get the attention of the pit boss, who hands out these comps, is to buy in for large sums of money, and play large bets. But, I don't want you to do that because it will affect your Money Management method. Don't let the prospect of a lousy $15 meal influence your play at the tables.

There are players who do have the heavy bankrolls, and you guys and gals can utilize your heavy play to get the comps that the casinos are offering. But don't just put your money on the table in bits and pieces. If you've decided to risk $750 at a session, pop it right out there in your buy-in. The pit boss will keep a record of your play, and more often than not he will come over and offer you a meal. If he doesn't, you could, in a nice dignified manner, ask him if there was a possibility of having dinner for two.

If he says no, and you feel you have been playing pretty heavily for a period of time, then you could choose to take your action elsewhere. Don't broadcast it to the world, just pack it in and open a line of credit at a casino where you will be appreciated.

Many times the pit boss will approach you at a table, usually if you're betting higher amounts, and ask for your name, saying he wants to rate you. What he does is put your name on the computer to see if you have credit in other casinos, and if you have a history of heavy betting. When he asks for your name for rating purposes, he's looking to keep your action. At that time, you could very courteously tell him: "Sure, I'd be happy to give you any information you'd like, but in return I'd appreciate a breakfast (or lunch) for my wife and me."

This has to be done in a classy way, and only if he requests information from you. If you warrant a meal, the casino will probably reciprocate, but if it doesn't, you're really not out anything.

The reason I am spending so much time on this subject is because of the interest that is generated by these comps. But my concern for you people reading these pages is more pointed in the direction of winning at the tables and not being bothered with the side nonsense.

If comps are your thing, and you want to insure your being treated to some extras, let me give you some moves you might follow:

1. Your buy-in must be very good, perhaps $1,000, but at least $500
2. Your play should encompass $25 per roll, or hand
3. Your play should be over a period of time, perhaps two or three hours
4. You have to do this in the same casino for a period of time, not just one day

The above is geared for the player who is looking for rooms, meals, shows, etc.

For the player looking to pick up a meal, the following is a guide:

1. Your buy-in should be decent, perhaps $200 or $300 per session
2. You must bet at least $10 per roll, or hand
3. You also should be in action for several hours, and each pit boss, at the different tables you play, should get the chance to rate you, otherwise how would he know you've been playing for some time
4. You must frequent the same casino over a period of months

But come on, a lot of the above is against the grain of what I am harping about as to controlled play. If you can, put the idea of comps out of your head for awhile. If I can get you to play intelligently, win some decent sessions, and cut your losses, it will be only a matter of time until you will be playing with higher amounts, and the comps will come often. You won't have to beg for them.

For you people who are obsessed with comps, try and tone down your quest for them. Accept the drinks, handle yourself in a dignified way, and stop acting like you're there just to pick up freebies.

A comp is a gift, and you don't beg for gifts.

ODDS AND ENDS 3

Etiquette

I don't give a rat's tail if you've never been to the tables, or if you're a daily visitor. there is a way to conduct yourself in the casino. It's called class. And baby, those with it carry a glow about them.

The dealers, floor people, pit bosses, anybody, can spot it. It's how you handle yourself with the casino personnel. They can read each player in a matter of minutes. They know when you're playing scared, playing stupid, or playing smart, within a few rolls of the dice.

If you need information or change or a number to be placed, do it in a courteous, quiet manner. Know how to ask for a bet or how to make change. Always say please, and try not to antagonize the dealer or other players at a table.

It will work wonders when it comes time to receive a comp or establish a credit line with these houses. You will be treated in the same dignified manner in which you conduct yourself.

At a craps table, here are a few tips to follow:

1. Don't force yourself in at a crammed table. There are usually eight people on each side of a table, depending on the width of two or three of the players.
2. Chart a table before you enter the game. Make sure the flow is in favor of the way you will be betting.
3. When buying in, wait for the dealer to be free before placing your money down.
4. Drop money in front of you, and be sure it is the session amount I've laid out.

5. When he gives you the chips, count them, and then drop two $5 chips on table and tell him: "Change, please," or "Break it down, please."
6. When you get in the game, make your bets as soon as possible.
7. If you were to place some numbers, drop chips toward dealer, and say: "Place the six and eight, please" (or whatever numbers you desire).
8. Proposition bets are tossed in front of the stickman, not the dealer.
9. When shooter is throwing dice from the far part of table, get your hands out of the way. (When the dice hit somebody's hands, it infuriates everyone at the table.)
10. Don't leave your hands dangling over the side of the table.
11. When it's your turn to throw the dice, don't be a "fixer." (Don't feel you have to position the dice a certain way—it doesn't work—honest!) Just toss them casually to the other side of the table.
12. Try not to throw the dice so hard that they bounce off the table.
13. Both dice must hit the far wall of the table.
14. Don't take dice off the table, out of sight of the dealers.
15. Don't touch dice with both hands—this is a no-no. (You would be suspected of being a mechanic, someone who can switch another set of dice into the game.)
16. Know the correct odds to lay and the correct odds to take.
17. Learn the correct jargon of the table (see Place betting chapters for explanations).
18. If you win, take your chips as soon as you're paid.
19. Don't keep resorting to asking the dealer the correct odds or payoffs, or bothering him. If he wants to talk, let him take the initiative. (You shouldn't play if you don't have the rules down pat, anyway.)
20. Don't be a crybaby if you lose or a braggart when you win.
21. If you're losing, don't start burdening your neighbor

about how bad things are going. He's probably got enough problems of is own.

22. Don't start begging for a comp. You're being watched. If you deserve it, based on your play (amounts you bet), you'll be offered it.
23. If you've been making some healthy bets, maybe $30 or $40 per shooter, and up (including Place bets), and the pit boss starts a conversation with you, then you could question him as to the possibility of getting a meal. In this case, he's made the first move in talking with you.
24. I know you want the world to know when you've won. (The world doesn't care—honest, it doesn't.) See if you can't win or lose without broadcasting it. Remember, there are a lot of losers at that table who don't exactly share in your good fortune, especially if they're going bad that day.

These are a few of the basic rules of conduct at a table. I know you feel it's part of the fun to "let it all hang out," so to speak. But, I'm trying to cover all the things that will come up in the course of a day, and if you can adopt this "class act approach," I think you'll find yourself being noticed more, and it may prove beneficial to you some day.

ODDS AND ENDS 4

Crooked Dice

What would a book on Craps be unless it had a chapter on the use of crooked dice in a casino. You hear the wails, usually from the losers, that a certain game is fixed. It is an excellent way of offsetting the fact that this boob got beat. Right away, he yells: "Fix"—"Cheats"—"Call the Cops"—"I wuz robbed." I'll list the complaints that come from the players of the various games:

1. CRAPS ....The dice are loaded
2. SLOTS ....The house adjusted the machines to avoid payoffs
3. FOOTBALL ....The quarterback deliberately threw the game
4. BASEBALL ....The pitcher was on the take
5. BASKETBALL........Every game has the points shaved
6. BLACKJACK..........................The cards are marked
7. POKER........................He's dealing from the bottom of the deck
8. BINGO ....They don't have all the numbers in the machine
9. HORSE RACING ....The jockey's in the tank
10. TROTS ....The driver intentionally broke that horse
11. ROULETTE ....The ball is magnetized to go in the zero slot

The stories go on and on about how someone "heard" about these fixed games. Well, will you please tell me why some dope would bet on a game or an event, if he even remotely assumed that there was the chance for a fix?

I have honestly had people say the above things to me over and over. They believe these things happen every day. I tell them they see too many movies, and that it is an easy way to explain the fact that they got whacked.

Does cheating exist in our world today? Of course it does. In isolated instances all of the above "may" be true, but not like people are led to believe. There have been proven instances of shaved points, fixed cards, loaded dice, in fact most of the things I've mentioned.

But it is not a common occurrence. People still talk about the point shaving of the 1950s, in basketball. Good grief, based on that situation, and the millions of games that have been played since then, the possibility of fixed games is infinitesimal.

Will you find loaded dice in a casino? You have a better chance of getting a date with Miss World. It is very amusing to watch the action at a craps table in Atlantic City. The dice go off the table and the boxman suddenly reaches panic stage, waiting for the six-headed monster to be returned to the layout. He then goes through the ritual of checking the dice to see if a loaded die has been slipped into the game. He is on center stage for a few minutes, and I always get the feeling that he loves the attention this draws to him. It just seems to me that the ceremony is dragged out a little too long, and if a bogus die was indeed returned to the table, could this fellow detect it? My opinion is . . . but that's another story.

Years ago, I was working at a craps table out west, where a shooter was in the midst of a scorching roll. For over an hour, he held those dice and was absolutely cleaning up. So was every "right" bettor at that table.

As fate would have it, I was on the opposite side of the table, but the dealer next to that hot shooter was raking in tip after tip. Naturally, he got to keep such tokes, as they are not shared by all the dealers at the table.

Anyhow, the hot roll went on and on, and this guy had some load of chips in his rack. Suddenly, on a subsequent roll, I couldn't believe my eyes. The shooter threw the dice across the table, and three dice, not two, stopped in front of me. The guy was a mechanic (dice sleight of hand expert), and as great as they are, they're still susceptible to mistakes.

This poor guy must have had a slippery hand, because he mistakenly let the bogus die come out. The silence was deafening, but the mechanic was as quick as lightning. In the instant that it took me to turn and look at him, he had grabbed a handful of chips and was tearing out the door. (Incidentally, it was the $100 chips that he had the foresight to grab.)

The attempt to find that guy was fruitless, but you can bet he laid low for a long, long time. This thing has happened many times, in various casinos throughout the country, but that was the only time I actually saw it occur. To be honest, it was a source of discussion for the next couple of weeks.

A point I would like to make is that a lot of cheating is done by an individual "against" the casino for personal gain, and not the other way around. The stories of cheating dealers are where they're attempting to steal money from the casino, while working with an outside contact. If, in fact, that dealer is working with an accomplice in an attempt to get money across the dice or Blackjack table, he actually isn't bothering you. He is not taking money from your pocket. His cheating is against the casino. Because of the lack of really good gamblers, the casinos do not have to cheat. The dopey players dig their own graves and usually dive right in.

The bottom line is to put that garbage about fixed or crooked dice from your mind. And finally, if you leave a table after getting whacked for $400, and start complaining that the dice were fixed, you make a bigger fool of yourself.

If you thought the dice were crooked, why the heck did you stay at that table? Do you want me to buy the nonsense that you didn't know they were fixed, until the last roll? And if you knew sooner that something was going on, why would you be so stupid as to stay at that table?

The dice in the casinos are not fixed. The reason you lost was probably a lack of the Big 4, and your own erratic play.

ODDS AND ENDS 5

Luck in a Casino

I hear it one hundred and thirty-two times a week. I hear it from $5 bettors, and $100 plungers. The words come from the mouths of young people, men and women, Craps players, Blackjack players, Roulette players, slot players and horse players. The list goes on and on. The words still drive me up a wall.

"Oh, I'm very lucky in gambling, I win all the time." The second part of the sentence, right away, labels these people as liars. Nobody wins all the time, and that is *nobody.* The people who claim that they do are not worth a retort.

It is to the people who bellow the first part of that sentence that I address this chapter. If you think luck is enough to make you a winner at gambling, you're kidding yourself. Luck is a wonderful thing to have, and I have as much luck as anybody. The only problem is that sometimes it's good and sometimes it's bad. I never know which will show, so I don't think about it or allow it to affect anything I do. My good luck begins when I am able to get up in the morning. My bad luck will take over when I pass away during the night and am not able to get up. But since I won't know about it, I won't worry about bad luck.

I surely do not count on luck in gambling, and certainly don't blame my losses on the lack of same. I beg you to get that nonsense, of luck being able to help you, out of your head. Gambling requires the skill and Discipline of the Big 4 and nothing else.

If you are losing, it is because the way you are betting is against the trend of the dice, and no supernatural factor is working against you. If you honestly think luck works in gambling, there'd be no need for learning anything about a certain game. It would depend on who is lucky and who isn't.

I believe the term "luck" is grossly overused. It is a terrific excuse to fall back on when you lose, but hardly the type of foundation you can expect to use, to build a strong attack on the game you play.

Luck is a figment of one's imagination and is really used to explain the way things happen to be going for each individual, at a certain point in his or her week. The next time a person starts a conversation with the words: "I'm really a lucky person in gambling, and never lose . . ." look him or her straight in the eye and say: "You're a rotten liar."

See if you're *lucky* enough to duck a left hook. Now that's where luck will come in.

ODDS AND ENDS 6

Streaks

Way back in the explanation of the Little 3, I mentioned an important part of gambling. I call it trends, and for the life of me, I cannot explain why trends occur, but they do.

Take a typical craps table in any casino you name. During the course of a certain day, all things being equal, the total number of "games" played that day might number 3,000 on one table.

Since we're talking about a simple Pass Line bet, with single odds, we're covering a part of the game that shows a vig in favor of the house of only .8%. Assuming that the laws of probability stayed in effect that day at that particular table, we could assume the Pass Line would win 1,530 times, and lose 1,470 times. Pretty close to 50%.

But you can bet the mortgage it won't appear, win/lose/win/lose/win/lose/win/lose, all day long. No, there will be streaks occurring both for and against the Pass Line bettors, and that is where the term gambling pops in. Since you do not know what will happen, you are risking your money on these outcomes, so you'd better have a game plan.

It's how you manage your money, that will determine your overall profits and losses for that day. That's why I *beg* you to be aware of these streaks or trends or whatever you call them. Follow those streaks. All that can beat you is a choppy table, but you can walk if that starts to show.

My concern is getting you to look for streaks, wait for streaks, play only with streaks. Someday you'll realize what I'm telling you is sound advice. These streaks will come. Until you get into a streak, bet small. As the dice heat up, you can reinvest the major portion of your winnings, and take advantage of that trend. But wait for it to start. I guarantee this'll happen:

1. You'll hold your losses down.
2. You'll be on the side (either right or wrong) that is prevailing.
3. You'll miss only the initial few rolls of a hot streak (digest this one).
4. You'll have the bankroll to play with—when that big roll does occur.

If you manage your money properly, you'll need only one scorching run per day to make your profit. And that hot roll will show. I want you to be there!!!

ODDS AND ENDS 7

Intimidation

Here is a common malady, suffered by many, many people in a casino. It's the matter of being scared, frightened, awestruck, intimidated: you name it, people go through it. And don't tell me it never hit you. You feel it when you enter a roomful of people, and think everyone is staring at you. You feel it giving a speech before strangers, or meeting your girlfriend's parents for the first time. It's a common fear and we all get affected by it at one time or another.

I give lectures two or three times a week on radio, TV, before clubs, groups, students, whatever, and I never feel intimidated, because I'm used to it, so I got to thinking I'm immune to being uneasy. Baloney!

Last July 4th, my daughters, Lori and Colleen, and I were looking to kill an afternoon. It happened to be a rainy, dreary day, and we decided to go to a movie and perhaps by the time we got out, the storm would have passed and we'd go to the fireworks display.

The show we picked was playing at a nearby house, so we rushed down there and I remember walking in about fifteen minutes after the show was due to begin, but it hadn't started yet. The reason it hadn't started was that nobody was in the place—that is until we sat down. Immediately, the lights went out and the show started. There we were, the three of us, in this huge theater, getting our own private showing. Were we intimidated? You better believe it. In fact, it was downright embarrassing. But the worst part, we knew, was when we had to leave. And when the time came, all three of us felt very, very conspicuous. And yet, all we had to do was walk past about four or five employees in the theater. That was a long walk. Where was all my cockiness? In my left ear. And Lori and Colleen admitted they felt very awkward too. Isn't that awful? You go to see the show *Annie* where Daddy Warbucks hires the whole theater, and you think how great that must be. But when it happens to you in real life, you have trouble handling it.

My associate, Lynn Niglio, has been with me a number of years. To say she is a knockout would only touch on her appeal. If I put her picture on the cover of the book, we'd double the sales. She can walk into a room, know she will be the center of attention, and never let it bother her. She is at home in such a situation, and used to it. In fact, she revels in the attention.

Now, we take her to Atlantic City and have her stand outside the Baccarat pit. Do you think she'd go in there alone? No way. It intimidates her. She admits it. Blackjack tables and Craps games do not bother her, but her Achilles' heel is walking into that Baccarat pit. Lynn could take a bathing suit that was smuggled into this country underneath a postage stamp, and parade down Broadway, without blinking. Oh, some of you guys out there would blink. In fact, you'd lose your eyeballs. But the point is that there are these hang-ups that we have, that cause a panic to develop within ourselves, when we feel out of place.

How many of you are scared of the Craps game, or the speed of the Blackjack tables? You're even scared to buy in at the Roulette wheel. You're scared to make certain plays at the craps table because you think it will antagonize the dealers. Well, these hedge bets and rules of pulling down your bets after two or three hits call for you to bother the dealer, so you'd better change your thoughts as to competing at gambling.

A very good friend of mine, Howie Goldstein, is a joy to be with. Howie is a great player in every part of gambling. He is a card counter, Craps expert, just an out and out good player. He is in Vegas now, but we keep in touch every week. Howie's Discipline is excellent, as is his Knowledge of the Game. Anyhow, one day we were in a Craps game, and enjoying a very profitable run of the dice. It was a small house, and the pit boss for that section was a little perturbed at the method we were using—a very advanced system of hedging, after the come-out, and leaving ourselves open for losses on only scant occasions.

At one point, the dealer neglected to pay Howie for a bet. Howie called his attention to it, was ignored, and turned to the boxman for a decision. He also waved Howie off. This did not sit too well with my friend, who demanded the pitboss intercede. Howie was in the right, but received no sympathy from these guys. The pit boss motioned the stickman to send the dice to the shooter. Howie, seeing that his pleas were going to go unheeded, did what any red blooded crapshooter would do. He climbed up over the rail and laid across the table. Somehow he managed to get everybody's attention. Picture if you will, this ex-football, basketball player over two hundred and twenty-five pounds sprawled over a four-foot wide craps table, his legs hanging over the side.

I almost split my sides laughing. I had pains in my jaw for hours, just roaring at that sight. Howie got his way, won his appeal, and got paid. Was he intimidated? Nothing intimidates Howie in a casino, and it shouldn't bother anyone who plays there.

I'm not suggesting you take up scaling craps tables, but don't let a mistake by a dealer, where you are positive you are right, turn you into a scared mouse. If you're right, stop the game until you get the proper results.

I know a lot of you are in awe of the casino, and the ingrown fear of going up to a certain table. Be yourself. Don't let anything bother you. If you completely understood all of the aspects of the game, you would not be intimidated. So, learn about the game you compete at and you'll be able to handle yourself.

We'll make a quick list of resolutions that we'll all promise to follow:

1. I won't be scared to go into an empty theater.
2. You won't be intimidated by anything at all in the casinos.

3. Howie will find softer places to park his carcass.
4. Lynn will start wearing clothes that fit.

Damn, I hope one of those things don't change. . . .

ODDS AND ENDS 8

The Ultimate Goal

So You Wanna Be a Gambler!! OK, you've got a few suggestions from me as to what to bring to battle. The Big 4 and the Little 3 will give you an excellent chance to compete on an even keel at the tables.

Just remember what the Ultimate Goal is. It's winning, not playing. Winning is what gambling is all about. If you can't win, or don't know how to win, you are taking on an exercise in eventual, possible, complete ruin, if you persist. I kid you not.

The decision is now yours, as to how you want to approach the craps tables. All the knowledge about the rules and the promise of excitement won't be worth a hill of beans if you keep losing.

Psychologically, the constant losses, large or small, will begin to eat at you. The consistent wins, albeit small, will give you a positive approach to the games, and the results will become so pleasing, that accepting percentage wins, will be all you'll look for.

When I lose, I hurt, and anybody who tells you it doesn't hurt has a cavity in his power plant. When I win, regardless of the amount, my goal has been accomplished and the feelings of satisfaction carry over to the next session.

Losing is for losers, and I don't want you to be one. The thrill of victory is almost as good as—ah, but that's another story. . . .

Finally, let me wish you the best in whatever game you play. It is possible to win at Craps, maybe not the fortunes you dream about, but a steady return on your starting bankroll.

How you will love the feeling of victory. My sincere best wishes; and since I abhor the word luck, let me wish you. . . .

Happy Winnings

JOHN PATRICK

Gambling Books Ordering Information

Ask for any of the books listed below at your bookstore. Or to order direct from the publisher, call 1-800-447-BOOK (MasterCard or Visa), or send a check or money order for the books purchased (plus $4.00 shipping and handling for the first book ordered and $1.00 for each additional book) to Carol Publishing Group, 120 Enterprise Avenue, Dept. 40554, Secaucus, NJ 07094.